A Couple of Soles

TRANSLATIONS FROM THE ASIAN CLASSICS

The lovers in a fishnet. (Woodblock-printed illustration by Cai Sihuang 蔡思璜, from *Wusheng xi he ji* 無聲戲合集, a Shunzhi era [1644–1661] imprint, reproduced with permission from Liu Xin and Xiao Jieran, eds., *Zhongguo gu banhua: Renwu juan, Xiaoshuo lei* [Changsha: Hunan meishu chubanshe, 1998], 186)

比目魚

A Couple of Soles

A Comic Play from
Seventeenth-Century China

Li Yu

TRANSLATED BY

Jing Shen & Robert E. Hegel

Columbia University Press
New York

Columbia University Press wishes to express its appreciation for
assistance given by the Wm. Theodore de Bary Fund and
the Pushkin Fund in the publication of this book.

Columbia University Press
Publishers Since 1893
New York   Chichester, West Sussex
cup.columbia.edu

Copyright © 2020 Columbia University Press
All rights reserved

Library of Congress Cataloging-in-Publication Data
Names: Li, Yu, 1611–1680? author. | Shen, Jing, translator. |
Hegel, Robert E., 1943– translator.
Title: A couple of soles : a comic play from seventeenth-century
China / Li Yu ; translated by Jing Shen and Robert E. Hegel.
Other titles: Bimuyu. English
Description: New York : Columbia University Press, [2020] |
Series: Translations from the Asian Classics |
Includes bibliographical references.
Identifiers: LCCN 2019025146 (print) | LCCN 2019025147 (ebook) |
ISBN 9780231193542 (cloth) | ISBN 9780231193559 (trade paperback) |
ISBN 9780231550369 (ebook)
Classification: LCC PL2698.L52 B5613 2020 (print) | LCC PL2698.
L52 (ebook) | DDC 895.12/46—ac23
LC record available at https://lccn.loc.gov/2019025146
LC ebook record available at https://lccn.loc.gov/2019025147

Columbia University Press books are printed on permanent
and durable acid-free paper.

Printed in the United States of America

Cover image: Royal Asiatic Society, London,
UK/Bridgeman Images

Cover and book design: Lisa Hamm

*To Cyril Birch (b. 1925)
and to the memory of
James I. Crump, Jr. (1921–2002),
master translators of China's great plays*

TRANSLATIONS FROM THE ASIAN CLASSICS

EDITORIAL BOARD

Paul Anderer

Allison Busch

David Lurie

Rachel McDermott

Wei Shang

Haruo Shirane

For a complete list of books in the series, see page 331.

CONTENTS

Acknowledgments ix

Note on the Translation xi

Introduction by Jing Shen xiii

Dramatis Personae and Their Role Categories xxiii

Preface by Wang Duanshu

1

Scenes

5

A Couple of Soles

13

*Appendix: The Playwright and His Art
by Jing Shen* 239

Notes 271

Bibliography 323

ACKNOWLEDGMENTS

Our thanks to the librarians and scholars in Beijing, Taipei, and elsewhere who helped us find old editions of the text we translate here, and to the Chapin Fellowship at Eckerd College, which funded the research trip. We also thank the many colleagues who commented on earlier versions of the introduction and appendix at annual meetings of Chinese Oral and Performing Literature, particularly Professor David Rolston. Dr. Hua Wei's kindness in clarifying some technical aspects of the play is greatly appreciated.

Thanks, too, to Christine Dunbar and her colleagues at Columbia University Press for their enthusiastic support from the moment we first mentioned the project to her. Christian Winting's guidance of the manuscript through the editing and publication process has been exemplary. And we must acknowledge with gratitude Irene Pavitt's meticulous copyediting and her tremendous patience and the care with which production editor Susan Pensak saw this project through to print.

Finally, we are especially grateful for the painstaking efforts of the two anonymous reviewers enlisted by the press. Their attention to detail revealed their thoughtful consideration of each aspect of the manuscript, while their erudition was clear throughout their many helpful suggestions. Particularly felicitous turns of phrase from their suggestions have strongly influenced this final version, making its current degree of polish a reflection of their generous devotion of time to this project.

Translating humor and conventions of theatrical performance across the centuries into an unrelated language—and through a screen of scholarly annotations—can only be challenging. But it has been enjoyable and, of course, informative for both of us. Although we gladly acknowledge the assistance of others, all remaining shortcomings we humbly accept as our own.

NOTE ON THE TRANSLATION

We have based this translation on the edition of the play in volume 5 of *Li Yu quanji* 李漁全集 (Hangzhou: Zhejiang guji, 1991), with reference to the annotations by Huo Xianjun and Zhang Guopei in *Liweng chuanqi shizhong jiaozhu* 笠翁傳奇十種校注 (Tianjin: Tianjin guji, 2008). Jing Shen also consulted the rare editions of *Liweng shizhong qu* 笠翁十種曲 from the reign of the Kangxi emperor (1662–1722) in the collections at the National Library of China in Beijing and at National Taiwan University in Taipei. Both libraries have given us permission to use the illustrations from those two editions in this book. The translation was a collaboration, although the research behind the notes and the first draft of the translation were entirely the work of Jing Shen.

Readers can easily distinguish the three different components of the play text in translation—arias, verses, and prose dialogues—as shown by tune titles and stage directions. In an aria, extrametrical words are printed in a smaller font. The lines of arias are indented farthest and are introduced by the tune titles given in romanization and enclosed in parentheses. Recited lines are indented less far and, following the convention of the text, are not preceded by any stage direction. These lines may be parallel-prose couplets, comic doggerel, more formal *shi* poetry in lines of equal length, or *ci* poems (lyrics) written to matrices bearing the names of the tunes to which those poems were originally sung. Although the melodies had been lost for centuries by Li Yu's time, *ci* poems are conventionally identified with these lost tune titles, here enclosed in parentheses.

INTRODUCTION

JING SHEN

A Couple of Soles (*Bimuyu* 比目魚, 1661) is a comic opera in the Chinese romantic tradition of *chuanqi* 傳奇 drama by the late Ming–early Qing period playwright and impresario Li Yu 李漁 (Li Liweng 李笠翁, 1610–1680). Li Yu had a reputation for writing tales that tested social limits. His short stories narrate illicit affairs, the adventures of a peeping Tom, and the devotion of a gay married couple, and he is almost certainly the author of the erotic—and comical—parody of a young scholar's "education": the novel *The Carnal Prayer Mat* (*Rou putuan* 肉蒲團). His comic plays were very popular during his own time; several were adapted from his own short stories.

A Couple of Soles develops in theatrical form the plot of the story "Tan Chuyu Declares His Love in a Play; Liu Miaogu Dies for Honor's Sake After Her Aria" (Tan Chuyu xi li chuanqing, Liu Miaogu qu zhong sijie 譚楚玉戲裡傳情, 劉藐姑曲終死節), from Li's *The Combined Volume of Silent Operas* (*Wusheng xi he ji* 無聲戲合集).[1] The suicide here is a rewriting and parody of a climactic scene from an earlier classic of Chinese *nanxi* 南戲 (Southern drama; the predecessor of *chuanqi*),[2] *The Thorn Hairpin* (*Jingchai ji* 荊釵記). Li's slapstick humor contrasts fairly violently with the earlier melodrama; it also innovates by stretching contemporary conventions of performance.

THE PLOT

As the play begins, the poor but handsome young scholar Tan Chuyu falls in love at first sight with Liu Miaogu (Fairy), the beautiful daughter of an acting family. She acknowledges his flirtation by returning shy glances of her own. To be close to her, he responds to an advertisement for a martial role and joins the theater troupe owned by Fairy Liu's father, Liu Wenqing. Most of the characters Tan actually gets to play do not allow him to act opposite Fairy. Having proved that he is clever and capable, he follows Fairy's advice and threatens to leave the troupe if his role does not change. The elder Liu complies with Tan's wish and lets him play the romantic male lead opposite Fairy, including in scholar–beauty love stories. He takes the opportunity to woo Fairy Liu onstage—though they are forced to keep their distance when offstage.

But then a local country squire, Qian Wanguan (Moneybags Qian), offers to buy Fairy Liu as his concubine. Her mother, Liu Jiangxian (Fallen Angel Liu), wants this bride-price as a nest egg for her declining years and tries to force Fairy to agree to marry Qian. The young woman expresses her unwavering devotion to Tan Chuyu onstage by performing the famous scene from the play *The Thorn Hairpin* in which the heroine drowns herself—and then Fairy commits suicide by throwing herself into the river over which the stage extends. Grief-stricken, Tan follows her into the water. But the local river deity, Lord Yan—in whose honor these plays are being performed—rescues the lovers from death by transforming them into a pair of flatfish, or soles, to be caught by Murong Jie, who has resigned from office and become a fisherman. As fish, they are pulled up in the net of Murong's servant. Then the river god restores them to their human form.

Back at the acting troupe, Moneybags withdraws his offer, but the silver is already in Fallen Angel's hands. This provokes a comic lawsuit, with bribes paid all around. But in the end, the local governor finds ways to appropriate all the cash in circulation surrounding the case.

After the young couple recover from their aquatic adventure, Murong hosts a rustic wedding ceremony for them to fulfill their amorous attachment. Then young Tan heads off to take the civil service examinations. Upon receiving top marks, Tan is rewarded with an official post. Later, Tan renders meritorious administrative and military service, his brilliant career ensured by exterminating a band of highwaymen.

These bandits are central to the second plotline of the play; the two stories alternate throughout. Murong Jie is introduced in scene 5 as an accomplished administrator who, now aging, longs for retirement and peace of mind. To that end, he leads a military force to defeat a group of mountain bandits that threatens local communities, and then he quietly leaves office. He and his wife live simply, and incognito, fishing for a living, until one day his servant nets the coupling soles—which then transform into Tan Chuyu and Fairy Liu. When Tan passes the examinations and takes Murong's former position, the retired official conceals in Tan's luggage a handbook with detailed advice on how to defeat the bandits and to pacify the land. However, when a bandit spy pretending to be Murong leads government armies into surrendering to the bandits, all the evidence makes Tan believe that Murong is a traitor to the state. He sentences Murong to execution, not letting personal gratitude impede the fulfillment of his public duty.

After this disruptive and nearly catastrophic case of mistaken identity, the truth comes out, and their friendship is restored. Murong convinces Tan to withdraw from officialdom to enjoy married life in retirement before the chance to do so slips away. The play ends with a cheerful renunciation of wealth and rank in favor of a life spent deep in the mountains.

PERFORMANCE AND MUSICAL STRUCTURES

Suppressing the bandits not only serves a thematic purpose but also offsets the romantic adventures of the leading man and lady. Conventionally, by the seventeenth century, *chuanqi* plays alternated between a love story and military or comic action to provide variety for the audience and to rest one set of players before bringing them back onstage later. These plays were long; many extended to around fifty scenes, taking as many as two or three days to perform. To hold the attention of the audience, it was necessary to design episodes that contrasted with one another in terms of theme, singing style, and mood—whether that was lyrical or full of action, the latter often including acrobatics or martial arts displays. This convention also led to the staging of selected scenes from one or more plays during any one presentation, as seen in the performance of highlights from *The Thorn Hairpin* in scenes 15 and 28 of *A Couple of Soles*.[3] *A Couple of Soles* seems structured to be performed in two days, leaving the audience in suspense about the fate of the young lovers after they are transformed into paired fish at the end of the first day.

Chuanqi plays such as *A Couple of Soles* consist of arias, spoken parts, and minimal stage directions. Plays in this form begin with a brief scene in which a respectable-looking male figure gives a general outline of the plot—usually through hints rather than by explicit explanation—to pique the interest of the audience. This figure can take the role of a character in the play, a knowledgeable friend of the playwright, or the dramatist himself.[4] Most scenes rely heavily on poetry, both recited (often comic) and sung (which can be quite powerful emotionally). Scenes generally close with a short verse recited by one or more characters.

To create arias, playwrights had to be versed in lyrical poetry and prosodic rules. The arias are structured as sets of tunes, each written in a specific musical mode; playwrights composed poems to given tunes instead of creating new ones. Musical modes determine the pitch-collection of melodies and facilitate the expression of emotions, as different modes represent various moods—at least according to traditional critics. A set of tunes written in the same mode can form a suite. Suites may repeat the same tune, alternate between two tunes, or form a cluster of tunes. Conventionally, suites may include introductory and coda musical passages as well.[5]

Tunes are often role-specific. Role types in *chuanqi* drama include *sheng* 生 (young male lead), *dan* 旦 (young female lead), *jing* 淨 (painted face), *chou* 丑 (clown), *wai* 外 (older male role), *mo* 末 (supporting male role), *xiaosheng* 小生 (extra male lead), *laodan* 老旦 (old female role), and *tie* 貼 /*xiaodan* 小旦 (extra female lead).[6] The secondary roles *jing* and *chou* would not sing melodious, slow tunes such as *Jin luosuo* 金絡索. By contrast, the *Jin luosuo* suits romantic leads—*sheng* and *dan*. Its consecutive uses (same tune) in scene 10 ("Becoming Leading Man") provide delicate music for Fairy Liu to convey her feelings for Tan Chuyu in a subtle way.

THE SIGNIFICANCE OF *A COUPLE OF SOLES*

In *Silent Operas*, Patrick Hanan called the story "Tan Chuyu Declares His Love in a Play; Liu Miaogu Dies for Honor's Sake After Her Aria" the "finest romantic comedy," but in some ways, Li Yu's treatment of this material in dramatic form in *A Couple of Soles* is more complex and imaginative.[7] With the play, Li Yu added a layer of complication by telling a theater story in a theater form: the audience watches actors playing actors or, in Tan's case, an actor playing a scholar playing at being an actor. The lovers communicate not with their own words, but through their lines. In scene 15, Fairy Liu's suicidal performance of the highlight from *The Thorn Hairpin*, "Clasping a Rock and Plunging into the River" (a play within a play within a play), is the central event with which the dramatic conflicts in *A Couple of Soles* reach their climax.[8] Fairy is not the only one who acts a part; almost all the major characters in Li Yu's play—even those who are not themselves actors—impersonate others at one point or another.[9] Consequently, the contrast of appearance and reality becomes an underlying theme through the drama.[10] The opposing pinnacles of those two values—Moneybags Qian and Old Fisherman Mo—serve as foils to each other, explicitly in scenes 11 ("The Fox's Might"), 12 ("Luxuriant Escape"), and 13 ("Throwing Money Around"). Thus Li Yu ingeniously uses the *chuanqi* convention of alternating and varied scenes in *A Couple of Soles*.[11] In Eric Henry's words, "Li Yu was never more thoroughly the master fabulist, never more happily absorbed in his craft, than he is in this play."[12]

A Couple of Soles also stands out among Li Yu's plays for its balance of comedy with very serious issues.[13] Li Yu is often criticized for the vulgar content of his drama, but *A Couple of Soles* makes "the loyal husband and chaste wife" its protagonists. In fact, Tan Chuyu's and Fairy Liu's moral stature is mentioned repeatedly until scene 19, interestingly, when they officially get married. Their total devotion to each other is what persuades the deity Lord Yan to rescue the young couple from drowning. When they recover human form, the account of their suicide to preserve their moral standards wins praise from Murong Jie, who also regards them as loyal husband and chaste wife. The song of celebration at their wedding confirms that they have earned these moral titles. This theme is reinforced through references to *The Thorn Hairpin*, whose protagonists are regarded as the most exemplarily faithful couple among all the characters of *nanxi* classics.[14]

That earlier play portrays the virtuous Qian Yulian, who is devoted to a poor scholar, Wang Shipeng. After succeeding in the civil service examinations, Wang is assigned to an official post far away. The wealthy Sun Ruquan secretly rewrites Wang's letter home, changing it to a writ of divorce in order to take Qian for himself. Greedy for Sun's money, Qian's stepmother presses Sun's proposal upon her. To remain loyal to her husband, Qian throws herself into a river but is rescued and adopted by an official on his way to his post. Learning about her "death" later, Wang and his mother offer a sacrifice at the river where she has attempted to commit suicide. In the end, Qian Yulian is reunited with Wang Shipeng. The story of Tan Chuyu and Fairy Liu is similar, even though Li Yu's play utilizes conventional ethical language to depict a romantic story with visual charm.[15]

Highlighting the moral stature of Tan Chuyu and Fairy Liu serves to uplift the image of the acting profession; this intention is clearly stated in the play's prologue and in the concluding poem of the last scene. In her first appearance in *A Couple of Soles*, Fairy voices her wish to perform only in plays that advocate virtues. Fairy's noble purpose enables her to fit in with the *chuanqi* convention of a proper female lead and also asserts the positive role of theater in upholding integrity and honor in society. Tan's firsthand observation of the rules that govern the opera troupe in scenes 7 and 9 makes it known that actors have to live according to strict codes of conduct and cannot be too familiar with actresses in the same class, which contrasts markedly with the remark, in scene 3, made by the experienced Fallen Angel Liu on how to flirt with patrons for money. This separation of the genders is certainly disappointing to Tan, since he has joined the troupe in order to be close to Fairy.

The preface to *A Couple of Soles*, included in this translation, reveals much about Li Yu's social circle. Li Yu was noted for his love of women and had a number of concubines. Meanwhile, he admired strong, talented female artists and writers, and engaged them in his work. He asked the woman scholar Wang Duanshu 王端淑 (1621–after 1701) to compose the preface to *A Couple of Soles*, which is dated 1661.[16] Writing a preface for a major work was normally an honor reserved for the author's superiors.[17]

Wang Duanshu, daughter of scholar-official, Ming loyalist, and drama critic Wang Siren 王思任 (1575–1646), was well versed in poetry, calligraphy, and painting. In addition to publishing her own writings, she compiled and edited a large anthology of women's works, *Classics of Poetry by Famous Women* (*Mingyuan shiwei* 名媛詩緯). Around the mid-seventeenth century, she socialized with notable poets, artists, and writers in Shaoxing and Hangzhou, where she met Li Yu.[18] Her preface to Li Yu's *A Couple of Soles* demonstrates her great knowledge of history and the classics through allusions to a number of philosophical and historical works. It first cites *The Book of Changes* (*Yijing* 易經) to assert that the union of man and woman accords with the Way of nature, highlighting the theme of passion in the play. Tan Chuyu and Fairy Liu's sincere devotion to each other has the power to bring them back to life after drowning, which makes *A Couple of Soles* a successor to Tang Xianzu's 湯顯祖 (1550–1617) remarkable play *The Peony Pavilion* (*Mudan ting* 牡丹亭)—about the archetypal young lady who dies of lovesickness and later comes back to life through love.[19] This emphasis on feeling affirms the affinity of Li Yu's play with the romantic ethos of late Ming drama. Quotations in the preface from the Daoist texts *Daodejing* 道德經 and *Zhuangzi* 莊子 bring out the key images—eyes and fish—of the play and foreshadow their transforming magic in the romantic story.

At the end of the preface, Wang Duanshu compares Li Yu with Xu Wei 徐渭 (1521–1593), a writer admired by her father, affirming Li Yu's achievements in drama, as Xu Wei was an original *zaju* playwright and wrote the first treatise on *nanxi*: *A Review of Southern Drama* (*Nanci xulu* 南詞敘錄). The Northern-style variety show (*zaju* 雜劇) of the Yuan dynasty (1271–1368) traditionally incorporated the tunes of robust Northern music, so different from the more delicate Southern tunes. A Yuan *zaju* play includes four acts, with a prologue or an introduction termed a "wedge," and only one leading character sings in each act.[20] In his *zaju* drama, Xu Wei broke free from these formal and musical conventions while defying social, religious, and gender norms in content.[21] The presence of such an eccentric figure in the preface, doubly noticeable in contrast to the many classical allusions, emphasizes Li Yu's own unorthodox nature.

LI YU

Li Yu came from a rural family of pharmaceutical merchants. His relatives did not include any high government officials, and his only experience of the civil service was attaining a position of the lowest grade, working as a secretary for the sub-prefect of his hometown, Jinhua, in Zhejiang around 1645. Of the limited career options in the Qing dynasty (1644–1912), he chose to become a professional writer and impresario living in the cities of Hangzhou and Nanjing, while periodically going on tour with his family and troupe. Little was written about him in local gazetteers, and he largely fell into oblivion in modern China, even though he was a well-known author and entrepreneur of his time who enjoyed the patronage of Chinese and Manchu high officials and socialized in diverse circles of scholars, artists, recluses, Ming loyalists, and those who served the new Qing regime. During his two decades in Hangzhou and Nanjing, he composed fiction, drama, and essays that were immensely popular. Skilled in conversing with his readers and audience, he created intriguing narratives and knew how to package his works for the market at his own bookshop. It was unusual that Li Yu published his own plays in separate editions and as an anthology claiming exclusive authorship. (These printed editions often appeared with extensive commentary, prefaces, and fine illustrations.[22] Images that accompanied an early printed edition of this play are included in this volume.) The books that he wrote and published display not only his original, humorous storytelling talent, but also his expertise in the art of living—he wrote on clothing, food, housing, daily activities, women, and sex—although he often complained about a lack of financial resources. The popularity of his work also attracted negative attention that intensified after his lifetime. Li Yu's unconventional style evoked controversy and his works were sometimes banned, but his individuality, mobility, innovative spirit, and pleasure-seeking nature—not to mention his role in the popularization and commercialization of literature—make him an excellent representative of the embryonic modernity of seventeenth-century China.[23]

DRAMATIS PERSONAE AND THEIR ROLE CATEGORIES

Interlocutor of the play in the prologue	*mo* (formal male)
Young scholar Tan Chuyu	*sheng* (young male lead)
Actress and Tan Chuyu's wife, Liu Miaogu (Fairy Liu)	*dan* (young female lead)
Fairy Liu's mother, Liu Jiangxian (Fallen Angel Liu)	*xiaodan* (extra female lead)
Retired official-turned-fisherman Murong Jie	*xiaosheng* (extra male lead)
Murong's wife	*laodan* (old female role)
Local powerbroker Qian Wanguan (Moneybags Qian)	*jing* (painted face)
Deity Pacifier-of-Waves (Lord Yan)	*wai* (older male role)
Fairy Liu's father, Liu Wenqing	*fujing* (secondary painted face)
Murong's servant (later, fisherman's boy)	*mo* (supporting male role)
Wife of fisherman's servant	*chou* (clown)
Group of people acting audience members	*wai* and *fujing* (men), *laodan* and *chou* (women), *xiaodan* (young child), and *jing* (monk)

Tan Chuyu's theater-going friends	*mo* and *xiaosheng*
Members of the Dancing Rainbow Troupe	*wai*, *xiaosheng*, *jing*, and *chou*
Maidservant of Murong's wife (Plum Fragrance)	*jing*
Members of the Jade Sprouts Troupe	*wai*, *mo*, *jing*, and *chou*
Instructor of the Jade Sprouts Troupe	*xiaosheng*
Bandit chief	*fujing*
Generals of the left and of the right	*wai* and *mo*
Local heads of households	*wai*, *fujing*, and *laodan*
Moneybags Qian's maidservants (Plum Fragrance)	*fujing* and *chou*
Moneybags Qian's boy servants	*mo* and *wai*
Judge in the Underworld	*fujing*
Local earth gods	*jing*, *chou*, and *mo*
Almsgivers	*xiaosheng* and *laodan*
Daoist priests	*mo* and *chou*
People who redeem their vows to the deity	*sheng* and *xiaodan*
Diviners	*jing* and *mo*
Assistant county magistrate	*chou*
Yamen runners	*xiaosheng* and *dan*
Magistrate's runner	*mo*
Old woodcutter	*wai*
Old farmer	*jing*
Old gardener	*fujing*
Shepherd boy	*chou*
Bandit chief's military adviser	*jing*

DRAMATIS PERSONAE

Traitor who assumes Murong's identity	*chou*
Yamen runners	*wai* and *jing*
Subordinate officials	*mo* and *fujing*
Fairy Liu's maidservant (Plum Fragrance)	*fujing*
Tan Chuyu's steward	*wai*
Tan Chuyu's servant	*jing*
Heads of the re-formed theatrical troupe	*mo* and *fujing*
Elderly men	*wai, mo, chou, fujing,* and *laodan*
Children	*dan* and *xiaodan*
Other subordinate generals	*jing* and *chou*

Gang of scoundrels; impersonators of tigers, bears, rhinoceroses, and elephants; rank-and-file soldiers; servants and conscripted laborers; retinue of deity; impersonators of shrimp, snail, crab, and turtle generals; impersonator of the paired fish; voice backstage for Wang Shipeng's mother (from *The Thorn Hairpin* scene) unspecified; executioners.

PREFACE

After all things appeared on Earth, there were created man and woman,[1] which were the first human ties since Heaven and Earth came into being.[2] The relationships between ruler and ministers and between friends inherited and followed the model of the relationship of husband and wife. Liweng [Li Yu] reposes the ideal of loyal ministers and true friends in the relationship between husband and wife, man and woman; he further reposes the hope of faithful husband and chaste wife in the class of actors and performers. Thus the play praises the Confucian ethical code. These basic matters are obvious, but they contain profound truth. The *Laozi* says: "Sages satisfy their stomachs rather than their eyes."[3] Excellent point! When [Hua Fu] Du of the state of Song came across Kong Fu's wife, he gazed at her walking toward him and followed her going past with his eyes, saying: "Beautiful and gorgeous!"[4] King [Li of the Western Zhou dynasty] dispatched masters of sacrificial rites and priests to watch for people who censured him. Thus the people exchanged glances when meeting on the road [not daring to speak openly].[5]

Tan Chuyu and Fairy Liu first fell in love through their eyes, then developed their relationship by speaking with their eyes, and in the end turned into a couple of eye-paired soles. Eyes have such great power that they can even revive the dead. Zhuang Zi says: "You are not a fish—how do you know the happiness of fish!"[6] How do I know that fish have this miraculous power to bring the dead back to life! When I consider this from the transformation of things, non-feelings can transform into feelings, as an age-old Chinese sweet gum becomes a winged immortal and rotten wheat becomes a butterfly. Feelings can also transform into non-feelings, as a virtuous woman turns into a solid rock and a mountain earthworm becomes a lily.[7] The couple love each other so much that they suddenly lose their graceful bearing and become emaciated; they abruptly put aside their refined restraints and swim away into the distance.[8] "Absolute sincerity can affect even pigs and fish, thereby bringing good luck."[9] How would the words from *The Book of Changes* deceive us?

Liweng embodies Murong Jie with the divine power to enlighten, but, in fact, Murong stands in for Liweng himself. It is said that fine writing faded by the time of Yuan drama, but Liweng alone uses the Way of voice and music as an avenue for [the characters'] nature and feelings. The highest development of their feelings is the highest revelation of their nature. Fairy Liu grew up in an actor's family, and yet Chuyu does not feel ashamed to humble himself, which is simply a story of secret feelings between a man and a woman. However, sincere passion reveals their inherent nature, which is the basis for the relationship of husband and wife and the connection that makes the relationship between friends. This nature motivates [Tan Chuyu] to eliminate his gratitude toward his benefactor [Murong Jie] over affairs of state and [Murong Jie] to enlighten [Tan Chuyu] on withdrawing from officialdom to live among hidden orchids.[10] We should just regard the play as a model and admonition to serve the ruler and trust true friends.[11] My fellow townsman and late sage Xu Wenchang wrote *The Four Cries of a Gibbon*,[12] a poetic masterpiece for the ages. But after that, *A Couple of Soles* ranks first!

Wang Duanshu, a woman scholar from Shanyin,
in the leap ninth month of 1661[13]

SCENES

Scene 1: Making a Start
Scene 2: Burning Ears
Scene 3: Organizing a Troupe
Scene 4: Special Appreciation
Scene 5: Punishing Bandits
Scene 6: Deciding on a Plan
Scene 7: Joining the Troupe
Scene 8: The Bandits Set Out
Scene 9: Drafting A Letter
Scene 10: Becoming Leading Man
Scene 11: The Fox's Might
Scene 12: Luxuriant Escape
Scene 13: Throwing Money Around
Scene 14: Extortion
Scene 15: Together in Death
Scene 16: Divine Protection
Scene 17: Scrambling for Profit
Scene 18: The Return to Life
Scene 19: Rustic Nuptials
Scene 20: The Secret Dispatch
Scene 21: A Parting Gift

Scene 22: A Cunning Plan
Scene 23: The Make-Believe Hermit
Scene 24: Departing in Glory
Scene 25: A Pretend Deity
Scene 26: Presenting the Book
Scene 27: Deciding on the Players
Scene 28: A Coincidental Reunion
Scene 29: Grabbing the Cart Shafts
Scene 30: Winning the Battle
Scene 31: Mistaken Arrest
Scene 32: A Shocking Reunion

FIGURE 1 The brigands attack with their beast army. (From *Bimuyu chuanqi er juan* 比目魚傳奇二卷, in *Liweng shizhong qu* 笠翁十種曲, Kangxi era [1662–1722] edition; National Library Rare Book Collection, Beijing)

FIGURE 2 Shedding official cap and phoenix coronet. (Illustration by Hu Nianyi 胡念翊 [or 翼], and carved by Wang Junzuo 王君佐, from *Bimuyu chuanqi er juan*, in *Liweng shizhong qu*, Kangxi era [1662–1722] edition; National Library Rare Book Collection, Beijing)

FIGURE 3 Fairy Liu throws herself into the river. (From *Bimuyu chuanqi er juan*, in *Liweng shizhong qu*, Kangxi era [1662–1722] edition; National Library Rare Book Collection, Beijing)

FIGURE 4 Life of leisure in retirement. (From *Bimuyu chuanqi er juan*, in *Liweng shizhong qu*, Kangxi era [1662–1722] edition; National Library Rare Book Collection, Beijing)

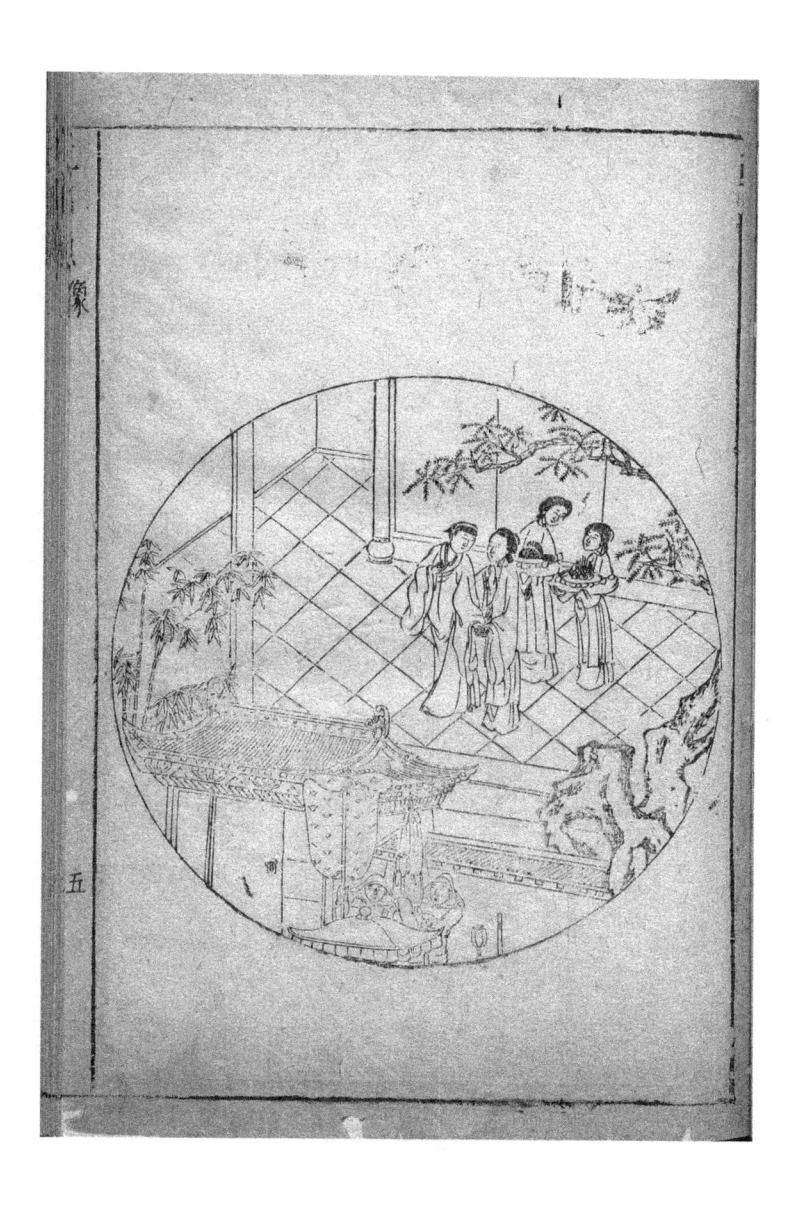

FIGURE 5 Before her suicidal performance, Fairy Liu with Moneybags Qian, who has sent a party to escort her to his home for the wedding. (From *Bimuyu chuanqi er juan*, in *Liweng shizhong qu*, Kangxi era [1662–1722] edition; National Library Rare Book Collection, Beijing)

FIGURE 6 Tan and his wife watch *The Thorn Hairpin*. (From *Bimuyu chuanqi er juan*, in *Liweng shizhong qu*, Kangxi era [1662–1722] edition; National Library Rare Book Collection, Beijing)

SCENE 1: MAKING A START

MO (*enters*):[1]
   (Pastiche: *Lian Qin E*)[2]
      (Tune: *Die lian hua*)
      Plying writing brush whenever idle for a year,
      Through texts both old and new
      I have searched everywhere for a marvelous tale.
      Since I could not find a play within others' plays,
      Searching has cost me effort all in vain!
      (Tune: *Yi Qin E*)
      To have actors act a play about an acting school,
      Their true features—how could they be lost?
      How could they be lost:
      A leading lady and a leading man,
      Form a match that's made in Heaven!
   (Pastiche: *Qinlou meng*)
      (Tune: *Yi Qin E*)
      Wooden clappers softly tap,
      Rainbow skirts[3] gently sway;
      But this is not a play like any other.

Its leading man the "seed of passion,"[4]
Its leading lady the model chaste wife:
They add luster to us in theatrical professions!
(Tune: *Ru meng ling*)
With thanks,
With thanks:
Each with voice and appearance repay your grace.
(Pastiche: *Shuangyu bimu you chunshui*)
(Tune: *Yujia ao*)
Leading lady Liu since birth has embodied enchanting grace;
Leading man Tan falls deeply in love when once he sees her face.
Their secret pledge to be man and wife is known to no one else.
Her mother presses her,
Out of greed, to be mated to another suitor.
(Tune: *Mo yu'er*)
Performing *The Thorn Hairpin*,[5]
The lovers drown themselves in deep water—
Who would expect a deity to intervene?
Through divine aid, they are steered into the hermit's net,
Not merely to complete a successful marriage.
(Tune: *Yu you chunshui*)
Honors for himself nearly turn due gratitude into resentment;
When laws of the land apply, personal feelings are suppressed.
Confronting danger, surviving peril—
Only then does our play reach its end.

Tan Chuyu falls so much in love, love enters his very marrow.[6]

Fairy Liu's going straight[7] leads her straight into the river.

Pacifier-of-Waves[8] in saving lives saves them into marriage.

Old Fisherman Mo in helping out helps them to the end.

SCENE 2: BURNING EARS

SHENG (*enters, costumed in scholar's hat and gown*):
>(Tune: *Man ting fang*)
>An immortal from Heaven,[9]
>A wanderer here on Earth,
>Who knows where I can find a home?
>A poor and humble scholar,
>I roam far to the ends of the Earth.
>But better to suffer wind and snow in strange lands,
>Than have relatives and friends
>Let me feel their heat!
>Forlorn,
>Living alone without a mate,
>Wasting away the best years of my life.

(*Recites: Hua tang chun*)[10]
>Fresh flowers bloom on limbs that bend to catch the sun;
>In seclusion, I wonder that spring's so slow to come.
>Even Heaven's Lord can favor those in power;
>He's surely partial to some!
>
>He gives out wealth and honor late or soon,
>But marriages ought not to be delayed.
>Why must you in the case of one so lovelorn
>Begrudge me finding a fair mate?

I am Tan Chuyu, given name Shiheng,[11] and I'm a native of Xiangyang.
>My chest's filled with talent,
>But I am poor to the bone.
>Member of a distinguished line,
>Although ashamed to claim its glory;

> Despite having relatives in high places,
> Too embarrassed to ask for their aid.
> In infancy, I learned how to read,
> Garnered fame as a child prodigy.
> At a young age, I entered the prefectural school
> And was recognized among the best in the land.
> My early brilliance I've not lost a bit;
> I read the rarest of books as old friends.
> Uniquely endowed with such talent,
> I write as if the gods inspired my brush.

Unfortunately, I lost my parents at an early age and am forever deprived of having brothers. The world as it is, fawning on the influential and snubbing the less fortunate, my hometown relatives and friends can only see me as poor as if scrubbed clean of all wealth and judge me superficially, their undiscerning eyes unable to recognize my worth. Hence, I left my native soil and roam the world's four corners, imitating the Grand Historian's[12] method of study: I take famous mountains and great rivers to be my wise teachers and helpful friends, my brush unconstrained and my spirit vast within me. Toting an umbrella and carrying a case of books, I come and go between Wu and Yue,[13] selecting examination essays for bookshops to publish and also selling some of my poems and essays when I have the chance. The remuneration I earn by my writing brush is sufficient for me to eke out a livelihood. But since I have already come of age[14] and have not yet been betrothed to a wife, I can't help feeling forlorn and alone. Know-nothings all say that because I have no money, I can never get married. How could they know that any wife whom I, Tan Chuyu, would take cannot be easily found with money? I am not bragging, if she were not one of the world's real stunners,[15] how would she be suitable for me, a genius of our times? But such a perfect match is hard to meet, hard to find!

(Pastiche: *Ying sheng xue huamei*)
> (Tune: *Huang ying'er*)
> The tree of jade awaits the humble reed.[16]
> It is not that I Lean on the empty balustrade,
> And pine for an exceptional bloom;
> Some charming vine will definitely grow toward
> This Branch of fine jade.[17]

One should know that any woman a man marries only by spending a large sum of money will certainly not be a True Beauty. When a True Beauty meets a Truly Gifted Scholar, if even the silk thread can be dispensed with as betrothal gift, there would be no use at all for gold, pearls, and other treasures.[18] Therefore, the things that are rare in the world are called priceless valuables; who could put a price on the most valuable treasures under Heaven?

> If Family property serves as matchmaker,
> and money is given as betrothal gift,
> Even A thousand in cash is worth only a thousand in cash!
> (Tune: *Huamei xu*)
> It's no boast:
> Because of my Reputation for talent,
> I will definitely have A lady knight who loves the orphans
> and the poor for my wife.

In order to see the sights at Mount Ke and Nine Dragons Lake, I recently came here to Sanqu.[19] I have heard that this place is famous for its many actresses who perform only local opera.[20] This morning, several friends of mine invited me to see a performance with them, but I had some writing commissions to complete and told them to go on ahead. Now I have finished writing, and I must go along as well. (*Walks.*)

(Pastiche: *Ying zu dai feng shu*)
> (Tune: *Huang ying'er*)
> Bolt the door and cover the window with gauze.

> This place where I'm staying has merely Clouds from atop my inkstone
> And flowers from my writing brush—[21]
> That is nearly all the property that I own.
> I expect that No thief would take them
> Even if I left the door wide open for him.
> I Should have no worries about being away.

(*From backstage, extras cry out in unison "Bravo!"*)

> (Tune: *Yi feng shu*)
> All that ruckus
> Sounds like A swarm of agitated bees.
> Why Is there such clamor amid cries of praise?

The performance must be over, and the spectators will all be leaving. I'll just stand aside and wait for them to pass by. (*Stands at the side.*)

(WAI *and* FUJING *are dressed up as men,* LAODAN *and* CHOU *as women,* XIAODAN *as a young girl, and* JING *as a monk; all enter, jostling one another and making a lot of noise. Sing in unison.*)

> (Tune: *Bu shi lu*)
> Jostling one another and raising a ruckus,
> Noble with lowly, men with women, nobody bothers to check.

(WAI *steals a glance at* LAODAN.)

LAODAN: Why on earth are you gawking at me instead of walking along?
> Don't go looking for trouble!

WAI: I was not looking at you on purpose; it is just that
> Rubbing shoulders and touching backs stirs the sprouts of love.

(FUJING *moves up behind* XIAODAN *and pats her buttocks and giggles.*)

XIAODAN: Keep your distance; don't go bumping and patting me to try to take advantage.
> Keep your hands off!

FUJING: When I saw you were unable to keep up, I pushed you along like I was pushing a cart, but you make accusations;

> You move slowly just because your cart lacks a rudder,
>> But luckily I, a Dry land helmsman, had the rudder of your boat.

(JING *looks down and picks up a woman's large shoe.*[22] *He turns aside to look at it; overjoyed, he hides it inside his sleeve.*)

CHOU: Somebody bumped me and stepped on my shoe, and my shoe came off. Let me put it back on before we go any farther. (*Looking down to pull on her shoe, she suddenly cries out in alarm.*) Oh, no, my shoe has disappeared! All of you, help me find it. (*All search for her shoe.*)

(JING *smiles at* CHOU.)

ALL (*except* CHOU): This bald donkey[23] has a suspicious look about him; he must have picked up the shoe. So bring it out at once!

JING: It wasn't I who picked it up.

ALL: Since it wasn't you who picked it up, just let us search you. (*They find the shoe.*) Isn't this a shoe? You bald donkey, under the blue sky and in broad daylight, you take liberties with a woman right in front of all of us—that's so disgusting! Let everyone join in and beat this bald donkey to death! (*They grab him and hit him.*)

JING (*cries out*): Gentlemen, do not make such a fuss. This shoe is of use for me, so I was unwilling to return it to her.

ALL: What use? Let him get up and explain. (*They release him.*) So what were you going to do with it?

JING: It does not have any use other than after I "meditate facing the wall for nine years," I will hang the shoe on my staff as I "return to the Western Paradise with a single shoe."[24] (*Exits hurriedly.*)

(CHOU *puts on the shoe and stands up.*)

ALL: If we had not found your shoe for you, how could you have been able to walk back?

CHOU: I didn't worry about that. If the shoe had not been found, I would have had that bald donkey carry me home on his back!

> My energy exhausted,
> I was ready to ride that ass;
> Who could have guessed My loss would turn out a gain,
> Just like the old frontiersman who gained a horse at last![25]

(*All exit together.*)

SHENG (*laughs*): Those men and women were really indiscreet; what could have been so good about that play? They jostled one another and acted like buffoons. (*From backstage is heard again the cry, "Bravo!"*)

Here come my two friends, the ones who invited me to go see the play with them. I will just ask them what was so good about the play.

MO and XIAOSHENG (*enter, wearing scholars' hats and robes*):
(Pastiche: *Ying hua ji yulin*)

> (Tune: *Huang ying'er*)
> We praise her beauty to the skies,
> Her voice that "circles the rafters"[26]—
> All so fine indeed—
> And her charming looks no painter's art could match.

SHENG (*uses a fan to tap his friends on the back*): Was it really that good?

MO and XIAOSHENG (*turn around to see him and smile*): So it's Elder Brother Tan. I ask you, when there was such a fine play, why didn't you come along? Why wait until now?

SHENG: I was writing out some texts for pay, so I had to come late. May I ask what is so good about this troupe that you, brothers, should praise them like this?

MO: Everyone in the troupe is good, but the leading lady is most exceptional.

SHENG: Which troupe is this? And what is the name of the actress?

XIAOSHENG: It is the Dancing Rainbow Troupe, and the main actress is called Fallen Angel Liu.

SHENG: Since naturally actresses can all sing a few arias, there is no need to talk about her voice; I am interested in only her looks.
MO:
>(Tune: *Shui hong hua*)
>Even if I Could talk flowers out of the sky,[27]
>I could not explain How totally charming she is.
>But several Ready-made phrases might tell you why.

SHENG: What phrases?
MO: She would look too white if she wore powder and too red if she wore rouge; she would look too tall if she were one inch taller and too short if she were shorter by one.
SHENG: I am afraid that description is overblown. Where in the world today could you find such a woman?
XIAOSHENG:
>(Tune: *Ji xian hao*)
>Feigning a worried look, she decorates her graceful
>   bearing.
>I admire the way she wears but sparing makeup,
>Both refined and enchanting.

If you do not believe me, brother, there will be another performance in a day or two. Why don't you come earlier then and see for yourself?
MO and XIAOSHENG:
>(Tune: *Cu yulin*)
>Get your eyes ready
>To appraise her up and down—
>You'll see that your objections have no grounds.
>We just fear that like a Glutton, when you see the food,
>You'll open your mouth especially wide!

SHENG: All right. On the day of their next performance, may I trouble you two to come by and remind me again?

XIAOSHENG: Brother, I am afraid that I'll be busy and will not be able to keep you company.

MO: Since I am a man of leisure, I will come with you, brother.

SHENG: An outstanding beauty has never been easy to find:
Her flower-like features you will not see if you use a flowery vision.[28]

MO and XIAOSHENG: We forgive you for applying only the loftiest standards,
But we fear that Laying eyes on this flower will correct your naive mind.

SCENE 3: ORGANIZING A TROUPE

XIAODAN (*enters*):

>(Tune: *Zi su wan*)
>
>Both in singing and in appearance, I am beautiful onstage;
>
>To get the finest rewards,[29] I have other special skills.
>
>And yet My only child at home possesses even greater charm;[30]
>
>I worry that she does not know our traditional family secret.

I, Fallen Angel Liu, am the *dan* actress in the Dancing Rainbow Troupe. My husband, Liu Wenqing, also performs in the troupe, and ever since he married me, I've helped him with all my heart and might to build up a family fortune. Today when there are so many *dan* actresses in the world that none of them can get rich, why am I alone good at making money? It is just because I was born with good looks, and thanks to the god Erlang's blessing,[31] when I appear on the stage I have the grace of a fairy descended to Earth from Heaven. Besides, I have an extraordinary memory. When first I learned a play script, I memorized the lines of both *sheng* and *dan*. Once I'm on stage, it doesn't matter what the role is—I can be *sheng* if I am asked to play a male role, and I can be *dan* if asked to play the woman. My performances are different from others'; seeing mine, the most virtuous men become infatuated with me, and even stingy fellows lavish me with gifts. I have taken up with several of them who are particularly willing to spend money; at most they give me half of their family property, and at the least I get several years' worth of their savings. That is how, in less than ten years, I have built up a very substantial family fortune. Who would have thought that my own daughter, named

Miaogu [Fairy], now just fourteen *sui*,[32] would outdo me in both appearance and memory? She has only been taught to read and has not learned any plays yet. She mastered writing, painting, and calligraphy long ago. But she does not yet know how to profit when it comes time for her to appear onstage. Today I am at home with nothing to do, so I will just call her out and pass on to her our secret of earning money. We'll see how it goes. Fairy, where are you? Come here right now.

(*From backstage*): Coming!

DAN (*enters*):

> (*Same tune*)
> My family's degraded and of awful repute;
> I've thought it through fully and can find no escape.
> Only If I use the stage to perform chastity,
> Could I face that shame with a clear conscience. (*Greets her mother.*)

XIAODAN: My child, you are fourteen years old now; you're not a baby any more. Your dad wants to organize a juvenile troupe so that you can all learn plays together. I'm not worried that you won't learn how to sing and dance; it's just that a *dan* actress has another way to earn money, which is not in play scripts and must be learned from childhood.

DAN: Mother, a proper woman should learn only women's roles like needlework, and with that she can earn a living. Playacting is not a woman's basic duty, and I do not want to learn it.

> (Tune: *Guizhi xiang*)
> Such arts destroy one's moral heart,
> And good looks invite seduction.[33]
> To muddy oneself just in order to become rich
> Is far worse than being pure minded and going hungry.

If I must learn plays, it would be best to earn an honest penny simply by my skill in acting and let that be the end of it. If I must lose my sense of honor and ruin my reputation and integrity by doing those other things, that's something I refuse to do.

If I must Follow in your fragrant track,
Follow in your fragrant track,
I only fear that It would be hard to follow your "virtuous example."
You hope for it in vain!
I myself will respect The proper rules for women.
Do not say that Only the thick-skinned family can be rich.³⁴
How could you not know that A lost reputation is a true loss!

XIAODAN: Your father and I had hoped to use you as the means to build up a nest egg; but instead, you give me this high-sounding nonsense. What kind of reputation can women like us expect? What sense of shame can we hold on to? We only need to make up our minds: when making connections with men, we must simply act as if we were performing in a play. Even if he is serious, we just pretend and consider both lovemaking and sentimental attachment with indifference. This is maintaining chastity for us. Why must you be so rigid!

(*Same tune*)
From a family of courtesans,
How could you be such a stickler?
Just pretend a little false interest, some empty affection,
And he will give you real wealth and favor in return.
Besides, this Way to earn a living is comparable,
Way to earn a living is comparable—
Treating Phoenix quilt and lovebird pillow,
As just An extension of the stage.
After your "wedding night,"
Even if your Student Zhang cannot bear to leave you,
Your Yingying need not be as faithful as Miss Cui.³⁵

As your mother, I would not ask you to go so far as to receive every man you meet. I have three secret formulas to pass on to you. If you follow these guidelines, you will enjoy both fame and fortune in return, be appreciated by both talented men and fools, and benefit from them your whole life.

DAN: What are the three secret formulas?

XIAODAN: They are: allow them to look but not to taste, go along with them in name but not in reality, and allow them to scheme but not to succeed.

DAN: What do you mean by "allow them to look but not to taste"?

XIAODAN: When you act on the stage, people can look you over from head to toe, missing nothing. When you are offstage, you can still play and flirt with men all the same. And yet this fragrant wine will never wet their lips. This is called "allow them to look but not to taste."

DAN: There is some sense in that. Then what about "go along with them in name but not in reality"?

XIAODAN: If a rich merchant or an heir of some noble family desires to do the real thing with me, I promise him in words but stall on some pretext and do not let him get his hands on me. This is called "go along with them in name but not in reality."

DAN: This shows a bit of resolve. Then what about "allow them to scheme but not to succeed"?

XIAODAN: When there are young men who are deeply infatuated with me and who are willing to pay out a lot of money to make me an honest woman, I agree enthusiastically so that they should spend whole days in planning and spare no expense in getting together with me. After all that planning, I just treat it as a spring dream for them, and I would never agree to actually marry them for real. This is called "allow them to scheme but not to succeed."

DAN: Since you would not let them have your body, why not tell them straightaway instead of setting so many snares for them?

XIAODAN: When the average man associates with a woman, the deepest affection and truest feelings for her are not to be found after they have had physical contact, but only at the stage of exchanging amorous glances. A man is like a glutton coming across food and drink. He should be allowed only to smell the fragrance but not allowed to lift his chopsticks; as soon as he starts eating, his desire will be over. He'll be nowhere near as devoted as when he was panting and drooling with desire!

DAN (*laughs coldly*):

> (Tune: *Chang pai*)
> Tricks upon tricks,
> Tricks upon tricks,
> And snare after snare,
> Make me Even as plotter afraid for the victim!
> What crime has
> He Committed to merit such punishment,
> That I should Deceitfully spread a net of love
> To ensnare his bewildered soul?
> Even if I succeed in Keeping chastity intact,
> My remaining fragrance and shattered jade[36]
> Will have been wasted for no reason.

Mother, according to what you say, have you told lies just to fool others all your life, never actually doing anything to defame yourself and defile your chastity?

XIAODAN (*laughs*): This child is being silly again. The three secret formulas are used only to get small sums of money without doing anything; for large sums of money, if you do not do the real thing with him, why would he give it to you? But be choosey and get acquainted with only the extremely rich who throw money about like dirt. To those patrons who spend merely small sums, just repay them with some flirtatious conversation.

DAN (*shakes her head*): How could you get away with this?

People are still wary of empty reputation and hearsay,[37]
Especially when in reality
They've been taken advantage of.
Just hearing my parent's lesson makes me feel ashamed.
A good reputation among others,
Once lost, can never be recovered.

FUJING (*enters*):
I've inquired all around the theater circles
In order to build a troupe with talent.
I worry that the music of the Heavens
Cannot be performed among mere mortals.

DAN: Dad's home! (*Greets her father.*)

XIAODAN: Father, where have you been so long that you have come back so late?

FUJING: In order to put together a juvenile troupe and round up some young actors, I've had to visit a number of places.

XIAODAN: Then have you got all the actors you need?

FUJING: We have filled all the roles except for only a *da huamian*.[38]

DAN: Of the male roles, the most difficult to fill is the *zhengsheng*.[39] What's so hard to learn about performing the *huamian* roles?

FUJING: Unlike the *xiao huamian*, the *da huamian* does martial arts and absolutely must have some heroic spirit. (*Sings.*)

(Tune: *Duan pai*)
Even though his face is painted on,
Even though his face is painted on,
He must be a man of heroic mien,
Whose dashing spirit must inspire awe!

XIAODAN: Then what's to be done if we can't find a *da huamian* now?

FUJING: It's easy. I'll just write an announcement and post it on the entrance gate, and sure enough somebody will come for the role. It is just that we should give a name to the juvenile troupe. My child, you are extremely bright: think of a name.

DAN (*thinks*): Since it is a juvenile troupe, I will choose something that means just beginning to grow—how about calling it the Jade Sprouts Troupe?[40]

XIAODAN: What a nice name, Jade Sprouts Troupe!

> This Name will attract some wealth,
> By suggesting It will be active and full of life.
> I only hope each stalk will grow into a bamboo
> Of a secluded and dense forest
> To lure the glorious phoenix in to rest!

FUJING (*writes*): "This house has newly organized the Jade Sprouts Troupe, which has filled every role type except for a *jing*. Should anyone desire to join the troupe, please be so kind as to make a quick reply." Let me go put this up. (*Puts up the poster.*)

DAN: Dad and Mother, since you want me to learn plays, I dare not disobey. However, as long as they are Confucian plays concerning the virtues of loyalty, filial respect, chastity, and righteousness, I will learn them; I absolutely refuse to learn any obscene lyrics and amorous arias that would ruin my sense of honor and cause me to lose my reputation and integrity!

FUJING: That is easy to arrange.

DAN (*aside*): Even so, I do not know what kind of person the one playing the *zhengsheng* roles will be. If by any chance he has a rough and clumsy appearance and a low disposition and cannot make a fit match with me, what should I do?

> (*Coda*)
> Even though it's only Playacting,
> Still I care for cardinal guides and constant virtues.
> What I worry about is That the man is the Jing
> and the female is the Wei.[41]
> When people neglect even nominal standards,
> This may lead to Failure in moral conduct!

FUJING: The fine name of Jade Sprouts we certainly will not change.
XIAODAN: The youthful troupe will outperform their elders.
DAN: Even if she has consummate skill onstage,
Still this is not appropriate for women.

SCENE 4: SPECIAL APPRECIATION

(SHENG *enters with* MO.)

  (Tune: *Lan hua mei*)

MO:
> I called on my friend to go hear "a voice that circles the rafters,"[42]
> Leaving books and zither[43] in my humble room.

SHENG:
> Ever since I heard of this, my ears have burned so long,
> I find it hard to rest in peace while sleeping alone.

TOGETHER:
> Seeing this play will compensate for our deep admiration!

MO: Here we are at the stage already. There is no one onstage yet; I suppose the troupe has not arrived. Let's just stand here beside the road for a little while. When Fallen Angel Liu passes, we will first relish her graceful steps—like tripping across the waves—and then we'll follow her to watch her perform. How does that sound?

SHENG: Just right. Those actresses' charm onstage and their appearance offstage can be markedly different. By standing here, you and I can discern the truth of the matter.

MO: How could the same person have two different kinds of charm?

SHENG: How they manage that is rather hard to understand. That felt rug on the stage[44] makes the most mischief; it can bring humiliation to ugly women while boosting the beauties. Once they step onto that rug, the ugly ones look even uglier, whereas pretty ones look even prettier. If you do not believe me, brother, please see for yourself.

MO: Right you are.

(WAI, XIAOSHENG, JING, *and* CHOU, *each wearing attire of style and color appropriate to his original role type, enter with* XIAODAN *and* DAN.)

  (*Same tune*)

WAI and XIAOSHENG:
> Walking along silently as if we were mute,

JING and CHOU:
> We must, In order to sing beautifully, now give our throats a rest.

(SHENG *gazes at* XIAODAN *and then at* DAN.)

DAN (*bashfully casts amorous glances at him*):
> At Tanlang's glimpse, I feel ashamed![45]

XIAODAN:
> Don't miss your chance to rake in fine rewards!

TOGETHER:
> Soon we will mount the stage, and all will do our best.

(DAN *looks back at* SHENG *and exits along with other actors.*)

MO: What do you think? Wasn't my praise justified?

SHENG: Is the one called Fallen Angel Liu the woman in front?

MO: Correct.

SHENG (*shakes his head*): She is just so-so.

MO: Any woman who looks this good must be considered beautiful. Could there be anyone else more beautiful than she?

SHENG: Yes, yes, yes!

MO: So, where is she?

SHENG: Right before your eyes.

MO: Since she is before our eyes, why don't you point her out for me to have a look at her?

SHENG: That girl walking along behind with the short drooping hair—isn't she just a superlative beauty?[46] How can you not appreciate the world's most priceless treasure and praise someone of ordinary appearance instead?

MO: That is her own daughter, named Fairy, who is learning plays from her. Fairy is good enough looking, to my eye, but she is not necessarily any better than her mother.

(*Same tune*)
> Those who love beauty are always of like mind;

Only you have An eye for discerning treasure of an unusual kind.

SHENG:

To appreciate a different style it takes an insightful friend.[47]

This girl is just like a bright pearl hidden in the womb or a marvelous piece of jade embedded in rough rock just waiting to be carved out. How could a man lacking unique insight even recognize her beauty!

MO:

Even if she were A bud that will bloom like brocade in days to come,
How could she compare with One whose famous beauty is now in fullest flower?![48]

SHENG (*aside*): Not only is this standard generally unknown, but others should not be allowed to know. If it becomes known by others, then the world's treasure would be shared by the world and I could not get her all for myself! I will just go along with him and mention Fairy's weak points, as long as I know the truth in my own heart. This being the case, if I want to get acquainted with her, I will have to get to her before her melon's been cracked.[49] I'll just follow the crowd to see the play, and when the performance is over and they go back, I will tail along behind to find out where she lives. Then I will think of a way to introduce myself to her. What's wrong with that? (*Turns back.*) After all it is you, brother, who are able to tell good from bad. Just now, that girl seemed attractive at first glance, but when I think about her again, there is nothing about her that is worth a second thought. We'd better stop wasting time and go in to watch the play.

(*Same tune*)

One moment at the play is worth a thousand plus in gold;
Let's not waste a minute's time, with merely idle words.

(*A flourish of gongs and drums from backstage announces the performance.*)

MO:
> Hearing this Flourish of gongs and drums really Makes hearts itch.

SHENG (*aside*):
> I am Like the old drunkard who does not delight in wine;[50]
> Instead, Far greater is my pleasure from drumbeats concluding the play.

MO: I take my friend to see a play to relieve his boredom,
Judging women and critiquing songs has boosted his mood.
SHENG: I don't care that throughout the world few have discerning eyes,
When Heaven suddenly presents me with this rare little darling.[51]

SCENE 5: PUNISHING BANDITS

XIAOSHENG (*wearing the three-part beard and an official's hat and belt, leads his attendants onto the stage*):

(Tune: *Po zhenzi*)
My heart is with tall trees and luxuriant grass,
Even as I sit under the black canopy of my official cart.[52]
I sigh to myself that these robes and hat are like fetters and shackles,
In vain made old by anxieties in my heart.
O, when can I lift this burden from my shoulders?
A lonely official at sea, I sigh in my despair,[53]
Though not advanced in years, my sideburns have turned gray.
All heroic goals unfulfilled, I cannot retire from my post,
And face ridicule both at the court and in the mountain forest.[54]

I am Murong Jie, courtesy name Shigong, a native of Xichuan. Since earning the metropolitan examination degree, second grade, I have served successively as historiographer and remonstrator and have been transferred from the capital to fill the post of military defense circuit intendant in Zhangnan.[55]

Talented and unyielding,
I have no worldly desire and can be firm.[56]
A "pedantic scholar"[57] for half my life,
I have often aroused the disapproval of my peers;[58]
A proud official for ten years,
I have weathered many storms in the seas of officialdom.
Even though I value a simple life and despise showy luxury,
The Creator of the Universe has not been benevolent,
Taking away what I value and giving me what I despise instead;

I suffer from social formalities and enjoy the sweetness of solitude,
But unfortunately, I was born out of my time,[59]
Which has brought me suffering aplenty and very little happiness.

I have repeatedly submitted to the Throne my requests to resign but have still not received permission to retire. Today I have returned from troop training in the field, and I am bound for my studio in the *yamen*[60] to eat and drink a bit with my wife. What's wrong with that? (*To the attendants.*) All you court runners may withdraw. Steward, ask my lady to come out.

LAODAN (*leads* JING *onto the stage*):

> (*Same tune*)
>
> The imperial mandate with the honorary title fills me with fear,
> For I, too, am steadfast in my resolve for the Gate of the Deer.[61]
> This time I am confident I can encourage him to retire,
> Even more resolved than when I urged him to accept this post.
> When can we sleep free from anxiety?

LAODAN (*meets her husband*): My lord, surely you must be exhausted from training your troops in the field. How have the might of your army and the strength of your generals grown since you have taken this post? Do tell me all about it. Plum Fragrance,[62] prepare the wine and wait on us.

JING: The wine is ready. (*She brings in the wine.*)

XIAOSHENG: My lady, please have a seat, and hear what I have to say.

> (Tune: *Yu furong*)
>
> The soldiers' might greatly surpasses before,
> The feeble and weak all now healthy and strong.
> The army observes discipline with more rigor,
> And is conversant with clever tactics.

LAODAN: If it is as you've said, the army is much stronger than before. Recently, those bandits in the mountains have not been seen to sneak out. Could it be that they have disbanded?

XIAOSHENG[63] (*shakes his head*):

> They Conceal their schemes and harbor ill intent—
> Dammed up water we must prevent from bursting through a rent.
> To guard against an unexpected uprising,
> We must prepare for every possibility;
> I scorn those mediocre officials, who
> Every time They face danger, lose their lives to hide their incompetence!

LAODAN: My lord, you have experienced all the hardships and difficulties of an official career, and storms on the seas of officialdom are very hard to predict. Since you have such noble aspirations, why don't you decide on a plan soon, instead of merely muddling along? Just think: if at some point you are impeached and convicted, will you still be able to just float away?

> (*Same tune*)
> Do not lose on the very first move:
> Plan your long-term benefit while there's still time.
> Consider that storms like the sea
> Have no bottom and know no bounds.
> To tow us through our peril there's no line,
> Only myriad skiffs to fill our boat with stones.[64]
> Don't be troubled by those ties,
> Ties that give but meager pay;
> You must also bear in mind
> That the stench of an official salary attracts the flies!

XIAOSHENG: How virtuous you are, my lady! I am well aware of all these concerns. It is just that I have repeatedly handed in my resignation, but the Court has not approved it. The day before yesterday, I again went to implore the provincial governor and regional inspector to sign off on my petition for sick leave; with luck, they may approve my request. Just one problem: until those bandits are annihilated, they will eventually cause trouble in this area. As long as I am here, I am still willing to do my duty for the imperial court: I spend all day training troops, developing their combat readiness, and amassing provisions and weapons for them. Even though I have not achieved any merit in battle, I have made the bandits know that we are prepared. I only fear that after I leave this post, those local officials will say that so long as the beacon-fires have not been lighted and the battle drum has not been beaten, then all is at peace. They hardly realize that an unexpected calamity is the greatest calamity. Once it begins, I fear that prayers to the gods of earth and grain[65] will be of little use and that they will be caught unprepared, which will cause this region great suffering! It would be better to take advantage of my presence, so that when the bandits in the mountains do make a move, I can roll out the finest strategies of my life to rid this region of that scourge, and then hang up my official hat and leave. Only then will I have achieved satisfaction both for myself and for the age. However, those insignificant demons, those petty worms, are reluctant to launch their campaign, leaving me no way out!

(*Same tune*)
Burning incense, I silently entreat Heaven
To fulfill my humble wish soon.
I fear that hiding myself and leaving my post
Would be to commit a grave fault.
They'll say, like a Green scholar worried about the test I
throw away my papers,
Or having no capacity for drink, I cleverly avoid the feast.
Tell me How I can explain?
If I want to save both life and name,

I'd better

Eliminate the threat to the state before returning to the fields.[66]

(*Drums beaten backstage.*)

WAI (*enters*): Commander, someone is beating the drum outside and says he has an urgent military dispatch to deliver.

XIAOSHENG: Bring it in.

(WAI *exits and reenters with the dispatch.*)

XIAOSHENG (*reads the dispatch*): Oh! Just as I was hoping to render meritorious service, I didn't expect to see this alarm: the bandits in the mountains are planning a raid. Steward, fetch an arrow of command[67] and pass it to the adjutant. Ask him to call the roll of men and horse, prepare provisions for the march, and wait for my command to dispatch the troops within the hour.

(WAI *responds and exits.*)

XIAOSHENG: My lady, I am now going to roll out the finest strategy of my life.

LAODAN: May I ask what stratagems you will employ, my lord?

XIAOSHENG: I have been planning two stratagems for a long time that I have kept secret. With my first, we will defeat the bandits by a surprise move, killing half of them and leaving the rest to scurry off like frightened rats, before they can plunge the people into an abyss of misery. With the second, we will burn the bandits' nest and smash their den to destroy them root and branch, sparing none of the remaining bandits.

LAODAN: But what are the two stratagems? Please explain, my lord, so that I may also make some trivial comments.

XIAOSHENG: How could I consult a woman about such important matters as using military forces! Moreover, top secrets and important information must not be let out, even to you, my lady. Do not inquire about them.

LAODAN: What you said is right. Thus I will say nothing about other matters, but only that you should avoid massacres when you use military force. Let me offer you a piece of advice, my lord: employ only the former stratagem to protect the region and save lives; with this, you will accumulate some hidden merit in the next world for your good acts. To burn the bandits' nest and smash their den, you will not only take a risk yourself but also cause heavy losses of life; it would be better to leave some leeway instead!

(*Same tune*)

I urge you to treat The garrison land as a field of merit,[68]
Fierce fighting loses out to winning hearts.
Remember the basic truth about using military force—
Subduing the enemy will comes first.
Those commanders,
Only know that Bringing in chopped-off heads adds to
    their record of merits,
And give no thought to the fact that Losing their own heads
    also Costs them their capital.
All depends on your Showing mercy,
So that the people's will with Heavenly laws conforms;
Always keep in mind—
The two words, "treasure life," are still the norm!
When directing troops, all must be planned in advance,
Being fervent on the battlefield leaves you few worries.
It's not that currying favor with your lord you crave,
Tying on your official hat simply to put it away.[69]

SCENE 6: DECIDING ON A PLAN

SHENG (*enters*):

>(Tune: *Po zhenzi*)
>I seek the fairy realm in far Lanqiao,
>There by all means to beg agate nectar.[70]
>How strange that dogs should bark even in the clouds[71]
>But Student Pei could only stay by the side of the road.
>How can I endure this thirst?

Ever since I met Fairy Liu, without my realizing it my soul has flown away. Such an exceptional beauty[72] is not only rare nowadays—I fear that through the ages, few like her have ever been born. I, Tan Chuyu, am a romantic type: How could I be willing just to let her brush past me? That day I tailed her as she was going home and learned where she lives; from her neighbors, I learned that although she is from a family of low status, this girl cherishes lofty aspirations. Learning plays is not her own idea; if she meets me, I have no doubt that she is fit to become my wife. There is just one problem: I have heard that although they want her to learn plays, her parents keep her under sharp supervision—not to maintain her reputation and integrity but simply to protect their investment. Their intention is just to hide her safely away and wait for a good offer.[73] I have also tried by every possible means to find a way to promote myself to her, but I have discovered none. I have only one plan by which to advance my case, yet I think it a low strategy, not something that a scholar should do. They have posted a notice on their gate to recruit a *jing* actor. If I am willing to join the troupe and learn plays together with her, our marriage would be 90 percent certain. However, how could a man like me enter such a trade?

>(Tune: *Jin chan dao*)

> I suddenly realize
> That I am a fool in love
> And cannot care How my reputation and integrity would suffer.
> But the moment that I want to step onto the stage,
> Quite wrongly My infatuated guts churn,
> By Former worthies and ancient sages held back.
> Just about to Repel the demon of love and follow the proper way,
> Weeding the field of my heart to wipe out the sprouts of distress,
> I cannot restrain The horse of my mind when given free rein.[74]
> Slipping its bridle of propriety, it Heads off in another direction.
> This makes me Hardly able to distinguish sage from madman;
> In a flash, different thoughts crowd my mind,
> And I fear that this demon is too much for Buddha to suppress!

Although learning plays is contrary to the Confucian code of ethics, words of true love have been excused by the ancients. Now I have no other choice; if I abandon this route, I think I will never be able to get close to her. If I do go ahead and join the troupe, perhaps even before I have learned plays, I will be able to get my hands on this happy thing. As soon as I get a grip on the situation, I may be able to extricate myself from the troupe without even having to paint my face. I will just pack my things and go there!

> (Tune: *Zhu nü'er*)
> Having just made up my mind, my heart's begun to itch;
> Zither, sword, and bookcase I will temporarily ditch.
> It is not that I Abandon the old and go after the new in too much of a rush;

I fear that If I wait a bit my heart might change again.
My soul now resides
There with her at her side,
Where I will stay even should some demon barrier arise![75]
Bitter orange and brambles are not where the phoenix rests,[76]
Yet he might lose his way when seeking his phoenix mate.
For her beauty, lowering my status I would not resist,
Using as excuse that a worthy penned "The Powerful."[77]

SCENE 7: JOINING THE TROUPE

FUJING (*enters*):

>(Tune: *Shuidi yur*)
>My family's wealth not easy to accrue,
>My wife adds support, and my daughter helps, too.
>I only seek to make my family rich,
>For good reputation I care not a stitch.

I am Liu Wenqing. Lately, I have been organizing a juvenile troupe; now I lack only a *jing* actor. The day before yesterday, I pasted up an announcement, but no one has come forward yet. I have already engaged a famous teacher and arranged for him to start training them today. We cannot afford to wait until all roles are filled; we'll just start with instruction for those recruits we do have. When the *jing* actor arrives, it will not be too late for him to catch up. Ask the youngsters to prepare the three sacrificial meats so that we can hold our opening-day ritual as soon as the teacher and everybody come.[78] (*A response from backstage.*)

SHENG (*enters*):

>(Tune: *Jin jiaoye*)
>My heart in a flurry, feet in a hurry,
>I rush to "warmth and tenderness village" as if I were going home.[79]
>From afar I look for the acting teacher's high walls,
>Yearning more for that place than for the Dragon Gate.[80]

Here I am already; I might as well go straight in. (*Enters.*) Might this be Master Liu?

FUJING: I am. May I know your name, sir? What do you condescend to teach us?

SHENG: I, a humble student, am Tan Chuyu. Hearing that your honorable establishment has recently organized a juvenile troupe yet lacks a *jing* actor, I have come especially to join your troupe.

FUJING (*surprised*): What? You are a scholar, a man of culture, and yet you come to learn plays? From what you say, this is good fortune for our juvenile troupe. Since this is the case, when the rest arrive, you can all start the lessons together.

WAI, MO, JING, and CHOU (*enter together*):

> (Tune: *Shuidi yur*)
> Happily wearing official hats and robes
> Following the master into the classroom we go;
> We can become officials in a flash
> Without having to study by cold window.[81]

(*They greet* FUJING *and bow.*) Who is this?

FUJING: He's our new *jing* actor.

GROUP: If so, then we'll all be studying together. Our welcome to you!

(*Together, they bow with folded hands.*)

May we ask whether you will teach us the plays yourself, or have you engaged someone else?

FUJING: I have no time myself, and so I have engaged a famous teacher, who will be here any time now.

XIAOSHENG (*enters*):

> (Tune: *Rao honglou*)
> I am expert in strings and winds, in singing and in voice;
> All the famous performers have trained within my halls.
> Not one word is ever wrong,
> As thousands all applaud;
> My work would meet even Master Zhou's standards.[82]

FUJING: Ah, you're here, Master. (*To backstage.*) Tell the servants to invite the young mistress to come out and pay her respects to the teacher. And have them fetch the three sacrificial meats so that we can burn our paper invocations to the god Erlang as well.

SHENG: May I ask you, Tutor: What is this god Erlang?

XIAOSHENG: Every school of study has its own patron god. The god Erlang is the patriarch of actors, as is Master Kong of the

Confucian school, Tathagata of the Buddhist school, and Old Lord Li of the Daoist school. This first master of ours possesses infinitely unusual powers and is also extremely stern, unlike the patriarchs of Confucianism, Buddhism, and Daoism who all practice self-restraint and take no notice of their followers' minor transgressions. Whenever one of our students does something dubious, he is sure to detect it; if it is a major issue, disaster will befall that person, and if it is a minor issue, he will fall ill and develop boils. You should all keep this firmly in mind and never violate his prohibitions.

SHENG: Then what must we avoid? I beg you, Tutor, to tell us a bit about them.

XIAOSHENG: The most serious prohibition is that classmates should maintain discipline and not commit blasphemy against the gods: through either the older dallying with the young, or men fooling around with women. These are what he is most concerned about.

SHENG (*aside*): If this is the way it is here, I have again taken the wrong path. But I am here now, and there's no going back. How should I deal with this?

DAN (*enters*):

> (Tune: *Jin jiaoye*)
> The boundaries between women and men—
> From now on all dikes broken, the barriers removed:
> How could I possibly avoid the shame?
> How do I block off men's prying gaze?

FUJING: My child, this is the tutor, and these are your fellow members of the troupe. All of you come over to become acquainted. (*They all greet one another.*)

DAN (*startled to see* SHENG; *aside*): Oh, this is the young scholar I happened to see on the road the day before yesterday. Why did he come here to learn plays? (SHENG *pauses and gives her a meaningful look.*) Oh, now I understand!

FUJING (*to* SHENG): Brother Tan, if you want to join the troupe, you will have to wear our clothes and colors. You'll have to get rid of that scholar's hat.

SHENG: Now I am just learning the plays; I've never acted in one. When the time comes for me to take the stage, it will not be too late for me to change then.

FUJING: That seems reasonable. (*Sacrificial offerings are delivered from backstage.* FUJING *burns paper money and kneels and bows at the head of the troupe.*)

> (Tune: *Zhu yun fei*)
> For defending the rules like metal and boiling,[83]
> Bow to Erlang to show our devout reverence:
> May you assist my pupils in silence,
> And secretly help their cleverness grow.
> Ha!
> May they sing from the first all in tune
> Without need to imitate others;
> May all their stylized movements on stage
> Be performed to meet proper standards;
> May their reputations be known far and wide.

Master, please have a seat, and allow them to pay their respects to you.

XIAOSHENG: Although I am the one who teaches acting, since they all depend on you, the manager, for support and care, you and I should receive their respects together. (*He pulls* FUJING *over, and they stand side by side. All pay their respects to them together.* SHENG *and* DAN *stand side by side, casting glances at each other when they pay their respects.*)

TOGETHER:

> (*Same tune*)
> Formally becoming pupils to the Master,
> We pray that You will be the Erlang present here on Earth:

May you manifest to us your assistance,
And gradually help our cleverness grow.
Ha!
We cannot sing in tune unless we're taught,
And we will imitate most diligently.
We beg you: Of stylized movements on stage,
To perform standard models,[84]
So that our reputations may be known far and wide.

MO: Have the roles been assigned?

FUJING: They have.

XIAOSHENG: Then please distribute the scripts.

FUJING (*distributes the scripts*): For today onward, I will assign their seats, each one will sit in his own place, and you will not be allowed to put your heads together to whisper ear to ear. If anybody breaks the rules, I ask you, Teacher, to punish them.

SHENG and DAN (*both aside*): May Heaven grant that we may sit together!

FUJING: Of all the roles, only *sheng* and *dan* have the major part of each play and frequently need to perform dialogues with each other, so they must sit together. Other roles should take the seat that I assign. (*To* CHOU.) You will play the *zhengsheng* roles and should sit beside my daughter. (FUJING *pulls* CHOU *over to make him sit beside* DAN. *Both* SHENG *and* DAN *look flustered.*)

FUJING (*assigns seats to* WAI, MO, JING, *and* SHENG.): Now that your seats are assigned, I will just go inside. A cup of weak wine has been prepared in the main hall. I entreat you, Teacher, to introduce how to sing a few lines to suit the auspicious day, then please come in right after that.

I've arranged a drink to mark the start of class,
A wine banquet for your taking on my pupils. (*Exits.*)

XIAOSHENG: Everybody follow me and sing a chorus together. (XIAOSHENG *picks a song randomly, and the students tap out the rhythm with chopsticks. After they finish singing, an invitation comes from backstage.*)

XIAOSHENG: All of you enter together, too; everyone must have a drink on this happy occasion.

> Classmates may seem like kin,
> The men and women are not apart like strangers.
> Remember, no distinction between the sexes backstage,
> As God Erlang is always standing guard.[85]

(*They exit together.*)

DAN (*lingers onstage*):[86] I think this scholar not only looks refined and elegant but also deports himself in a calm, unhurried manner. How could he be just someone ordinary? He certainly could not have joined the troupe and be willing to learn plays without reason. That day when we met on the street, he looked at me with great intensity; it must be that he came here today because of me. (*Sighs.*)

> My Tanlang, my darling!
> You know to love me only for the beauty of my youth,
> And do not feel we actors are lowly;
> Wishing for us to study in the same classroom,
> You are willing to act the painted face.

From this, it seems you must be the greatest romantic of all time! How could I turn my back on you? Having a father and mother like mine and having to perform in this kind of profession, I never thought I would be able to rise above this background. Best I should set my mind on him as my lifelong support. What could be wrong with that?

(Pastiche: *Zhu ma qi*)

> (Tune: *Zhu ma ting*)
> We are a pair of phoenixes joined in Heaven.
> Those acts of respect we made today!
> They can be regarded as Secretly tying us together in preparation for our marriage.

> Those people—we can take them as Relatives who help prepare the bride,
> A matchmaker who accompanies the bride,
> And a maidservant who helps the bride bow.
> Oh! Father—if he had not Taken you for his father-in-law in his heart,
> How would he have been willing to Kneel before you for no reason!

Be that as it may, young scholar, since you have a mind to learn plays, you should play the *zhengsheng* role, so that you and I might address each other as husband and wife. Then others would not be able to take advantage of me with words like these. Why must you act the painted face?

> (Tune: *Qi Yan Hui*)
> How will I be able to Often portray Lady Yu in *Thousand Pieces of Gold*,
> And get to Marry "Double Pupils" and let *jing* and *dan* form a pair![87]
> No wonder that most marriages are mismatched;
> Even pairing *sheng* with *dan* on stage can turn out wrong.

SCENE 8: THE BANDITS SET OUT

FUJING (*dressed as the Great King of the Mountain,*[88] *with the face of a tiger and grotesque in shape, leads a gang of villains onto the stage*):
    (Tune: *Xinghua tian*)
        Deep among ten thousand mountains I have made a kingdom,
        My state, you ask?
        It's enveloped in clouds and by mist obscured.
        Defense always ranks first in every battle plan,
        Long ago, I took over this dragon's lair, this phoenix cave.
    I look just like a Heavenly demon, by nature I'm like a bear;
    My prodigious strength to lift mountains few could ever match.
    Say not that dolts like us possess no special skills,
    Apelike arms have always served to draw a mighty bow.
We[89] are the Great King of the Mountain.
    In form monstrously strange,
    By nature truly ferocious,
    Born among tigers and leopards,
    Raised with foxes and wildcats,
    I eat raw flesh[90] and drink blood,
    I'm a modern who's taken up ways of the distant past.
    Pillowing on rocks and sleeping in the clouds,
    A mountain sprite enjoys the good fortune of immortals.
  We had no parents when young and do not know who gave us birth. We only heard our old wet nurse say that before I was born, a very strange man appeared in these remote mountains who not only had the skill to tame tigers and subdue monsters but also regularly had sex with female beasts. Suddenly, one day, she caught sight of a blood-stained child in the thick forest who looked

monstrously strange. We were that child. This old woman knew that We were that strange man's son, given birth by a beast of prey, and that in the future We would turn out to have some good points. So she took me back home with her and raised me. I grew up to have a frame and movements that were similar to those of beasts. Whenever I ran into jackals, wolves, tigers, and leopards, they treated me like close kin; not only did they not harm me, but they regarded me with tenderness. I have heard that a couple of decades ago, there was a simple children's folk rhyme that said:

"When the heart of a beast has a human face,

The world will fall to chaos and waste;

But a human's heart that wears the face of a beast,

Will quickly bring tranquility and peace."

This prophecy will most obviously be fulfilled by my humble self. That is why among the ten thousand mountains I have gathered troops and bought horses, stored up fodder and stashed away grain, and trained my army for over twenty years, and finally the time is ripe. Because We were born in the mountains, We use the word "Mountain" as the name of Our state. Above I follow the will of Heaven, and I comply with the wishes of the people here below; for now I have taken my place as the Great King while making deliberate plans to achieve the honor of Son of Heaven. I have always wanted to rouse my troops and move out of the mountains. But because a circuit official with the compound surname Murong, a master of military strategy, spends all of every day training troops and storing army provisions, even though I do not know their actual situation, the might of my glorious army has been taken away from us by his empty reputation. Lately, I have heard that he is losing interest in being an official and he is anxious to retire. It would be best to take this opportunity and stage an uprising, in order to force this official to resign, and settle his indecision for him. There's just one question: the art of war has always valued the extraordinary. How could I realize my grand aspirations if I relied on only some rank-and-file soldiers? Happily, since We actually belong to the beastly tribe, We've regularly built up several regiments of special forces, all consisting of beasts of prey from the mountains. They will fight in the vanguard—with them killing their way forward, who would I fear could block my way? Generals and field officers, sound the bugle to call up the four regiments of tigers, bears, rhinoceroses, and elephants to lead the way. (*Subordinates respond and blow the bugles.* FUJING *mounts the platform, holding flags of command to signal his orders. Those dressed up as tigers, bears, rhinoceroses, and elephants enter one after another and dance. After each group has danced,* FUJING *waves the flag of command and then they exit.*)

Get the troops in order and move them out here and now. (*Everybody responds.* FUJING *steps down from the platform and leads everyone around the stage.*)

TOGETHER:

    (Tune: *Tuo huan zhao*)
    Hoist up that dragon flag,
    Hoist up that dragon flag!
    Tigers and leopards charge ahead,
    Rhinoceroses and elephants show their might,
    Jackals and wolves snap their jaws,
    While stags and foxes cover the plain.
    They are all our Extraordinary forces that will ensure victory,
    Unlike the might of human soldiers,
    Who can sometimes be timid.
    Our soldiers' pay and provisions, you ask—
    Are mountain vetch and wild bracken;
    And their weapons?
    Bows of peach with willow limbs.[91]

It is dangerous to rattle them.
Do not sigh in resentment.
We advise you To temporarily lend us
Your land of splendid rivers and mountains! (*All exit.*)

XIAOSHENG (*in martial attire at the head of the two generals* WAI *and* MO, *who each lead rank-and-file soldiers onto the stage*):

(Tune: *Xinghua tian*)

The golden goblet[92] should not be allowed to lose the smallest piece,
As a small ulcer can become a huge abscess.
Employing my strategies, I feel certain that we'll win;
Cherishing our land, I guard against any slip.
About to retire from office and leave but going into battle again,
I cannot restrain my fervent desire to win victory.
It isn't that the old official still craves a little action;
After this one success, there will no more for me!

I lead my troops to resist the bandits; traveling day and night, we arrived here, very near to the bandit army. I have heard that the enemy chief is a monster who is extremely quick and fierce and whose vanguard is all ferocious beasts. I figure that the only way to capture the enemy is by strategy, because I think it would be hard to take them by force. Generals, you all come near and hear my instructions. (*All respond.*)

I have heard that the enemy army is limited in number and relies instead on beasts of prey to protect them. If the beast soldiers win the victory, the enemy force will go on a rampage; but if the beasts are wounded and disabled, the enemy will naturally suffer defeat. There is no more excellent way to defeat the beasts than to attack them with fire. I have already had a deep trench dug at the main road, in which land mines and firebombs have been planted; when they trigger the mechanism, the mines will automatically explode. Following the explosions, sparks will fill the sky and cover the plain; exposed to flames, the hairy beasts will catch fire all over. The burns will cause such pain that they will naturally run away. You will lie in ambush at strategic points, and when you hear the sound of the cannon, rouse your troops to pursue and slay them. Once the victory is assured, we will discuss searching the mountains.[93] You must all carry out this plan carefully and not disobey my orders! (*All respond and march.*)

TOGETHER:

> (Tune: *Tuo huan zhao*)
> Set an ingenious trap,
> Set an ingenious trap!
> A clever strategy to subdue the tigers,
> A brilliant route to pursue the deer,
> An ingenious ruse to defeat the dragon,[94]
> They stirred up a fire just to burn themselves.[95]
> We guarantee to make you Shed your hairy garments;
> Stark naked, you'll turn a reddish brown.
> You cannot escape the moat fish's disaster,[96]
> While we can't entertain a guest with a burned head![97]

TOGETHER:

> Throw away long rapiers
> And discard that "Moye" sword.[98]
> Watch us sweep away their demonic aura,
> Without wasting an inch of our steel. (*All exit.*)

(*All the beasts enter together and dance. Suddenly a cannon is fired, and flames shoot up all over the stage. All the beasts flee helter-skelter and exit.*)

FUJING (*leads extras walking anxiously onto the stage*):

> (Tune: *Shuidi yur*)
> Raging flames are hard to block,
> I sigh in resentment as they burn all around.

> Beasts stampede, and horses flee;
>
> Even we wear out our boots in running.

Oh, no, oh, no! His fire attack burned all my beast soldiers to death! Now that I have lost my vanguard, the rest of my troops cannot advance! All I can do is withdraw my troops and retreat. (WAI and MO *lead troops onstage in pursuit and attack them. The bandit troops are defeated and exit.*)

XIAOSHENG: Since the renegade army has suffered a crushing defeat, we should take advantage of our victory to search the mountains. But after repeated battles today, both our horses and men are worn out, and I am afraid there might be mishaps. I remember that before I left, my lady repeatedly urged me to spare lives. We have killed enough today and can leave them some leeway. (*Turns.*) The enemy's force is depleted, and our army's strength is exhausted. Order the generals and field officers to stand down their troops. (*All respond and march off.*)

> (Tune: *Tuo huan zhao*)
>
> Withdraw all our Heavenly troops,
>
> Withdraw all our Heavenly troops!
>
> Extinguish all the beacon-fires,
>
> Store away the signal drums,
>
> The demon star[99] has suddenly disappeared.
>
> Food and drink brought to welcome our army now cover the plain,
>
> As the myriad folk all sing and cheer,
>
> Happily relying on the might of our arms
>
> To protect their lives and work.
>
> Shadows of the sun have moved across to mulberry and thorn bush;[100]
>
> Record the day of victory that brought peace to people and their state!
>
> (*Repeat together*)

Throw away long rapiers
And discard that "Moye" sword.
Watch us sweep away their demonic aura,
Without wasting an inch of our steel.

(*All exit.*)

SCENE 9: DRAFTING A LETTER

SHENG (*enters*):

>(Tune: *Fan busuan*)
>Because I'm obsessed by love,
>I have offended against my scholarly role.
>My precious pearl is thrown away, and the sparrow's hard to hit,[101]
>But in my heart, I have no regrets at all!

All for the sake of Fairy Liu I have not only thrown away examination success, rank, and wealth, but have even put aside my lifelong reputation. I just thought that after joining the troupe, like close kin we would not have to be separated by "inside" from "outside" or to worry about arousing suspicion. Who would have expected that the rules of the green room are different from ordinary families: among this extremely mixed group, there are clearly distinct spaces. Men everywhere can fool around with any actress—unless they are their brothers of the same troupe, in which case there's no fooling around at all! Who could have originated this miserable practice? It is also said that some god named Erlang is on the watch for this kind of business, which is even more ridiculous. Therefore, in this school, there are not only the teacher's restraints and her parents' precautions, but even classmates must all keep an eye on one another. For the past month since I joined the troupe, we have not even exchanged comments about the weather, to say nothing of how hard it would be to do other things. We can rely on only our eyes and eyebrows to express our feelings and to intimate something more. (*Sighs.*) The longing we feel when we meet so often is more difficult to bear than the longing of not seeing each other. This could be the death of me soon!

(Tune: *Yi jiang feng*)
My sickness is hard to cure.
I cannot stand that Our shadows may be close but our bodies far apart;[102]
My eyes cannot satisfy what's in my heart.
It's as if I were salivating over my food.
Even if Just unpolished rice, it would be hard to bear,
Let alone the jade nectar that is she.
I've become emaciated because of her—how could I still endure seeing her?
Before this, my waist was never fat,
And now it's become even thinner.
This is all because My falling in love was an unpardonable sin!

Now I have no choice but to write a secret letter about the great pains I took to join the troupe and my secret wish to propose marriage with her. I'll crumple it into a ball, and then when we are reading scripts and nobody else is watching, I will drop it in her lap. Once she reads the letter, she will naturally make a reply. But there's just one problem: If by any chance someone else picks up the letter, how should I deal with that? (*Thinks.*) I have a way! Although this group of fools can read a few characters, they cannot read proper literary prose. If I use poetic and allusive language in the letter and throw in some uncommon words, it goes without saying that our classmates could not understand it at all. And even if they take it as evidence and deliver it to Miaogu's parents, they won't be able to unravel it either. This will work; it will work! (*Writes.*)

(*Same tune*)
My yearning is recounted
Through an eccentric style
Using profound and poetic diction,

> Just like the graphs on old stone drums,[103]
> Even if They pay a thousand in gold per word,[104]
> They cannot Decipher their deeper intention.

I think that since I have a mind to learn plays, I should naturally study the *zhengsheng* role: in the first place, when smartly dressed, I will still retain some scholarly bearing; second, even if I have not been fated from my previous incarnation to marry her, we can both utilize the plays we act onstage to reveal our inner feelings; I can address her as "wife," and she can call me her "husband." It may not be a bad idea as a way to give some reality to our "spring dreams."[105] It is just hateful that the roles have been assigned and cannot be changed. Now I will write these thoughts into my letter and ask her to intercede with her father for having my role changed to *zhengsheng*. With a little Heavenly luck, he might just assent to my request. (*Writes again.*)

> I ask her to petition[106] her father in haste,
> So that he may consider my transfer,[107]
> Which will be the same as Giving up an empty title[108] to
>   take a higher post!

I have finished writing the letter. I will wad it into a ball and go to the classroom to wait for my chance.

> I crumple my letter into a ball,
> Not only to convey a secret matter,
> But in hope of knotting our hearts as one[109]
> And to hint at my wish for an ultimate union.

SCENE 10: BECOMING LEADING MAN

(WAI, MO, JING, *and* CHOU *enter together*.)

WAI:
    We study no *Poems* or *Documents*;[110] instead, we learn to act,

MO:
    Just because we seek our ease and like some time to play;

JING:
    Who'd have thought we, too, would suffer the teacher's switch,[111]

CHOU:
    And the master's rod[112] would find our heads all day.

WAI: We brothers have been studying scripts for a couple of months, but we're still not able to sing even one or two plays. Who would have thought that the *dan* actress Fairy Liu and the *jing* actor Tan Chuyu would both have extremely good memories and have learned many plays by heart now. We just can't catch up with them—so what can we do?

MO: Yesterday, our teacher said that he was going to give us a test today and everybody must take this seriously.

CHOU: It is all the *jing* and *dan*'s fault; the two of them want to show off how smart they are just to make us look not so good. Fairy is the master's daughter, so we should not give her a hard time, but we should not let Little Tan, that bastard, off the hook. If I don't get a beating today, then that will be that; but if I do, I will surely take it out on Tan.

JING: I could overlook everything else, but what irritates me most is that he wears that scholar's hat to pretend that he's so cultured. If you and I strike together, we'll just tear it off his head.

WAI: The master is about to come out, so we'd better take our seats.

SHENG (*enters*):
    I have tried every possible scheme

To avoid arousing suspicion.

I worry not if the blue simurgh brings no letter[113]

But I only hope the yellow dog fails in its mission.[114]

Greetings, all of you. (WAI and MO *make a proper salute;* JING *and* CHOU *take no notice of him.*)[115]

XIAOSHENG (*enters*):

(Tune: *Sheng cha zi*)

My disciples have no talent,

Merely wasting the teacher's time.

DAN (*enters*):

The role assignments were wrongly made—

You can't blame your students for that.[116]

(*All take their original seats.*)

XIAOSHENG: Bring over all the scripts you have learned. I'll choose a line at random, and then you must recite on through to the end. If you can recite your lines, that will be that; but anyone who does not know their lines will be severely beaten.

SHENG: I have learned ten scripts by heart and sang them all fluently yesterday without one mistake.

DAN: I have also learned ten scripts by heart and sang them all yesterday as well.

XIAOSHENG: Since the two of you have learned many scripts by heart and have committed them all to memory, you need not perform them now. I will just give the others a test.

WAI (*hands over his scripts*): I have learned only two scripts. Although I cannot say I have memorized them well, with an effort I can still sing them.

XIAOSHENG (*reads*): "In wind and dust, it is getting dark in the outskirts": Which script is this line from? What is the name of the tune?

WAI: It is from *Red Whisk*,[117] and the name of the tune is *Jie jie gao*.

XIAOSHENG: Go ahead. (WAI *sings to the tune mentioned.*)

You may go.

MO: I, too, have finished only two scripts. (*Hands over his scripts.*)

XIAOSHENG (*reads*): "The state destroyed, only mountains and rivers remain."

MO: This is from *Washing Silk*,[118] and the name of the tune is *Jiang'er shui*.

XIAOSHENG: Go ahead. (MO *sings to the tune mentioned*.) You may go. (*To* JING.) Bring your scripts here.

JING: I have learned only one script.

XIAOSHENG: Even the worst among the others have two scripts, but you have finished only one. All right, then; bring it here.

JING: I have memorized the script extremely well and so do not need to perform it.

XIAOSHENG: Nonsense! Quick, bring it over.

JING (*flustered*): What'll I do? (*Tugs on* SHENG's *back*.) If I forget my lines, please prompt me.

SHENG: It won't do if the teacher hears me.

JING: I have a way to express my gratitude. (*Points to* CHOU.) Just a few minutes ago, he said this test was all because you want to show off how smart you are and just to make him look bad, and he is going to take it out on you. If you will prompt me, I will help you beat him up; but if you don't, I will help him beat you up.

SHENG: In that case, just relax and perform your lines, and I will just prompt you. (JING *hands over his script*.)

XIAOSHENG (*reads*): "Entrusting the life of the orphan to the care of a subordinate will be written in the classics and histories." (JING *gives* SHENG *a look*.)

SHENG (*in a low voice*): This is from *Golden Pellet*,[119] and the name of the tune is *San xueshi*. (JING *repeats what* SHENG *has said in a loud voice*.)

XIAOSHENG: Then go ahead. (SHENG *sings to the tune mentioned in a low voice, and* JING *follows* SHENG *in a loud voice*.) You may go.

CHOU (*aside*): He got somebody else to prompt him. Can't I do the same? Since Fairy and I sit together, I can only beg her to help me.

(*To* DAN.) Good sister, I beg you to prompt me, and I will buy a handkerchief for you tomorrow.

DAN (*nods with a smile*): All right. (CHOU *hands over his script.*)

XIAOSHENG (*reads*): "Alas, parents pin their hopes on me."[120] (CHOU *gives* DAN *a look.*)

DAN (*aside, laughs*): I am dying to beat this fool to death so that my darling Tan can take his place. Why should I be willing to prompt him? (*Sits up straight and ignores* CHOU.)

XIAOSHENG: Why do you say nothing at all?

CHOU: I know the song thoroughly, but I can't remember the name of the tune.

XIAOSHENG: So dispense with the name of the tune; go on and perform the song. (CHOU *loudly sings the line "Alas, parents pin their hopes on me," and then stops.*)

What is this? I cued you with one line, and you also sang only that line. Can there be an aria that has only seven words?

CHOU: I originally knew the song thoroughly, but because I spoke a couple of words, I've lost the thread.

XIAOSHENG: In that case, I will cue one more line for you: "And teach me to read the writings of the ancient sages." (CHOU *sings the line loudly and stops again.*)

XIAOSHENG (*furious*): Such a fool! A *zhengsheng* who cannot remember a single line of an aria? (*Points to* SHENG.) He is a *huamian*, and yet he is so smart that he may even have memorized your songs! (*To* SHENG.) Do you remember this song?

SHENG: Yes.

XIAOSHENG: So sing it properly, and I will make him feel ashamed. (*To* CHOU.) Kneel down and listen to him sing. (CHOU *kneels, and* SHENG *sings aloud.*)

Good! You remember the song clearly and sing it well. (*To* CHOU.) Having heard him sing, don't you feel ashamed? Now get up and receive my beating. (CHOU *begs for mercy, but* XIAOSHENG *pays no attention and beats him.*) I'll spare you a few whacks for the time being. If you cannot recite your lines again the next time, I will beat you to death. Quick, go sit down and memorize. (CHOU *goes to his seat and makes faces, secretly cursing the* DAN *and then the* SHENG. SHENG *and* DAN *each laugh.*)

    I am going out to see a friend. Each of you must study diligently; do not put your heads together to whisper ear to ear and talk some nonsense.

STUDENTS: Yes, Master.

XIAOSHENG:

> I'd advise you people not to waste your time;
> The god Erlang hovers just above your heads. (*Exits.*)

(CHOU *leaves his seat, goes over to* JING, *and whispers in his ear.*)

JING: Let me think it over, and I'll let you know. (*Aside.*) He wants to beat Young Tan and has asked me to help him. But since Young Tan prompted me, how can I beat him? All right, I will just back him up with a few curses, but when they come to blows, I will actually help Young Tan and beat him up good. Wouldn't that be fair to both? This will work; this will work! (*He turns back and whispers to* CHOU. CHOU *is overjoyed.*)

CHOU (*to* SHENG): Young Tan, please come over here; I want to talk with you.

SHENG (*leaves his seat*): What do you want to talk about?

CHOU: You learn your plays and I learn mine, but why did you show off how smart you are in front of the master? I wound up getting a beating!

SHENG: The master instructed me to sing. What did that have to do with me!

JING: When the master told you to sing, you could have just said that you did not remember and that would have been enough. Why did you have to start singing the aria? It was your fault. (*He makes a gesture toward* SHENG, *and* SHENG *understands.*)

CHOU: Since you're learning plays, naturally you should wear a cap like ours. Why do you carry that tortoiseshell on your head? (*Hits* SHENG *on the head with a fan*) I bet you think you're better than us just because you can read a little? (*He stretches out to pull* SHENG'S *hat;* SHENG *dodges.*)

CHOU (*to the group*): This is a public nuisance that I'm taking action against; quick, brothers, join my righteous army!

JING: Right! Come on, everyone, thump his dog's head! (CHOU *grapples with* SHENG; WAI *and* MO *try to dissuade* CHOU; CHOU *does not respond.* SHENG *seizes* CHOU *and pushes him down to the ground.* JING *curses* SHENG *yet beats* CHOU.)

DAN (*aside*): I will pretend to stop them from fighting one another. First, this is in order to hold my darling Tan's hand so that I might have at least a little skin and flesh contact with him; and second, to help him by hitting that guy several times to vent my anger on his behalf! (*Squeezes* SHENG'S *hand, and they flirt with each other, while at the same time telling* JING *to beat him severely.*)

WAI: They do not stop when I ask them to. Let me go out and imitate our master's voice and shout at them a few times. That should scare them apart. (*Secretly moves to the back of the stage and coughs.*) Which of you animals are making such a racket inside? Quick, open the door and let me in.

MO: The master is coming! Let go at once! (SHENG, DAN, JING, *and* CHOU *disperse, startled; each goes to his seat and reads scripts.*)

WAI (*pretends to be the teacher, swaggers in*): Who made that racket just now? All of you kneel down here. (SHENG, DAN, CHOU, *and* JING *see* WAI; *all laugh.*)

MO: The teacher really will be coming. Let's do some reading. (*Each reads scripts.*)

DAN (*aside*): Just now while I was pretending to stop them from fighting, my darling Tan handed me something. I do not know what it is, so let me take a look. (*Looks.*) It turns out to be wadded up paper.

There must be something written on it. (*Opens the ball and reads, nodding.*) So this is what it is. Now I want to write a reply but have no way to pass it to him. What shall I do? (*Thinks.*) I know what to do! This bunch of fools are pretty stupid. I will write my reply to him into an aria and sing it out loud for him to hear. They will just think I am reading a script—how could they figure it out? This will work; this will work! (*Turns back in her seat and reads the script.*) These two songs seem interesting. I'll just sing them through.

(Tune: *Jin luosuo*)
The meaning in your missive is too abstruse,
But I know it's a precaution against the miscreants.
We are both like A lock and key that match each other—
What riddle could be so difficult to solve?
My heart has long been thine,
Secretly I wait for you;
Fear not that Heaven or man will thwart our plan.
All for me, you Needlessly ignore your ambitions, becoming wan and withered,
You have suffered unfair treatment to the full.
This makes it Hard for me to resolve—
Would that I could Fly to you on simurgh wings![121]
But my Pinions are all too weak,
And the way ahead remains obscure.
I will just have to Quietly wait until wind and clouds converge.[122]

(*Same tune*)
To let him be exchanged for thee
Would fulfill my heartfelt hope.
I want to persuade my father,
And yet fear arousing his suspicions.
I Have mulled it over and conceived a brilliant scheme
I wish to tell you:

> The stratagem
>
> For Our being together
>
> Lies in your leaving.
>
> Among this Flock of raptors none has a clear call;
>
> They rely solely on you, A single crane crying in the marsh, to shake a mighty city;[123]
>
> You must deliberately Abandon your fellows;
>
> Just say that Men of noble character disdain to engage the lowly.
>
> If You decline this post
>
> And cast aside all its files,
>
> Surely you will Ascend to a position worthy of your stature!

SHENG (*aside; is happy*): Such an intelligent girl who would think to intone her letter of reply aloud, in front of everyone! Only I could understand her; those foolish worms did not understand a bit of it. From this, it appears that she is even more intelligent than I! Her first aria was her acceptance of my marriage proposal; the second told me how to change my role from *jing* to *sheng*. She says that in this class, I'm the only good one and all the rest are useless. She asks me to say directly to her father that I am unwilling to play the *jing* and want to take leave of him and go home; without a doubt, he will keep me on as the *sheng*. This turns out to be an excellent plan! When the master comes back, I will put it into action.

XIAOSHENG (*enters*):
> From calling on a theater friend,
>
> I return to teach my theater pupils.
>
> Everything I do is theater—
>
> Only making money is for real.

Have you all finished with your homework?

STUDENTS: Yes.

XIAOSHENG: Then, it's getting dark; you may all go home. (WAI, MO, JING, CHOU, *and* DAN *exit*.)

Why haven't you gone?

SHENG: I have something to say, and that's why I have not gone. I entreat you to call the manager to come out. (XIAOSHENG *calls*.)

FUJING (*enters*):
>When the private tutor's cry is urgent,
>
>The manager's gloom is deep.
>
>If he's not pressing for holiday gifts,
>
>Then he's demanding to be paid for his keep.

Master, what instruction do you have for me?

XIAOSHENG: This student has something to say and requested you to come out.

SHENG: I salute you upon taking my leave, Master, and sincerely thank you, Manager. Tomorrow I will leave for home.

FUJING: Just when you have learned various plays and are ready to earn a living with them, why do you want to go back home?

SHENG: As a scholar, I should be reviewing the *Poetry* and the *Documents* in preparation for my advancement. Learning to act is just not for me!

XIAOSHENG: If that is so, why did you join the troupe in the first place?

SHENG: When I first came, I thought that I would play only major *jing* roles; if I weren't playing Guan Yu, then it would be the hegemon-king of Chu.[124] Even though my face would be daubed with paint, I could still show my true heroic qualities in impassioned and violent scenes. Who would have thought that out of every ten plays, there would be only one or two where I played the moral gentleman, and in all the rest I'd just play some petty character who has no dignity at all. How could a man play that sort of role?

>(Tune: *San huan tou*)
>
>All day long I bear the shame, the embarrassment,
>
>Of portraying Slave girls and maidservants;
>
>Even if sometimes I wear an official's hat and belt,

I do nothing more than Bring credit to some crafty sycophant.
I do not Fail in morals or in my acts;
Without rhyme or reason, my fine visage
Must suddenly change to one twisted with anger!
How could it be that I am especially given the flower-face roles[125]
Just because I have a lotus-like face.

TOGETHER:
This Fine name[126]
Could easily be turned over to that Scholar who's been lazy in his studies!

XIAOSHENG: If you don't want to play a *huamian*, why didn't you just say so openly? Why must you go away?

FUJING: If this is the way you feel, just choose any role you'd like to play. The *zhengdan* is reserved for my daughter,[127] which cannot be changed. So pick a role from *laodan* or *tiedan*.

SHENG: How could a man with whiskers and eyebrows maintain his stalwart manliness when playing a role with his hair up as a woman?

FUJING: So then, pick a role from *wai* or *mo*.

SHENG: Doesn't a young man lose his dashing spirit by playing a white-bearded old man?

XIAOSHENG: Well, if this is the way it is, why don't you act the *xiaosheng*.

SHENG: I could put up with this role, but for one question: the *xiaosheng* in a play either relies on others for his own success or assists others in achieving fame for themselves. He is never seen establishing a name for himself through his own efforts, which also does not seem like the role for me.

XIAOSHENG: When he speaks of it this way, clearly what he wants is to be a *zhengsheng*. I think in voice and figure he actually does have the makings of a *sheng*; it would be best to let him do as he wishes.

FUJING: Of all the roles, the *sheng* and *dan* have the most onerous work because they are onstage most of the time and offstage the least. There's not a one of the major arias that they don't sing. I'm just worried that a scholar like you could never bear such hard toil.

SHENG:
>Without painful effort to practice an art,
>Who ever gains wealth in this world?

If your daughter can endure the work, so can I; if there are hardships, she and I will just share them; if it's good fortune, we'll enjoy it together.

>(*Same tune*)
>Like body and image, outside and in,
>Joyous together though both overworked.
>When did you ever see The fish work when the water rests
>As the two roles sing their arias? (*Aside.*)
>I Envy him and yet Laugh at him:
>You should choose a good match for your beautiful daughter
>But I'm embarrassed to play Wen Qiao.[128]
>How could it be that I, With a face like a lotus flower,
>Would be matched to a freckle-faced wife?[129]

FUJING: Since this is the way it is, you will exchange roles with the *sheng* actor. You will play the *zhengsheng*, and he will play the *huamian*. Nothing more needs to be said about it.

>(Tune: *Dong Ou ling*)
>Do not shake out your sleeves and leave;
>Do not knit your brows.
>Changing *jing* to *sheng*, we comply with your demands;
>You and he Will trade onerous and simple roles, and
>Neither will have regrets.

> This troupe of mine Entirely relies on you to bring credit to us all;
>
> From now on The flies are not afraid of losing their way,
> As the tail of a thoroughbred takes all along.[130]

SHENG: Since this is the way it is, I can only force myself to stay. To be frank, when I first joined the troupe, it was in pretense; but now what was said in pretense will be fulfilled in earnest.

> (*Same tune*)
> My hiding like a phoenix,
> Perching like a simurgh,
> Amid thorn trees[131] will appear something rare.
> I have only one concern: As a scholar, I act only scholarly plays.
> As a clear break from theater ways.
> Henceforth I will act only as I wish;
> If you object, to my home I'll repair.

XIAOSHENG:

> (Tune: *Liu po mao*)
> A humble Teacher yields to the brilliant student,
> And must fulfill your every future wish.
> I allow you To perform stunts and play in special roles;
> As long as my Salary as teacher does not decrease,
> I might as well Receive instruction from my pupil!

SHENG: There is another thing to mention: Who does not know Tan Chuyu's reputation? Who does not recognize Tan Chuyu's face? Today I have joined the troupe to act in plays all because of my poverty, just as the chief minister of Chu played the bamboo flute and Han Xin begged for food.[132] Moreover, since time immemorial there have been worthy men who hid among actors, and spectators will naturally excuse me. This student's hat must stay on my head to retain a gleam of my scholar's dignity, because this must not be removed.

(*Same tune*)

For now, I'll leave off my black scholar's robe,

Leaving only this Chu captive's hat stuck on my head,[133]

To foretell my eventual official's black hat.[134]

On my body, I have no restrictions,

But with My head I preserve my righteous name.

FUJING: We have complied with every wish of yours—why mind this one? We will simply let you do as you like.

In the past, a *sheng* actor could be demoted to a *jing*,

But today, this *jing* is promoted to a *sheng*.

If we want to use the stage to satirize officialdom,

We can't restrict talent with regulations.

SCENE 11: THE FOX'S MIGHT[135]

JING (*wearing scholar's hat and robe, enters, leading* MO):
>(Tune: *Lihuar*)
>As a rich man, my mighty name dominates the region;
>My belly's so big it seems swollen.
>Without reading *Poetry* or *Documents* I still became an official,
>Ha! It's by wealth that I got the position.

I am none other than the number-one rich man and retired official in the market town of —— Wharf, and I am known as Qian Wanguan [Moneybags Qian].[136]
>My gold and silver pile up high as mountains;
>I store grain and rice until they are as stale as dirt.
>From my lush fields spread all across the land,
>From north, south, east, and west come more cash and cereals than I can take.
>I've lent capital and goods to people everywhere,
>In spring, summer, autumn, and winter flows in more interest than I can count.
>I employ strong-arm lackeys;
>I send out ruthless goons;
>It's not just that my greed could know no end,
>But that old saying really got it right—
>"Do not laugh if I'm bad at drawing tigers;
>Adding 'fangs and claws' can still give you a fright."[137]
>I've married beautiful concubines;
>I house seductive maids.
>I know this puts a drain on my vital energy,
>But I remember a story from the *Mencius*—

> The man from Qi who begged for food put up a good face for his family,
> So how can a rich man not lord it over wife and concubines?[138]

But that's just a minor matter. It has been said since ancient times: "Great wealth gives birth to official positions." Even if you have *juren* or *jinshi* degrees,[139] you still have to go to a bit of expense; the shops that make black gauze hats never give them away for free. I have also heard that it is certainly dangerous to hold a high government post, so that's not as good as my separate path of advancement: I'll never be a very high official, but you have never seen a memorial to the emperor specially impeaching a local functionary[140] for scraping the fat off the land. When you get right down to it, it is not bad at all to be a great rich man and still just a petty country gentleman. How could you keep me from sticking out my belly and swaggering around to toot my own horn? (*Laughs.*) Once I, Moneybags Qian, had bought an official rank with a contribution of grain, I chose an extremely rich and populous place, became its assistant magistrate for one term, and amassed myself a huge pile of silver.[141] In less than three years, I resolutely retired at the height of my official career, asked for a lifelong leave, and hastily came home in silken robes.[142] Now every time I pay a visit to the county magistrate, I use a card that calls myself his subordinate,[143] and he generally also comes to pay a return visit. When my tenants and debtors see this, they are so frightened that their hair stands on end; even if they owe me no more than a pint or a gill, a mace or a penny,[144] I will send him a note about it. So who would dare not to come and pay up? To sum up, I live well, thanks to nothing but to living in a good place, which is not in the city but in the country. If I still lived in the city where there are lots of provincial and metropolitan graduates, how could common people there think anything of the official rank I got through back channels? But there is a drawback to living in the country: those local "grandpas" and "moms and dads"[145] are unwilling to come out to the countryside without some good reason, so I get to show off my tiger's might only once or twice a year. My black gauze hat and round collar[146] are getting old on the shelf. Today I have heard that the assistant county magistrate will make an inspection tour of every village, organizing and inspecting the neighborhood-watch system.[147] As soon as he gets to this place, he will have to pay me a visit, and the locals preparing a banquet for him will have to ask me to keep him company. This power and prestige can be useful. Boy, take this opportunity to bring all the land rent accounts up to date, make a list of those behind in payment and hand it over to the assistant county magistrate, and entreat him to press them for repayment in person.[148]

MO: Yes, sir.

JING:

> (Tune: *Sibian jing*)
> I quickly seize this chance all my debtors to press,
> Unwilling to forgo either penny or mill.
> At my word, they could all face arrest—
> So who would dare resist?!

MO:

> Let them be eloquent as they can,
> Surely they'll lose all courage.
> They'll sell off property, their wives and the kids
> Just to pay off all their old accounts!

WAI, FUJING, and LAODAN (*enter together*):

> The magistrate's aide suddenly visits
> To check on our ten-household units.
> Although he is following past routines,
> He just wants to line his own pockets. (*Greet* JING.)

JING: Who are you people? What business brings you here?

ALL: We are the heads of hundred-household neighborhoods. We are here just because the county's Third Lordship is coming to check up on our neighborhood-watch system.[149] This is an old practice from former years, intended to obtain some customary gratuities, which we will have to come up with. Now all the money has been collected, but if we give it to him, he may think it falls far short and may not accept it. We ask Master Qian to send out your visiting card and then deliver the money to him; we feel this would add some face to it. Whenever officials come to the countryside, there is always a welcome banquet, which we have also prepared; we invite Master Qian to the banquet to keep company with the guest of honor. If we have been lacking in any way and the official starts to take account of it, we ask Master Qian to put in a good word and smooth things over for us.

JING: I have never agreed to send out my card rashly. Moreover, I am ill and unable to help entertain the official drinking wine. Go ask somebody else to do it.

ALL: You are the only gentry man in our little market town. Where is there anyone else?

JING: Just do it yourselves; there is no need for any gentry.

ALL (*smile*): Master Qian is making fun of us again. We are just common people; how would we dare use a visiting card? How would we dare keep the official company at the banquet?

JING: Heh! So there is some distance between the two words "officials" and "the people"? If that is the way it is, why on ordinary days are you so huffy and puffy as to take no notice of me?

ALL: We definitely dare not take liberties; we have the utmost respect for you, Master Qian!

MO: Sir, these people are either tenants or debtors; they all have accounts that have never been cleared.

JING: What? If you have such respect for me, why are you unwilling to pay me what you owe me? Now I was just about to make a list and hand it over to the official, to ask him to collect in person. I wish I could break your damned backs, and you still expect me to poke my nose into matters that don't concern me?

(*Same tune*)

Look at you A litter of piglets growing so nice and fat,[150]
In good shape to feel the magistrate's staff.
After a beating you'll pay me back;
Don't imagine that I would let you off free.

ALL: There is no need to hand us over to the official; we will just pay you back, for certain!

We hope you will Be free with your vast generosity:
Of course, we will clear our accounts.
Even though we've neither silver nor cash,
We'll mortgage our wives and our children.

JING: If this is the way it is, for the sake of the county I will keep up appearances for you. Leave all the silver you've collected here, and I will deliver it for you. Make certain the banquet for the assistant magistrate is proper; I do not feel like going out to attend your banquet, so bring it here too. Even if the local arrangements are inappropriate in some way, I will put in a good word for you; only be a little more sensible hereafter. You people, to say nothing of other uncouth behavior, even your forms of address are not in fashion. Can it be that the two characters, "Master Qian," are stuck together like glue and lacquer? Can't a word be simply added to "Master Qian"?

ALL: We have been thoughtless. From now on, we will just add a word and call you "Venerable Master Qian."

JING: In that case, call me that a few times more to make up the previous number. (ALL *call out repeatedly;* JING *answers each time.*) This is just the right thing to do. Have you said all you wanted to say? Now I feel tired and want to go in and take a nap. Those who have any business should present a memorial to me; if no one does, you may withdraw.[151]

ALL: There is yet another important matter to report to Venerable Master Qian: Lord Yan, the Pacifier-of-Waves, is the guardian god of this area.[152] This deity is extremely efficacious; the third day of the tenth lunar month every year is his birthday, and we must present a play as a gift. May we ask Venerable Master Qian, which troupe of actors should we hire?

JING: In former years, the plays were all put on by the Dancing Rainbow Troupe; furthermore, the actress Fallen Angel Liu and I have an affection for each other. I will just send someone to make the arrangements.

ALL (*respond*):
> Till now we've never known retired officials to be good,
> Now we finally realize the rich should be revered! (*Exit together.*)

JING (*laughs*): Wonderful, wonderful! If I, Moneybags Qian, didn't use my power and influence to intimidate villagers, what else would I use it for? Tomorrow when the assistant magistrate arrives, I will use their silver and their banquet to add to my own stature and might. This is excellent! But there is another thing: A business deal brought right to the door must not be let slip; when they bring the silver here, I will take half and give only the other half to the official. I just take a tiny little cut myself before finding an excuse.

> (Tune: *Da ya gu*)
> These are not Formal grain levies for taxes;
> It's a private gift given straight from the people—
> Why not let a bit stick to my fingers?
> This Practice I did not make up,
> It's quite common at the magistrate's court—
> A handling fee's no bribe if all share alike.

Boy! (MO *responds.*)

Find out where the actors of the Dancing Rainbow Troupe are performing so that I can send someone to go invite them over.

MO: Sir, the Dancing Rainbow Troupe is good, but the Jade Sprouts Troupe is even better known, and recently the local operas have all been put on by them.

JING: I want to use this as a pretext to talk with Fallen Angel about our former affection, not merely for the play. How could you know that?

MO: The Jade Sprouts Troupe also has a leading lady who is none other than Fallen Angel's daughter, called Fairy. She is even better looking than her mother. Moreover, in order to look after her daughter, Fallen Angel has recently left the adult troupe and joined the juvenile troupe as well.

(*Same tune*)
The girl's charm surpasses her mother's;
She is so naturally lovely
That she uses no makeup at all.
Onstage, she makes men's hearts pound wildly;
In addition, Though so sweet she stirs up their longing,
Not one glutton has yet had a taste.

JING: Right. She does have an extremely beautiful daughter; I saw her in the past. Now she has come out to act onstage? In that case, go quickly and book the troupe, and I will ask her mother to act as go-between so that I may also have a little get-together with her. What's not wonderful about that!

MO: I have heard of sisters who married one husband
But not mother, then child on the side.

JING: The husband is none other than daddy
And he serves both as father and as grooms.

SCENE 12: LUXURIANT ESCAPE

XIAOSHENG (*wearing official hat and belt, leads* MO *onstage*):
>The imperial mandate arrived that approves my resignation,
>Having rendered outstanding service I happily live at ease.
>Good sir, mention not any of my successes, please:
>I fear most a proclamation of imperial favor!

I, Murong Jie, resisted the rebels by a surprise move the day before yesterday and won victory by good fortune. I am also happy that the royal court had granted my petition for sick leave even before I dispatched the troops, which allows me to return to my hometown and to nurse my health. I think it is fortunate that this decree had been issued before the news of victory arrived; if His Majesty had seen the report and learned of these merits and achievements, he would have urged me to stay on without any leave—how would he agree to release me to return to my native place? Now if I do not leave very soon, I fear that another decree will be issued and I will be unable to get away. Servant, be quick and ask Madam to come discuss setting out. (MO *responds; invites her.*)

LAODAN (*leads* CHOU *onstage*):
>The day a husband succeeds
>Is the day wife and children are emboldened.
>Those two things are not worth celebrating;
>My greatest joy is that he resigns from his post.

My lord, as the imperial edict has already been issued, you should hasten to extricate yourself; why should you still hesitate or wait and see? Surely you are unafraid after enduring ten years of hardship? Are you waiting for yet more hardships to bear?

XIAOSHENG: My lady, it is not that I hesitate or wait and see. It is only because I have set my mind on resignation and must make it final;

I will not resign my official post and still leave some ties unbroken. When I go back to wearing my rush rain cape and bamboo hat,[153] that black gauze hat and round collar will also start to contend for a seat, which will make it impossible for me.

LAODAN: In that case, what do you think you should do?

XIAOSHENG: In my opinion, when His Majesty has seen the report of victory, he will definitely reinstate me. If I go back to my native place, how can the "grandpas, moms, and dads" there let me off? They will definitely urge me to set off for my post. It would be better to abandon the old home and sail away in a tiny boat[154] to follow the wind and go with the current wherever they might take us. When we arrive at some remote mountain location along a meandering river, we can build a thatched cottage with several rooms and live there. We'll enjoy the wind in the pines and the moon through wisteria while eating pulse leaves[155] and wild rice soup to live out our lives. Won't that be wonderful?

LAODAN (*smiles*): This is precisely the way it should be! From that point of view, we do not even have to arrange outfits for our return; we'll take only a few sets of everyday clothes with us, that's all.

XIAOSHENG: Exactly. Servant, come: first draw ten taels of silver and go some distance away and wait for us; buy a small fishing boat and prepare a rush cape and a bamboo hat. I will put them on the moment I get there.

MO: I understand.

XIAOSHENG: Quick, go out and hurry the conscripted laborers and drivers to come in. (MO *responds, exits. A group costumed as various servants and laborers enters.* XIAOSHENG, LAODAN, *and* CHOU *get on; horses and carriage move along.*)

> (Tune: *Northern Xin shui ling*)
> It is not that I Use the whip and depart too hastily;
> I am impatient to abandon
> This Black gauze hat—the root of disasters.

> I, who Have worn it out, complain of hardship;
> Those who Have not might still long for it.
> Now I will throw off these chains and these fetters,
> Still worried they Won't let me off and will hasten in pursuit.

(*A loud cry from backstage*): Gentry and common people must retain His Honor in his post much longer! We've already submitted a petition to the magistrate, and the magistrate is about to present a memorial to the Throne to request it, so we urge you, Your Honor, not to leave!

XIAOSHENG: Even hearing the word "retain" gives me a headache! You tell him: retaining officials has always been merely a formality; those who want to stay will stay, while those who want to leave will leave. Many thanks for their kind intentions. (ALL *pass it on.*)

(*From backstage*): In that case, please stop the men and horses, and wait for local elders to take off His Honor's boots.[156]

XIAOSHENG: Taking off the boots has always been a bad convention, and it is unnecessary. Moreover, if I am gone and my boots stay, I am afraid that taking leave and yet leaving loose ends becomes a portent of reinstatement in my former office, which is not a good omen. You tell them: I appreciate their kindness, but they do not need to do that. (ALL *pass it on.*)

Hurry up and get on with this journey!

ALL [servants and conscripted laborers]:

> (Tune: *Southern Bubu jiao*)
> Taking True feelings and deep wishes all as False pretense,
> You refuse them without exception.
> You think Leaving your boots behind is an ill omen—
> But how many Officials want to come back,
> When the common people wish otherwise!
> You fiercely resist all grandeur
> And do not allow it To embellish the journey.

MO (*enters, rowing a boat*): Your Honor, your small boat is ready.

ALL: This boat is too small, not at all like those that officials take. Your Honor, up ahead there's a government boat just waiting for you.

XIAOSHENG: A government boat is too large for me, not like the one I will use as an official who is leaving his post. This small boat is just what I need. You all go home. (ALL *respond and exit.*)

 Fetch the rush cape and the bamboo hat for me to put on.

LAODAN: I will also change into a plain raw-silk blouse and cotton skirt, and only then will I be dressed like a fisherman's wife. (*They each change clothes.*)

XIAOSHENG (*to* MO): Now I will change your title; you will not be called "house servant" anymore; instead, you will be called "fisherman's boy." Boy, hurry up and shove off. (MO *sets sail and sculls with* CHOU.)

 My lady, I have no more use for this black gauze hat now. Let me compose an elegy, hold a memorial service for it, and then commit it to the flowing stream. (*Holds the black gauze hat in his hand, looking at it while singing.*)

  (Tune: *Northern Zhegui ling*)

  I hold a memorial service for my black gauze hat but have no wine,

  Relying only on A few words of empty talk

  To replace Jade wine in a golden goblet.

  Many thanks for Adorning my rank and dressing me with glory,

  While expelling my poverty and lowly status;

  However, you have also Brewed me hardship and made me busy.

  I have never Relied on your might to appropriate some Yellow gold and bright silver ingots.

  I have failed to live up to your Two spread wings,[157] which seem Bared fangs and brandished claws.

Today, it is not that I am Perfidious or ungrateful,
Requiting kindness with resentment;
It's only that your Very nature brings wind and waves;[158]
For this reason, I Let you drift away, entrusting you to the Infinite!

LAODAN: Now that your black gauze hat has been committed to the east-flowing river,[159] this phoenix coronet[160] of mine should also go along with yours and keep it company. I, too, will say a few words at parting. (*Holding the phoenix coronet in her hand, she sings while looking at it.*)

(Tune: *Southern Jiang'er shui*)
I have already allied myself with gulls[161] and egrets;
Now it's hard to bear a phoenix coronet on my head.
How many women have Flicked the dust off their own hats[162] and Longed to put you on;
How many lazy ones Put aside their looms and wish you would be granted them;
How many caught in Downpours cannot wait for you to rescue them!
It is not that I Did not have the good fortune to enjoy you;
It is only because I worry about disaster and guard against danger:
Holding on to you is not as good as abandoning you.

XIAOSHENG: Go get the fishing rod and let me try my luck. (MO *hands him the fishing rod.*)
Heaven, if I, Murong Jie, am guaranteed exemption from honor or disgrace and can live out my life as a fisherman, let me catch a fish as soon as I drop in a hook. (*Drops in the fishing line.*)

MO (*to* CHOU): Here's the fishing net[163] I bought; let's cast it out.

CHOU (*helps* MO *spread the fishing net*): Heaven, as man and wife we have not had any children yet. If we can still have offspring, let us be blessed with a fish as soon as we cast the net. (*Cast the net.*)

XIAOSHENG (*lifts the fishing line and gets a fish*): Ah! As expected, I have caught one!
LAODAN (*takes out the fish and looks at it*): It turns out to be a perch. In the past, a man longed for watershield and perch[164] and became a hermit; the perch is an omen of living in seclusion. So it would seem that you and I will live peaceful and carefree lives.
MO (*lifts the fishing net and is delighted*): Ah! I've caught one, too.
CHOU (*takes it out and looks at it*): It's a soft-shelled turtle.
MO: There was no fish, but instead we got a soft-shelled turtle. This omen is not good enough.
CHOU: No, this is a very good omen, but you don't know how to interpret it. This predicts bearing a son, don't you know?
MO: How so?
CHOU: The Lord of Heaven instructs us by saying that if you want to bear a son, you have to put the turtle in the proper place.[165] If you don't know how to put the turtle in the proper place, how could you produce a son!
XIAOSHENG: Boy, let the boat come alongside the bank and go purchase a jug of wine for me and my wife to enjoy with this perch.
MO (*lets the boat come alongside the shore and says to* CHOU): While you cook the fish, get the turtle ready, too, and I'll buy another jug of wine for us to enjoy with it. (*Gets jugs and exits.*)
LAODAN: My lord, now that you have abandoned your post and fled from your reputation, you should choose another name so that you have an answer if someone asks you who you are.
XIAOSHENG: It has always been the case that really outstanding people not only do not reveal their proper names, but don't even have pennames; this is why so many books are attributed to anonymous authors. Now I will just take away a few strokes from the bottom of the character Mu 慕 to change my surname to Mo 莫. So if someone inquires, just call me "Old Fisherman Mo."[166]

LAODAN: What you say is right. Since this is how it is, even my form of address should be corrected, and from now on, you must not call me "my lady" any more.

XIAOSHENG: I'll just call you "wife."

MO (*enters with wine*):

>Rustic wine is really rich,
>
>The perch particularly fresh.

Here comes the wine; it was already warm and does not need to be heated.

LAODAN: So bring in the fish. (CHOU *brings the fish and pours wine*; XIAOSHENG *and* LAODAN *take seats on the ground and drink.*)

XIAOSHENG: There's a favorable wind now. Boy, raise the sail. (MO *raises the sail.*)

LAODAN (*to* CHOU): Just leave the wine here, and we will pour it ourselves when we need it. You, husband and wife, go have a drink yourselves. (MO *and* CHOU *sit in a different place and drink.*)

XIAOSHENG: Wife, you and I have become two immortals starting from today.

LAODAN: Exactly.

XIAOSHENG:

>(Tune: *Northern Yan'er luo* with *Desheng ling*)
>
>It is not that I become An immortal to glorify myself;
>
>It's only that leaving The sea of bitterness relieves my mind for the first time.
>
>If I had not suddenly Opened my heart and freely lifted the cup,
>
>How could I have felt Yesterday's cares have left my mind free tonight!
>
>This wine Enters my throat and falls into my stomach,
>
>Unlike what I had Chewed on before but was so hard to swallow.
>
>In the past, Sorrows that could not be dispelled

Fermented into greater sorrows;

But today, without Drinking even three cups I have forgotten all of that.

I boast

That such good fortune cannot be measured;

Now reckless,

I might even serve as a Minister in Yelang![167]

LAODAN: My lord, have a few more cups to drink.

(Tune: *Southern Jiao jiao ling*)

Tonight you have no documents to sign;

Tomorrow you will hear no case in court.

I urge you, sir, to regain your former ability to drink—

So that I can also drink myself drunk with you!

MO (*acting drunk, rises*): Good wine, good wine! Now I must not drink anymore, because I am afraid someone will be reporting matters from outside. I will just go stand by the box for bills of complaint for a little while.

CHOU: This is a boat, not the *yamen*. Stop your drunken talk. (MO *is about to fall over;* CHOU *holds him up.*)

LAODAN: He never drank much in the past; why has he gotten so dead drunk today?

CHOU: When he was at court, he was constantly on the lookout for official reports and was continually listening for the sounding block alerts. Official matters were always on his mind, so he dared not drink. Today, having left his burden behind, he feels completely relaxed and unexpectedly drank past the limit of his capacity, and so that's how he got this drunk.

XIAOSHENG (*laughs heartily*): Wonderful, wonderful! Even the official's assistant, with no more box for receiving complaints, feels relieved and happy and becomes a drunkard, to say nothing of how I as an official having left my post, feel unrestrained and unfettered, just like an immortal! Obviously, that black gauze cap had no small effect on people! Now I am even more satisfied. Pour me more wine!

>   (Tune: *Northern Shou Jiangnan*)
>   Ah! All seems so joyful—why Didn't I leave office before this
>   to drink myself drunk?
>   With my False grandeur, no substance and all name,
>   I harmed Family members and servants by making them
>   all bustle about.
>   Speaking of it makes me hurt and sad;
>   Hearing about it makes me ashamed and uneasy.
>   I end up by only Raising my glass to drink a forfeit and
>   cover my face in shame.

LAODAN: My lord, throughout our journey we have seen green mountains and blue waters, birds singing and fragrant flowers—really most delightful scenery.

>   (Tune: *Southern Yuanlin hao*)
>   Our fishing boat drifts amid bright mountains, bright
>   waters,
>   Our sails touched by the fragrance of flowers and blooms.
>   What is more, The cries of gibbons ring through mountain
>   valleys,
>   Far better than the music of drums and reeds,
>   Far better than the music of drums and reeds!

XIAOSHENG: Boy, ask the man on the bank: What is this place? (MO, *drunk, asks him.*)

(*From backstage*): This is the Yanling area, not far from Seven Mile Brook.

XIAOSHENG: To judge from that, Yan Ziling's Fishing Terrace is ahead;[168] I'll meet a true friend today. We may just as well build a thatched cottage with several rooms and stay here. What's wrong with that?

(Tune: *Northern Gu meijiu* with *Taiping ling*)
We will tie up our fishing boat beside this green stream,
And build our thatched cottage on emerald slopes,
To share the whereabouts of the Fishing Terrace recluse.
I did not seek to follow his trail,
Or come here to Mechanically draw a gourd by copying a model;
Who would have thought that Ancients and moderns with no thought to meet
Might suddenly come face to face though a thousand years apart?
It is not that I On entering the mountains seek some new connections,
Or rely on ancient worthies to build up my own fame.
It's only Because these hills are high and the rivers long,[169]
Ah! From ancient and present times These two men of leisure both settle here!

TOGETHER:

(Tune: *Southern coda*)
A decade of worry put aside in a moment,
I only fear I do not yet feel quite well tonight;
I cannot avoid Recurring dreams that bring back bitter thoughts!

SCENE 13: THROWING MONEY AROUND

XIAODAN (*enters*):

>(Tune: *Qi niangzi*)
>The child I bore wastes her flower-like beauty;
>Vowing to remain chaste, she is an unworthy daughter.
>By losing lots of money
>And vexing me deeply,
>She occupies my mind the whole day long.

I, Fallen Angel Liu, have borne only one daughter through half a lifetime of hardships. I had hoped that she would strengthen our clan and surpass our ancestors in helping her father and mother. Who would have thought that even though she is an extremely good actor, she has a peculiar disposition and cannot be talked round: she always insists on her sense of honor and considers her reputation and integrity. When she meets a man, she is unwilling even to pretend a frown or a smile, let alone do other things. Now we have come to perform at the temple fair in this market town; as its head is a rich man. Although he is stingy in other ways, he is very willing to spend money freely for our services, and he is an old "acquaintance" of mine. Having seen my daughter, he is totally infatuated with her and wants to patronize her. Yet she is unwilling to accept this fated match, and I cannot make her change her mind. Now I have no choice but to go as a substitute for her. (*Sighs.*) It's like this:

>The daughter is not like her mother,
>Nor does the son take after his father.
>Even when seeming as filial as crows,[170]
>Still they act contrary to their wishes. (*Exits temporarily.*)

JING (*enters*):

>(Tune: *Puxian ge*)

> I must admit I'm disposed to be horny,
> And the beauty I've met is so lovely;
> My heart all aflame with desire,
> I spent money as if it were shit,
> But my predestined love wants none of it!

I, Moneybags Qian, have whored around all my life and have seen so many women. I always thought that no one could beat Fallen Angel Liu's good looks, but who would have expected that her own daughter is many times yet more beautiful! Watching several of the daughter's plays has cost me half of my life! I have also tried every possible way to get it on with her, yet she completely ignores me. She must be wanting to pick a wealthy patron and do a wholesale exchange, and that is why she's unwilling to sell retail. Now I'm risking everything on a single throw by offering a large sum of money to take her home as my concubine. Her mother likes me a lot and so may not reject my proposal out of hand. As they always say, "the sight of money opens your eyes"; I've withdrawn a thousand taels of silver to put in front of her when we speak about this. Seeing the money will naturally heat up her greed, and after I sweet talk her with some fine words in addition, I am not worried that she won't agree. Plum Fragrance, warm some wine to serve.

XIAODAN (*enters*):

> I conserve my strength to perform new plays,
> And snatch some leisure to visit an old friend.

JING: Are you here? (*Greets her.*)

XIAODAN: I am. Is there something you wanted to see me about?

JING: I haven't seen you for a long time, and I would like to talk about our old feelings for each other, nothing else. Plum Fragrance, bring the wine for our guest.

> (Tune: *Liangzhou xinlang*)
> Flowers give forth their fine fragrance,
> As smoke curls up from the censer—

Both add greatly to our enjoyment.
To create a pleasant mood,
We must also fill our cups with strong wine.
I wonder how like jade you're unchanged year after year
And like the flowers each season anew—
Your beauty just seems not to age.
Our first meeting after long parting
Is so delightful;
One moment of private love is equal to a whole night long.

TOGETHER:

The jade wine jar drained,
And the golden goblets overturned;
Good Phoenix couples we must imitate whenever we can.
Our partings and meetings
May be hard to predict.

JING: The day before yesterday, I pleaded with you again and again over the matter of your dear daughter; why haven't I had any reply yet?

XIAODAN: What shall I say? It was all because I did not cultivate virtue in my former life that I gave birth to this odd creature who is always disobedient. I've tried to talk to her about it several times, but seeing me on the point of saying something, she just walks away. I can only conclude that unfortunate creature does not deserve your patronage. Now since I was unable to talk her over, I have come to take her place.

(*Same tune*)

The child declines a lovely date,
So mother must help entertain;
The fragile willow fills in for a flower's beauty.[171]
I advise you To imagine a supple twig
While hugging this withered stalk.

> Besides, she is not Some rootless magic fungus[172]
> Or a stemless flower on an agate tree
> Whose looks and charm are hard to match.
> If you want to see a rare pearl,
> Ask about her mother's womb:
> Tough or tender, we are not that different in nature.
> (*Repeat together*)
> The jade wine jar drained,
> And the golden goblets overturned,
> Good Phoenix couples we must imitate whenever we can.
> Our partings and meetings
> May be hard to predict.

JING: Fallen Angel, I have a good proposition to discuss with you, but I do not know whether you will be willing or not. If you are, it will not only bring you wealth and honor but also save you a great deal of trouble. I'm just afraid you do not have such good luck.

XIAODAN: If it is that wonderful, why would I not be willing? But I do not know what you have in mind.

JING: Your dear daughter is unwilling to receive men, which is also where her high aspirations lie: she is simply determined to go straight and marry a good husband. Why don't you go along with her wishes? Accept lots of money and send her away. Then use that money to buy a girl, teach her plays, and keep on with business as usual.

XIAODAN: I went through innumerable hardships teaching my daughter. Now she has learned many good plays, and I want to build up our family fortune with her. How could I be willing to give her up!

JING: Do not blame me for saying it, but if an actress depends only on acting in plays, the amount of money she can earn is limited. Like you, it's only when she acts in both real plays onstage and pretend plays offstage that she can earn lots of money. But with your daughter's temperament, if you expect her to build up the family fortune, I'm just afraid you're going to have a hard time of it!

XIAODAN (*nods*): You are not wrong there.

JING: Whether or not she is rolling in money, it doesn't matter much. I am just afraid she will also use even the money you have earned and waste your family fortune until it's gone. And then she will have to sell herself. The money you get from selling her will not be able to buy her substitute; it will only be enough to pay off your debts. You can't do business like that.

>   (Tune: *Jie jie gao*)
>   If not guarded fast, your family fortune
>   Will melt like ice,
>   And you will have to Search for one to take your precious
>   pearl in trade for rice.[173]
>   By then, She will not be young,
>   Her price will not be high,
>   And relatives may not help.
>   Pitifully she'll no longer qualify for pepper apartments,[174]
>   And with no smoke from her stove she'll have to get by.

TOGETHER:

>   Let us now pray to the gods on whether to go or stay,
>   That we might not wait and let lots of money slip away.

XIAODAN: Even though this is the case, we have not reached that stage yet.

JING: You don't seem to realize that those powerful sons of princes and nobles may let it pass if she ignores them with a bold manner, but if she deliberately spoils their fun and makes them lose face, they will want to bring you to court to make a fool of her, and they won't stop until you have to dissolve your troupe.

XIAODAN (*aside*): There is reason behind every word he has said; I can't treat them as pretense. (*Turns back.*) When you speak of it this way, I really must marry her off, but I do not know what kind of family I can send her off to.

JING: The two words "wealth" and "rank" are definitely essential. But there's just one concern: the family should not be too rich or too high in rank. When wealth and rank reach the extreme, first, I am afraid there might be misfortune in store, and they will not enjoy a happy life to the end; second, I am afraid that once he becomes a powerful official it's fine if he feels satisfied, but if he no longer feels satisfied, that may cause your daughter a life of suffering. He should be a rich man who is neither too big nor too small, and a retired official living in the country whose rank is half high, half low—only a man like me could make her a good patron.

XIAODAN: When you speak of it this way, it is you who wants to marry her.

JING (*makes a bow*): That would be too much of an honor! I do certainly have this wish, but I dare not act on my own. If you are willing to favor me with your consent, since it would be embarrassing to give just a little, I offer a thousand taels of silver as betrothal gift. Plum Fragrance, bring in the betrothal money that I have withdrawn. (FUJING and CHOU *enter, carrying a money chest.*)

Please look: fifty taels in each sealed packet and twenty packets altogether, all fine silver, without the slightest impurity.

XIAODAN (*examines carefully; aside*): From the beginning, not a single word he said was wrong. With this much silver, I can buy at least ten girls and train them as an all-female troupe. When each and every one of these actresses is bringing in money, how could my family fail to make its mark? Why should I keep this creature as a constant aggravation? (*Turns back.*) All right, I give my consent to your proposal. But after she's married into your house, you must treat her properly.

JING: I will just carry her around on my head—I'd never dare be disrespectful!

XIAODAN:

> (*Same tune*)
> The one I treasure I must ditch:
> Destiny is hard to escape—
> A beauty should embrace a man who is rich![175]

>   Your Money is surely good
>   And your lot has been superior;
>   Others could not compare.
>   This Flower star[176] shines only upon you here—
>   Who knows how many will die of envy?
>   (*Repeat together*)
>   Let us now pray to the gods on whether to go or stay,
>   That we might not wait and let lots of money slip away.

JING: Then, when will she be brought over to my house?

XIAODAN: There will be only one more play tomorrow for Lord Yan's birthday. When it's done, I will bring her over to you. Now let me take my leave for the time being.

JING: Since this is the way it is, I'll have two of my servant boys carry the silver and escort Aunt Liu home.

>   (*Coda*)

XIAODAN:
>   Just a few words and her lifelong contract is sealed;
>   How can I wait for this Gold to be in my hands in order to
>   clinch the deal?

JING:
>   What I fear is Without the [red] string,[177] the marriage will
>   not hold!

SCENE 14: EXTORTION

DAN (*enters*):

>(Tune: *Fengshi chunqian*)
>A private alliance has been formed:
>The very image of embroidered mandarin ducks.[178]
>Shared glances exchanged at every moment,
>Holding each other close is all we've lacked.

Since I agreed to marry my darling Tan, I just feel happy that I have chosen the right person and will have someone to depend on for the future. I am also happy that he has changed his role from *jing* to *sheng*, which is exactly what I wished for. What other actors fear is appearing on the stage, and what they like is going offstage because appearing on the stage needs great effort and it is easy to hide away and rest off-stage. Yet he and I are the opposite of the others: what we like is appearing onstage, and what we fear is going offstage because we must avoid arousing suspicion off stage while onstage we can be husband and wife. Once we get onstage, he takes me for his real wife, and I regard him as my real husband; all of our words come straight from the heart and pierce to the bone. Other people see it as a play; what he and I do is real. We take the script as true and always enjoy it, never tiring—how could we not reach the peak of perfection? That is why the reputation of this Jade Sprouts Troupe is getting ever more well known every day. Even though this is so, because being husband and wife onstage cannot be taken as real in the end, we must think of a plan to make it official. A few times I've wanted to speak to my mother, but I found it difficult to bring the matter up. Now I cannot consider this anymore; sooner or later, I will have to reveal the truth and risk becoming her sworn enemy to take this load off my mind!

XIAODAN (*leading* WAI *and* MO, *enter, carrying the money chest*):

(Tune: *Fengshi chunhou*)
My family fortune is suddenly increased by a thousand
    taels of silver,
At the cost of losing a family member.
But still my worries vex me. (*Arrives.*)

WAI and MO: Aunt Liu, please make an inventory of what's inside the chest; we would like to turn back.

XIAODAN: Both of you, return, please. There is no need to check the amount. Tomorrow I will have a modest gift to give you.

WAI and MO: Many thanks!
Plenty of silver we've carried here,
But a small amount in return for a person.

XIAODAN:
What I've gained is so much cold cash,
Yet what I will lose is a living treasure.

(WAI *and* MO *exit.*)

DAN: Mother, where have you been so long? What is inside this leather chest?

XIAODAN: My daughter, you are extremely bright, so make a guess.

DAN:
(Tune: *Hong na'ao*)
Could it be The old dark-red silks used to renew the
    rainbow skirt?[179]

XIAODAN: No.

DAN:
Could it be Spare silk ribbons[180] to adorn official
    costumes?

XIAODAN: Not that, either.

DAN:
Could it be A thousand poems in return for your clear
    songs?

XIAODAN: Even more wrong.

DAN:
>Could it be A roll of brocade awarded for your exquisite
>>dancing?

XIAODAN: All of your guesses are wrong.

DAN: Then I have guessed it.
>The word is on the tip of my tongue,
>But I fear that it's too embarrassing to mention!

XIAODAN: Since you have guessed it, what could be unmentionable?

DAN:
>Could it be that Because one moment with you is worth a
>>thousand in gold,
>You took daytime as a spring night
>And so Received a fine payment of a thousand pieces of
>>gold?[181]

XIAODAN: Wrong every time. What is in this leather chest is a replacement for you. Having this, your mother does not have any more use for you.

DAN: What? You do not need me to act in plays? Oh, thank Heaven and Earth!

XIAODAN: As your mother,
>(*Same tune*)
>I hoped that your Fair reputation would be a courier
>>bringing wealth,
>I hoped that your Frosty brush[182] would be a broom to
>>sweep in interest,
>And hoped that you Would earn a thousand in gold by
>>flirting and pleasant chat,
>Accompanied by The limpid glances that bewitch the men.
>Who would have thought that you Would be too bashful
>>even to meet someone
>And draw back your hand at the first sight of money,
>Making those Resentful butterflies and mournful bees

> All Hate our flower branch,[183]
> Until Your bright springtime has wasted into autumn.

DAN: Mother, I do not understand what you said at all—please explain it clearly.

XIAODAN: To be frank with you, because of your temperament I do not see in you the material for someone who can earn money; instead, you will simply court disaster in the future. It would be better for you to become a wife in a respectable family and to eat food already on the table. There is a local worthy named Qian here, who has a big family fortune and is generous as well. He fell in love with you at first glance and is determined to marry you as his concubine. As your mother, I have already given my consent. This is his betrothal gift, and when the play is over tomorrow, I will take you to him.

DAN (*greatly alarmed*): Ah! How could this strange thing be? I have a husband, and a virtuous woman does not marry two men—how could I remarry?

XIAODAN (*alarmed*): What husband do you have? How could you have betrothed yourself to someone on your own authority, without your father and mother's approval?

DAN: How would I dare to take responsibility for the decision? Daddy and you, Mother, gave your permission for this marriage. How could you break the pledge of marriage just because there were no betrothal gifts?

XIAODAN (*greatly alarmed*): When did I ever accept such a proposal? I am afraid you are only being ridiculous! But if this is the case, who are you betrothed to? Just tell me.

DAN: It is Tan Chuyu, who plays the *sheng* roles. How could you have forgotten?

XIAODAN: This is even stranger! When did I ever accept his proposal?

DAN: He is a young man from an official family; he is a scholar and enjoys unsurpassed talent. Obtaining appointment to an official position would be as easy as turning over his hand, yet why was he willing to come learn plays? Just because he has fallen in love with me and could not be close to me, he used learning plays as an avenue of approach. Then he feared that a *huamian* would not be able to make a match with a *zhengdan*, and that is why he wanted to have his role changed to *zhengsheng*. This was a crystal-clear statement of his seeking a marriage alliance: he could not speak plainly and so created a riddle for you to guess. Daddy and you have been *sheng* and *dan* and are people in the know; how could it be possible that you weren't able to solve the riddle? If you had not accepted his proposal of marriage, you should not have asked him to stay and learn plays. Even if you had asked him to stay and learn plays, you should not have allowed him to change his role from *jing* to *sheng*. Since you went along on both of these matters, obviously your intention was to consent to his proposal. Why do you suddenly start to change now? I think that this would be unreasonable.

XIAODAN (*clicks her tongue*): Tut-tut! What a shameless trick! As you tell it, you would let him trick you into giving your body away by relying nothing more than these few artful words?

DAN:

> (*Same tune*)
> He and I Made a pledge to each other long ago;
> He and I Have shared both joy and sorrow.
> He and I Drained nuptial cups[184] onstage;
> I to him Tossed the silk ball in public to take him as your son-in-law.[185]

XIAODAN: Then who is your matchmaker?

DAN:

> It is all you Who stitch scripts on wealthy families' brocade,[186]
> But you did not know this Paper matchmaker could also exist on its own.

XIAODAN: Even if you go to court with this, you still need a witness. Who bears witness for him?

DAN:
>Of those who have seen our plays—Ten thousand staring eyes—
>Who wouldn't say We are a phoenix couple matched by Heaven?
>How could we lack Strong chief witnesses to testify to our wedding!

XIAODAN: You are not mad or perverse, child; what you say is all just daydream. How could being husband and wife onstage be accepted as real?

>(*Same tune*)
>It is neither that You lack intelligence, dumb as a turtledove;
>Nor is it that You're pretending to be a fool and making a joke.
>Why when seen As a phoenix pair[187] you're ashamed to join hands,
>And obstinately imitate Mandarin ducks in paintings longing to be side by side?[188]
>How many *Sheng* actors become *dan*s' companions?
>How many *Dan* actors are faithful to their *sheng*?
>Only Shanbo and Yingtai
>Became husband and wife as classmates,
>But had to Await the next life to fulfill their butterfly dream![189]

DAN: Everything under heaven can be made into a play, only marriage cannot; what was done as make-believe must become reality. Other actresses who do not value a sense of honor or treasure their name and integrity may not need to be serious; I am one who does value my sense of honor and does treasure my name and integrity. I dare not treat a wedding onstage as pretending. I am determined to marry this husband![190]

XIAODAN: A fine scolding that is! When you put it that way, then your mother does not value a sense of honor or treasure her name and integrity? Since I do not value a sense of honor or treasure my name and integrity, what maternal feelings can I have? Even if I did force you to marry someone, no one would think it strange! I'm going inside to sleep, and when the play is over tomorrow, I will speak with you again.

> Even if you used a hundred mouths to obstruct this marriage,
> You must still pay me back a thousand taels of silver as my pillow.

(*Exits, taking the money chest.*)

DAN (*wipes tears, sighs deeply*): My darling Tan! My darling! With one heart you and I bore our suffering together, looking forward to our wedding day; who would have thought that halfway along it would come to naught? When my mother saw this sum of money, she was just like a greedy gibbon who finds fruit or a hungry dog who smells raw meat: Now that she has swallowed down the money, how would she be willing to throw it up again? There's no way to escape this calamity! My darling Tan has suffered immeasurable troubles and pains for me—how can I betray him? I might just as well find a way to end my life. (*Unties her girdle and ties it around her neck to hang herself, but suddenly stops.*) Wait a moment! Since I want to be an unyielding and virtuous woman, determined to die, I should clearly recount my resolution to maintain my chastity in front of people. On the one hand, my sweetheart who sees me dying could call back my soul[191] on the spot; on the other hand, men of letters who hear of my story could write some poems to make my deed imperishable. Why should I die in obscurity and become just another mute chaste woman?

(Pastiche: *Jiangtou jingui*)

> (Tune: *Wu ma jiang'er shui*)
> It is not that I want Other people because of me,
> To plunge into the swift current.

It's that I'd feel ashamed to Die like some ordinary woman,
Drinking resentment and swallowing sorrow;
As I am not Tongue-tied, simply a bell that does not ring!
(Tune: *Liu yao jin*)
Why should I Bury deep in the dirt and dust
My fierce courage and chaste heart?
When in death I reach the Yellow Springs,
Grieved and regretful I would want to speak out, yet have no way,
Still my romantic deed would become the stuff of tales.
(Tune: *Guizhi xiang*)
Besides, I Preserve the ethical standards,
Preserve the ethical standards,
And bring honor to my ancestors and posterity.
How could I be willing To choke my own self?
Do not deride performers' low state:
This Family tradition of mine is not all dishonest!

What would be a good way to commit suicide? (*Thinks.*) I have it! Our marriage was initiated onstage. Since we got married onstage, I should die for chastity onstage. The Temple of Lord Yan happens to face a big stream. Although the rear part of the stage is on the bank, the front part is over the water. It would be best if I selected a scene on suicide to preserve chastity and perform it seriously; then in the middle of it, I will suddenly jump into the river. Would this not be the most remarkable death to preserve female chastity in all of history?! This idea makes sense!

Mother holds a dagger-ax to drive away her daughter;
Human standards all defiled—what is there to do?
Postponing death for one more night is not without its points;
Preserving a good reputation has many benefits.

SCENE 15: TOGETHER IN DEATH

(*Erect a stage in advance.*)
SHENG (*enters*):

>(Tune: *Yi Qin E*)
>After fruitless yearning,
>The course of true love takes an unexpected turn,
>Takes an unexpected turn:
>Even onstage as man and wife
>We cannot realize our hopes.

I have suffered all kinds of shame for Fairy Liu, hoping for some opportunity to realize my heart's desire. Who would have expected that her mother would accept the betrothal gift of a thousand taels of silver and sell her to the Qian house as a concubine? I have heard that right after the play is over today, she will join his household. How could we let our fated romance come to an end here? How could this be! When we were first reading scripts, she sang this to me herself:

>"My heart has long been thine,
>Secretly I wait for you;
>Fear not that Heaven or man will thwart our plan."

How fervent these three lines were! If she did not even fear Heaven, how could she fear human interference? She must have made a decision: to say nothing of disapproving the marriage, she will be unwilling even to act in this play today. It will take a lot of forcing before she'll even go onstage. I will just go wait in the green room and see her expression when she gets there. In short:

>When she enters, don't ask her about rise or fall,
>The expression on her face will tell you all. (*Exits temporarily.*)

DAN (*enters*):

(*Same tune with a different beginning*)[192]
Her hateful words fill me with fierce resentment,
And my liver and intestines are shattered all to pieces.
Shattered all to pieces—
If I can reveal my heart to people,
I can die without resentment!

Yesterday I wanted to find a quick end for myself, but because I have not yet bidden farewell to my darling Tan, I still wish to see him one more time; second, I wish to reveal to everyone the anguish that fills my bosom, so I put it off until today. I did not sleep the whole night, revising a scene of an old play with a new plot. I will just go wait in the green room, and as soon as everybody arrives I can perform that revised scene. Just one problem: if I reveal any of my sorrow in front of everybody and they see through me, they will not let me die. I must act as usual and pretend to be happy, which will really be a surefire plan. In short:

A loyal official faces death with no signs of fear,
And a virtuous woman approaches peril with a smile.

SHENG, WAI, MO, and CHOU (*enter together*):
The rich man lusts after sex;
The beauty loves only cash.
When a thousand in silver touches her hand,[193]
Kindness and virtue go out with a crash.

Elder sister Liu, we have heard that you are engaged, and we want to congratulate you on your wedding today.

DAN (*smiles*): That's right. Having learned the art of plays, I can perform one more only today, but by tomorrow I will not be able to. I rely on all of you to support me; please do your best.

ALL: We'll do our best to help you with it.

SHENG (*aside, angrily*): What? Between Heaven and Earth, how could there be such a heartless woman? Such a shameless woman! Since she's not in the least bit upset, she might just as well go. And her skin is thick enough even to say things like that!

(Tune: *Da ya gu*)

> My Heart has been frying on a fire!
> I was going to Join our voices together
> To shout out our wrongs and resentment,
> > Yet who would have thought her Charming face would be brimming with cheer,
> And further, her red lips would reveal the truth.
> Now I believe that with starlets and whores
> Not one is fated to marry!

Perhaps she is upset in her heart and afraid others might spot her weak point, so she is deliberately acting like this—it's just so hard to know. I see that man Qian coming over there in the distance; it has been said since ancient times: When enemies come face to face, they are particularly sharp-eyed.[194] I'll just see how he treats me.

JING (*enters, with bright hat and gaudy clothes, swaggering*):

> (Tune: *Lihuar*)
>
> I have thrown away a thousand in silver to buy myself a beauty,
> All that romantic stuff is left to me alone.
> Thousands of eyes stare at me, envious of our match.
> Ha! I worry not that none will witness this "happy event."

(DAN *smiles and salutes with her hands.*)

JING (*points at* DAN *and turns to* SHENG): She's no longer what she was; now she's become my wife. You should both stand a bit farther away from each other; it doesn't look good to have you huddle up together.

(SHENG *shows anger.*)

DAN: As soon as the play is finished today, I am going to go over to your house. But I still wish with all my heart and might to perform some good scenes, to provide something special for everyone to see. Will you let me do it?

JING: If that is what you want, why shouldn't I let you do so?

DAN: Then you must comply with two wishes of mine.

JING: To say nothing of two, even if it were ten wishes, I would go along with you.

DAN: First, I will not put on a complete play; I'll perform selected scenes instead. Second, you must not request plays, and instead let me choose titles as I like, the ones that I can play the best.

JING: That's just as it should be. Then which scenes do you wish to put on?

DAN: Only the first scene is important: I have revised the scene, "Clasping a Rock and Plunging into the River," from *The Thorn Hairpin*; it is brand new and different from the old version. It should be staged at the outset, and for the rest of the program, we'll put on a few random scenes, that's all.

JING (*bows*): Thanks for telling me. I only beg you to appear on the stage soon.

SHENG (*aside*): Thus it seems she is actually willing to marry him. It's my fault: I was so blind as to misjudge her in the first place. Now it is too late for regrets; I'll just let her do as she pleases.

DAN: Gentlemen, hurry up and beat drums and gongs so that I can appear on the stage. (*All respond and exit first.*)

DAN (*to* SHENG): Elder brother Tan, do not worry; just watch my performance carefully!

SHENG (*angrily*): I am blind and cannot see you. (*Nominally goes offstage, but physically stays on.*)[195]

(*Drums and gongs are beating from backstage;* DAN *appears on the stage. A group acting as audience members enter, crowded together.* JING *brings a folding chair and sits down to watch, complacently.*)[196]

DAN:

>(Tune: *Wu yer*)
>Meeting with reverses,
>Suffering torments,

I Cannot help but shed tears!
I have no way to wash away my hatred,
No way to distance myself from disgrace.
Now my situation is urgent,
> I will brave death and become A wronged ghost in the Yellow Springs!

I am Qian Yulian. Because that thief Sun Ruquan secretly hatched a sinister plot and used a trick to write a bill of divorcement, then my cruel stepmother treated sham as reality and forced me to remarry. And yet, as a loyal minister does not serve two rulers, a virtuous woman will not marry two men—how could I wait upon another man? Of all the possible ways out, the best would be to die! I have no alternative but to go stealthily to the edge of the river and throw myself into the water to die. It's already dusk now. I must leave the door of life and go seek the road to death. What a cruel fate I, Qian Yulian, have!

(Tune: *Wugeng zhuan*)
Hard to testify,
To the deep pain in my heart! (*Faces* SHENG, *weeps.*)
My husband! Ever since you left for the capital,
Each day I have longed for your return to live with you in harmony.
Who expected that today,
We would be torn apart midway?
That mother of mine,
Believes in slander,
And does me wrong.
Mother—Single-minded in your greed,
Greedy for his rank and wealth.
To propriety and morals
You choose to pay no heed!

Here I am now at the edge of the river. I am happy that there is a rock here: I must clasp it in my arms and leap into the river. (*Clasps the rock and is about to leap.*) But wait a moment. Since I am determined to die, I should also give vent to my resentment! Those who force me to remarry are my natural parents—because of my obligations to them, I cannot defame them. I harbor an implacable hatred[197] for only the scoundrel who used a trick to write the bill of divorce. Why don't I curse him to vent my spleen before I die! (*Points at* JING.) Let me use this senseless stone by the river to stand in for him for the time being; I will point my finger at it and curse it. I will not stop until that senseless stone nods in agreement.[198] (*Temporarily puts down the rock.*)

 (*Same tune*)
 Truly, I gnash my teeth,
 Because it is so hard to bear! (*Points her finger at* JING.)

Vile-hearted thief, you do not read *Poetry* or *Documents* nor have any sense of morality, so I need not talk to you about ethical standards or moral integrity. I only advise you to go look at your face in the river and to see what it looks like. And you want to make a marriage with me, a woman of matchless beauty? When have you ever seen

 An evil owl became the husband
 Forcing a lovely simurgh or brilliant phoenix to be the
  wife?[199] (*Points again.*)

Cruel-hearted brigand, you seek only your own happiness, and separate another man from his wife! What if someone took your wife away by force, how would you feel? I advise you:

 Examine your own conscience,
 And put yourself in others' shoes:[200]
 Why do you give free rein to your lechery,
 Relying on your arrogance and wealth
 To do others harm? (*Points again.*)

Shameless tortoise![201] Since ancient times, they've said: "If I do not seduce others' wives, others will not seduce mine." While you are openly seizing another man's wife, how do you know your wife has not been taken away by some other man in secret? This other man's wife is unwilling to defile her chastity for you and would rather throw herself into the river to die—but I fear that your wife would not have this resolve!

> I advise you to turn your head toward home,
> Turn your head and take a good look at your bedroom door.
> I am afraid that you have Simply lost the hare behind you
> When you went to hunt a wolf!

JING (*nods his head and cheers*): Good cursing! Good cursing! This part of the plot is all new, and the revision is really wonderful!

DAN: Since the senseless stone has nodded in agreement, I need say no more. Now I clasp the rock and take my own way out! (*Clasps the rock and turns to look at* SHENG.) My husband! Your wife has never forgotten what we've said in former days: with all my heart, I want to marry you! Today it cannot be as I wished—I can only throw myself into the river to die. You must take care of yourself and need not think of me! (*Wails aloud, weeps bitterly;* SHENG *also weeps.*)

> (Tune: *Hu dao lian*)
> Offending public morals,
> Disrupting all ethical standards,
> My mother forces me to marry a man of wealth.
> I'd far rather meet my death in the Yangzi River,
> Than have my name disgraced!

(*Quickly leaps off the stage; exits stealthily.* JING, *alarmed, cries out:* "Drag her out." *Audience bursts into uproar.*)

SHENG (*stands at front of the stage, shouts loudly*): You do not need to make a racket. Fairy Liu is none other than the wife of mine—I am Tan Chuyu. Her death today was no accident, and she intentionally died for the sake of honor. In such a swift current, I doubt we could drag her out. Now that she has become the model of a chaste wife, I have no choice but to become a righteous husband! (*Beckons with his hand downward.*) My wife! Go slowly—wait for me to catch up!

>(*Same tune*)
>She upheld public morals,
>Maintained all ethical standards, (*Points at* JING.)
>And the murderer is none other than this man of wealth!
>She Preserved her chastity and sacrificed her life all for me,
>And I, too, will meet my death in the Yangzi River!
>(*Quickly leaps off the stage; exits stealthily.*)

AUDIENCE (*cry out in alarm*): Moneybags Qian took advantage of his position to seize the bride and hounded two people to death! You spectators—let's get him; let's beat him to within an inch of his life and then hand him over to the magistrate!

JING (*flustered*): What'll I do?
>Of the thirty-six stratagems,
>Running away is tops.
>Misfortunes never come singly;
>Blessings never come in pairs. (*Exits, running fast.*)

ONE PERSON (*shouts loudly*): The murderer has run away, but happily the county's assistant magistrate has come to the village to review and check the neighborhood-watch system. Let's all get together to write a joint complaint and then go denounce Moneybags Qian to the authorities as a criminal.

ALL: Right you are—we'll all go together!

TOGETHER:
>(Tune: *Da ya gu*)
>Call out to the magistrate to redress this wrong!

Make known far and wide the marvelous deeds
Of loyal husband and chaste bride!
They performed the play to express true feelings
And threw themselves into the river to end their lives for real.
This version of *The Thorn Hairpin*
Will be even more widely known. (*All exit.*)

SCENE 16: DIVINE PROTECTION

WAI (*costumed as the Pacifier-of-Waves, and* FUJING, *costumed as a judge from the Underworld, lead a divine retinue onstage*):
    (Tune: *Northern Dian jiangchun*)[202]
    Vigorously calming down great waves,
    That roll to the ends of the Earth:
    The mighty deity arrives.
    For pacifying the world, I've earned high merit;
        In setting aright disorder, I've had countless sucesses.
    My might in leveling the waves makes me worthy of the name,
    Even billows tall as mountains I level all the same.
    Great waves are no more dangerous than people's minds:
    Against the sight of which even I quail in my divine might!

I am Lord Yan, Pacifier-of-Waves; my fief is the watery realm, and my general duty is to manage what's dark and the yin. I oversee the work of making waves for Heaven and put right all disorder in the world. The area as large as all foreign states and our Nine Provinces, judged on the scales of our laws, is no more than a cup of water in our low-lying court. Yet, those with the vision at the level of mere insects and grass exaggerate, saying that water is far away and dikes are long, and they make distinctions among the five lakes and four seas.[203] To my divine eyes, the transformations of the seas into mulberry fields[204] are no more than trading a scoop of water for a pinch of dirt. Yet although as transient as mayflies, people cannot be stopped from transforming the world from deep mounds into high valleys and making all kinds of changes throughout the ages.[205] Today is the third day of the tenth lunar month, and it's my birthday. In the capital or in provincial cities, suburbs or rural villages, wherever there are my temples, surely there will be sacrifices held for me today. You must realize that even though there are many temples, I am only one deity after all. When it is time to hold the sacrifices, I have to ride the wind and drive the lightning to make my rounds to enjoy them everywhere. Infernal Judge, muster all my divine retinue to follow me on an inspection tour. (*All respond, walk in a column.*)

> (Tune: *Hun jiang long*)
> Master of cloud clears the path,
> Goddesses of wind and lightning help with divine steeds.
> My travels all over The Nine Provinces and to the ends of
>   the Earth
> Must be limited To this one day.
> It is not that I Everywhere delight in the incense and fill
>   my mouth and belly,
> Or just accept offerings and collect spirit money along
>   the way.
> It is just because I am touched by the depth of their piety:
> Attracted by the power of their vows.
> Their true feelings I can enjoy,
> Their sincere wishes I must appreciate.
> It is not An incidental invitation
> To the remains of a feast,
> Or any disrespectful treatment when I arrive
> That belittle gods or slight the offerings!
> If they are not respectful,
> Even though all the meat offerings[206] are in array, I am In
>   no hurry to respond;
> But if they are pious,
> Even before pure incense has burned away, My Carriage
>   will already be there.
> If I do not accept the invitation,
> Their talismans[207] are drawn in vain.

> If I am not properly escorted away,
> The paper horses[208] are burned for nothing.

(*Backstage, a drumhorn is blown.*)

FUJING: Your Highness, we have already arrived at one of your temporary palaces.

WAI: Rein in my horse and carriage.

JING (*enters, costumed as local earth god*): The earth god of this temple pays his respects.

WAI: Who are those people coming over there? What are those musical instruments they are blowing?

JING: That's the custom of this area: whenever they perform sacrifices for the gods, they play musical instruments called drumhorns.[209] Since today is Your Highness' birthday celebration, these benefactors have come especially to congratulate you on your birthday, and now they are at the gate. Your Highness, please ascend the altar to enjoy the ceremony. (WAI *ascends the altar;* JING *exits.*)

(XIAOSHENG *and* LAODAN *enter, costumed as almsgivers holding sacrificial offerings;* MO *and* CHOU, *costumed as Daoist priests, enter blowing drumhorns. Every time* MO *and* CHOU *sing and dance,* XIAOSHENG *and* LAODAN *offer wine to* WAI.)

MO and CHOU:

> (Tune: *Saishen qu*)[210]
> Kill a lamb and soak up the wine,[211]
> *di-du-di, duo-du-di,*
> As sacrifice to the god,
> *di-du-di, duo-du-di, duo-du-di, du-duo-du-di.* (*Blowing while dancing.*)
> Men, women, and children,
> *di-du-di, duo-du-di,*
> Are all sincere at heart,
> *di-du-di, duo-du-di, duo-du-di, du-duo-du-di.* (*Blow and dance.*)

They pray that the god,
di-du-di, duo-du-di,
May bestow blessings and protection,
di-du-di, duo-du-di, duo-du-di, du-duo-du-di,
That every family will be happy,
di-du-di, duo-du-di,
All enjoying peace,
di-du-di, duo-du-di, duo-du-di, du-duo-du-di! (*Blow and dance.*)
Kill a lamb and soak up the wine to thank the god;
Men, women, and children are all sincere at heart.
Praying that the god may bestow blessings and protection;
That every family will be happy and all enjoy peace!

The ceremony for the god is now completed. Please clear away the sacrificial offerings. (XIAOSHENG *and* LAODAN *clear away the sacrificial offerings;* MO *and* CHOU *exit, blowing drumhorns.*)

WAI (*descends from the altar and leads the retinue*):

(Tune: *You hulu*)
Rustic song and border music[212] are hard to comprehend.
Although it's not like The tripping dance
With clear and melodious sound,
Played with all sincerity It resembles the *Xiaoshao*.[213]
One hears from them No request for boon greater than peace,
And we know they are not Using shrimp to hook the divine fish.
I enjoy these local customs
So similar to the most ancient times;[214]
So simple and sincere,
And free from any cunning.
Here I Would grant generous recompense,
Not reduced by a fraction because they are modest.

(*Backstage, striking of gongs and beating of drums, singing of "li-luo-lai, luo-li-lai."*)

FUJING: Reporting, Your Highness: we have arrived at another of your temporary palaces.

WAI: Rein in the horse and carriage.

CHOU (*enters, costumed as the local earth god*): The earth god of this temple pays his respects.

WAI: Who are those people beating drums and striking gongs? What is that song they are singing?

CHOU: That's the custom of this area: whenever there is a calamity, people make vows in prayer to a god, and when they come back later to fulfill their vows they sing these songs called "fulfillment tea banquets." Today they are taking advantage of Your Highness's birthday and have all come to repay their pledges. We have already arrived at the gate; Your Highness, please ascend the altar to enjoy the ceremonies. (WAI *ascends the altar;* CHOU *exits.* SHENG *and* XIAODAN *enter, costumed as penitents holding sacrificial offerings;* JING *and* MO *enter, costumed as diviners beating drums and gongs. Every time* JING *and* MO *beat drums and gongs,* SHENG *and* XIAODAN *offer wine to* WAI.)

JING and MO:

>(Tune: *Chayan qu*)
>Having divine power and response,
>*li-luo-lai, luo-li-lai,*
>Are gods of Heaven and Earth,
>*li-luo-lai, luo-li-lai, li-lai-luo-lai-luo-li-lai.* (*Beating of drums and gongs.*)
>To bring the dead back to life,
>*li-luo-lai, luo-li-lai,*
>Needs no doctors,
>*li-luo-lai, luo-li-lai, li-lai-luo-lai-luo-li-lai.* (*Beating of drums and gongs.*)
>We use the money for medicines,

li-luo-lai, luo-li-lai,
To fulfill our vows,
li-luo-lai, luo-li-lai, li-lai-luo-lai-luo-li-lai.
We never waste money,
li-luo-lai, luo-li-lai,
On anything,
li-luo-lai, luo-li-lai, li-lai-luo-lai-luo-li-lai. (*Beating of drums and gongs.*)
Having divine power and response are the gods of Heaven and Earth;
To bring the dead back to life needs no doctors.
We use the money for medicine to fulfill our vows,
And never waste money on anything.

The tea banquet ceremony has been completed. Please clear away the sacrificial offerings.

(SHENG *and* XIAODAN *clear away the sacrificial offerings;* JING *and* MO *beat drums and gongs. All exit.*)

WAI (*descends from the altar and leads the retinue*):

(Tune: *Tianxia le*)

There they Spend wine and sacrifice meat with no diligent effort,
That makes it hard for me to accept their offerings.
Just like this, they request my favor without any merit.
Death and life are always up to Heaven;
Even prayers to the gods produce no guarantee.
I am ashamed to be imitating A quack doctor in demanding gifts in gratitude!

(*Backstage, beating of gongs and shouting*): Let's notify our neighborhood heads: a local tyrant has hounded someone to death. Everyone, come out and report to the magistrate.

FUJING: Your Highness, we have arrived at another of your temporary palaces.

WAI: Rein in the horse and carriage.

MO (*enters, costumed as the local earth god*): The earth god of this temple pays his respects.

WAI: Who are those people that are shouting? Is it true that someone has been hounded to death? Tell me frankly.

MO (*recites*): Your Highness, please listen to my report:

> Actress Liu held fast to her purity,
> Actor Tan was staunch and upright;
> Their troth with a few words they plighted;
> In Zhu Chen[215] no new match could be made.
> The affluent crook tried to buy her,
> But the lovers pledged devotion onstage;
> It was hard to tell reality from acting
> Until they threw themselves into the waves.

WAI: From what you say, they must be loyal husband and chaste wife. I am an upright and fair-minded god—seeing these virtuous people in grave danger, how could I not save them! Tell my divine retinue to mount the mist and ride the clouds and catch up with me as I race in pursuit! (*All respond and march.* SHENG *and* DAN *enter quietly and lie down on the floor, embracing each other.*)

> (Tune: *Nezha ling*)
> Driving a flying dragon,
> Riding a raging demon of floods,[216]
> Commanding a fierce wind,
> Rolling up swift billows,
> We dash across the vast and misty, roiling waves.
> If they Float, we will scoop them out of the water;
> If they Sink, we will dredge them from below.
> I assume The current could not have carried them far.
> Even if The one who's leaped over the Dragon Gate[217] can
>   move quickly,
> Without doubt Her footsteps[218] treading the fragrant dust
>   are tiny.
> This pair of souls can surely be summoned back.

RETINUE (*notice* SHENG *and* DAN): Your Highness: here are two dead bodies embracing each other; presumably, they are that couple.

WAI: Judge from the Underworld, you chase after and capture their souls so that I might revive them. At the same time, transmit my instruction to the watery troop to report at once for my order.

FUJING (*uses a flag to summon the souls of the dead and transmits the order backstage*): Hear the decree of His Lordship Pacifier-of-Waves: all units of the watery troop are to report at once to receive his commands.

TROOPS (*costumed as shrimp, turtle, snail, and crab generals,*[219] *enter*):
    My shrimp body can bend like a spirit,
    My turtle's head never sticks out,
    As a snail, I'm still light with my shell on,
    And as a crab, it is sidewise I run. (*Greet* WAI.)
    Watery troops at your command!

WAI (*points to* SHENG *and* DAN): That pair are a righteous husband and chaste wife who threw themselves into the river to die in order to maintain their integrity. I will display a bit of my divine prowess and transform their inseparable bodies into a couple of soles[220] to mingle in your ranks to follow the waves and drift away with the current. When they get to Yanling, there will be a man of noble character who has resigned from his official post and become a hermit among fishermen and woodcutters. Protect these fish and escort them there and into his fishnet. When he hauls in the net, the fish will change to their original shapes. Not only will the fulfillment of their marriage vows and the realization of their aspirations, even their future wealth and honor will all depend on that fisherman. Follow my orders carefully; do not disobey.

TROOPS: We have your orders. (SHENG *and* DAN *exit secretly, while one person, costumed as the paired fish, enters secretly, marching together with the crowd.*)

WAI:

>(Tune: *Jinzhan'er*)
>It is not that I, To help with the good and auspicious,
>Always take the whole thing on myself;
>It is just because they Followed the ethical code
>That I am willing to shoulder this burden.
>It appears that She went first to die, and he then laid down his life;
>When he found her
>He tightly embraced her dead body.
>It is thus clear that
>The strength of their will is like iron—
>Even death cannot force them apart!

FUJING: Your Highness: this man and woman have transformed into the shape of fish.

WAI (*points to the fish*):

>A couple of soles, a pair of flatfish!
>You had good luck to meet me;
>Had you never suffered while you still had breath,
>How could you find happiness after your death?
>If you want to become two separate trees with branches intertwined,[221]
>First merge your two fish bodies into one pair.
>If all the world's lovers were just like you,
>Who would not be willing to lose their lives in some ditch?

My divine retinue, stir up wind and drum up some waves while I accompany them part of the way myself.

ALL: Aye! (*Walk together.*)

WAI:

>(Tune: *Jisheng cao*)
>Why compare affectionate companions with mandarin ducks;

A COUPLE OF SOLES

Don't praise married couples using a phoenix pair.
How can they compare to these Bodies close together like
 stringed pearls or belts of jade,[222]
Bodies embracing tightly to indulge in joy and pleasure?
This is no False claim of belonging together like fish and
 water.[223]
Let the greatest fools for love that history has ever seen
Enjoy Such happiness that the world has never known!
(*Coda*)
Without burning incense that retrieves the dying soul,
Or prescribing some herb that restores life,
I have preserved two spirits that were only dimly seen.
I am not Taking over the chopping board and chasing
 away the chef,[224]
By taking the place of the matchmaker and replacing Old
 Man of the Moon.[225]
You may well ask Whose billows are these in this vast
 expanse of foam.
To say nothing of The frontiers that lie under my control,
Even When winds arise and tides spread across the land
And waterfalls spring from your eyes,
They are also from me, The humble Pacifier-of-Waves,
 lacking sincere contributions!
(*Exit together.*)[226]

SCENE 17: SCRAMBLING FOR PROFIT

CHOU (*enters, costumed as an officer of the court, followed by* XIAOSHENG *and* DAN, *costumed as* yamen *runners*):[227]

>(Tune: *Zhao pixie*)
>I am a county *yamen* officer charged with making arrests,
>But in three years as an upright official, I've gained only
>>Five thousand taels of silver.
>
>My district superior deserves far more praise than I;
>It took him only Half a year to skim the county dry!

I am none other than the assistant magistrate of this county. I entered government service via status as a clerical official, and I was not promoted to this imposing post of assistant magistrate until I had been a police chief for six years. Having been at this post for three years, I have harassed all the rich men, big or small, in these parts. One may well say that my clerical talent is extremely fine, yet who would have thought my newly arrived district superior would be even ten times better. Nothing profitable in these parts can escape his notice. Before we can even get started, quite unexpectedly the silver and cash has already found its way inside his bootlegs. Now he handles everything in town himself, leaving nothing for us assistant magistrates to have a hand in. There's nothing I can do about it, so I have come to the countryside on a pretext. In former years when I went to the countryside, I could definitely receive several petitions to the authorities and skim a little fat[228] for myself, but this time it is so quiet that I haven't seen a single piece of paper. (*To the* RUNNERS.) You runners should go around everywhere, making it known that you are soliciting complaints.[229] Once you get petitions, I will dispatch you with warrants.

RUNNERS: We have in fact received a petition, but we are just afraid the accused is so powerful that our *yamen* is too small to get any money from him.

CHOU: What is the case about? Just tell me.

RUNNERS: There is a rich man in these parts named Moneybags Qian who drove two people to their deaths because he tried to marry an actress by force. Local headmen are about to come file a complaint against him as a criminal.

CHOU: Is that rich man named Qian the one who helped entertain me at the welcome banquet?

RUNNERS: Indeed he is.

CHOU: That son of a bitch, I really hate him! The local headmen collected money to give to me, but he kept half of it for himself. I have been looking for an opportunity to implicate him in something but I didn't expect it would be such a major matter! Hurry up and go solicit the complaint; you must not wait for the county magistrate to learn of this and let the case go to his court!

RUNNERS: Master, set your mind at rest. The magistrate is not in; he has gone to see his superiors in the provincial capital.

CHOU: Good! Even so, I am still afraid that local headmen will have been paid off and will not come to submit the complaint. You should, after all, go solicit it.

RUNNERS: We'll go right now.

CHOU:

>(Tune: *Sibian jing*)
>Don't intimidate them with your might—
>Villagers so easily take fright.
>Tricking them out of their complaint,
>Will give me the knife with which to kill.
>I'll make the complaint into a major case,
>Exaggerate the claims from what's at base;
>Say we will report it higher up,
>Even if that isn't quite the truth. (*Exit together.*)

XIAODAN (*enters, holding a complaint*):

>(Tune: *Zhao pixie*)
>Don't brag about your virtuous nature

> To an old hand at being greedy and unfeeling.
>
> For money, I cast aside all considerations of face,
>
> Regardless of Having shared his couch in past days!

By nature, I, Fallen Angel Liu, love only money and pay no mind to personal feelings. My daughter was unwilling to get married and so was hounded to death. Although it was my fault as her mother, it was also Moneybags Qian's rotten luck. I cannot take into consideration any former affection; instead, I want to cheat him out of some money. It was for money that I sold my daughter the day before yesterday, and it is also for money that I sue my old lover today. If he says I am unfeeling, I will recite the two lines of this old saying as evidence:

> If even my own flesh and blood I treat like this,
>
> How much more would I do so to a stranger.

I see the local headmen coming from a long way off; I'd better wait and go in together with them.

WAI (*holding a complaint, enters with* LAODAN):

> (*Same tune*)
>
> When enemies meet on a narrow way,
>
> Confrontation will be hard to avoid.
>
> Now power is in our hands, we cannot let him off;
>
> Does he Remember now how much he used to boast?

XIAODAN (*meets* WAI *and* LAODAN): All of you have come, too. Can it be that you are going to bring a charge of murder?

WAI and LAODAN: Yes, we are.

XIAODAN: Then take me along with you.

JING (*hurriedly leads* MO *onstage, holding the money chest*):

> (*Same tune*)
>
> Only because of one wrong move,
>
> I let her perform *The Thorn Hairpin* play.
>
> Two violent deaths when added together
>
> Made this Retired official worse off than common folks!

Over a mere trifle I, Moneybags Qian, have provoked an enormous disaster! Hearing that the local headmen and the family of the victim have all gone to file a complaint against me, I have no alternative but to bring silver and try to catch up and delay them. (*Walks hurriedly and catches up, grasping* XIAODAN *with one hand and* WAI *with the other.*) Gentlemen, my distinguished relatives and worthy cousins, please don't do this. I, old Qian, am to blame, and I should not have caused deaths for the sake of a woman's beauty. Now I both apologize and give you presents as a way to beg you not to take up paper and pen. (XIAOSHENG *and* DAN *quietly enter and eavesdrop.*)

WAI (*turns away and says to* LAODAN): If this is presented to the assistant magistrate, he will get this money and we will get none of it. It would be better to loosen the rope a bit instead.

LAODAN: I am just afraid the family of the victim will not agree. (*To* XIAODAN.) Aunt Liu, what are your thoughts on the matter?

XIAODAN: Even if all of you do not bring charges against him, I am determined to take him to court.

JING: Fallen Angel, Fallen Angel! Even if you do not make allowances for our former affection, you should do so for the sake of the thousand taels of silver. I have not asked you to return it, and you still want to take me to court? This main road is not a place for doing business. There is a wine shop behind us. Let's go there and have a few drinks. Then we can talk. (*Pulls on them, exit together.*)

XIAOSHENG: Now that they have gone in to settle the matter privately, this complaint will never be filed.

DAN: That is not a problem. Let's just wait here, and when they come out, we will seize them and accuse them of settling a murder case privately and take them in chains to His Honor. I expect they have both the complaints and the silver with them; with bribes and evidence in hand, when they are tortured, have no fear—they will confess!

XIAOSHENG: Just right, just right!

XIAOSHENG and DAN:

>(Tune: *Sibian jing*)
>Let him pass out money as freely as he pleases;
>We Will arrest him with the law on our side.
>When we have both evidence and bribes,
>No more investigation will be needed.
>The bribes he'll offer to avoid punishment,
>When divided, we'll still get our cut;
>Only Our officer has the unmerited advantage,
>And will end up With a nice bit of wealth!

JING (*from backstage*): All of you go on ahead. I will take care of the bill and so cannot escort you very far.

WAI, LAODAN, and XIAODAN (*from backstage*): Many thanks! Please don't take offense at what we said before!

(WAI, LAODAN, *and* XIAODAN *enter together.*)

XIAODAN: With the matter settled like this, it's a great advantage to him.

WAI and LAODAN: The money is a minor matter, but letting us give vent to our anger has been a great relief.

XIAOSHENG and DAN (*secretly move behind them and tie them up with rope*):

>When you're happy, so happy—
>Be on guard against disaster!

Now that you have this ill-gotten wealth, let's see you trying to avoid that charge at the *yamen*!

WAI, LAODAN, and XIAODAN (*alarmed*): Ah! What are you talking about?

XIAOSHENG and DAN: You tried to settle a case of murder privately and obtained fine silver illegally. His Honor invites you in to have a talk with him.

WAI, LAODAN, and XIAODAN: We did not do it, so don't arrest the wrong people!

XIAOSHENG and DAN (*take them away*):
>Whether right or wrong
>We'll find out before long!
>We have arrested you in accordance with the law
>And would not dare to untie this rope on our own. (*Bring them to* yamen *and cry out:*) We have arrested the criminals! Your Honor, will you come out?

CHOU (*enters*):
>The complaint is not yet here,
>But the criminals have already come;
>To see me, you need not be arrested,
>Yet of gifts, you know the trick to give some!

(XIAOSHENG *enters first, greets* CHOU, *and whispers in his ear.*)

CHOU (*overjoyed*): Wonderful, wonderful! Hurry up and bring them in. (DAN *brings them and greets* CHOU.)

I, your assistant magistrate, have gone on an inspection tour in the countryside in order to investigate corrupt practices among the people. You bastardly men and women, having obtained people's money, would go so far as to conceal a major crime like murder without reporting it. What's the reason for this?

XIAODAN: It is true that my daughter threw herself into the water; because of some unfortunate words between mother and daughter, she took her own life, but nobody forced her to do so.

WAI and LAODAN: We are local headmen of neighborhood-watch units. We have always abided by the law and would never settle a case of murder privately. Where did this idea come from?

CHOU: When you speak of it this way, is it I, His Lordship, who has arrested the wrong people? (*To* XIAODAN.) Let me ask you, how many months are you pregnant?

XIAODAN: I am not pregnant.

CHOU: If you are not pregnant, why do you have such a big belly? (*To* WAI *and* LAODAN.) Are the two of you both bloated?

WAI and LAODAN: We are not bloated.

CHOU: If you are not bloated, why do you both seem rather full and obstructed between your chest and belly? You cannot play tricks on me, your magistrate! Let me give you some medical treatment. You runners: quick, rub their bellies for them. (RUNNERS *are about to rub their bellies, but* XIAODAN, WAI, *and* LAODAN *resist.*)

CHOU (*furiously*): Pah! Don't you bastardly men and women know me—seeing how impartial I am, you still want to play tricks? To say nothing of the bribes you have in your pockets, I will not allow you to hide anything: even the bribes you have eaten, I will pour watery dung down your throats to make sure that you throw them up! Attendants: Quick, search them!

ATTENDANTS (*discover the silver and the complaints*): Your Honor, we have discovered one complaint and two hundred taels of silver on this woman; we have also discovered a complaint and fifty taels of silver on each of the local headmen.

CHOU: How about that? Wasn't I right to arrest these three criminals who had been under investigation?

XIAOSHENG and DAN: You were right to arrest them—you truly are an impartial judge!

CHOU:

>   (*Same tune*)
>   Don't be surprised that I have seized the real bribes;
>   I use Methods that immortals have taught.
>   Let you try some cunning deception,
>   But I, The impartial judge will ensure you are caught.
>   Even though all has been discovered,
>   You need not feel such alarm;
>   If you merely confess to the original complaint,
>   I will put you aside to look for that instead!

Now it's no good trying to deny it any more. Just tell the truth.

XIAODAN, WAI, and LAODAN: It is a homicide case in fact; we dare not pretend that it is otherwise. We wish to give the two complaints to you, Your Honor, to show our respect and only beg you to reward us with the original silver and to let us take it away.

CHOU: You are going too far with your cheating. You should be grateful that I did not ask you to take out more; you want to take away even the spoils I've found? Well, then, attendants: put the finger squeezers on that woman and use the ankle press on those men to find out where they have hidden the remaining bribes!

XIAODAN, WAI, and LAODAN (*flustered*): We wouldn't accept any more, not even a bit of it!

CHOU: Then escort them out to get somebody to go bail for them. At the same time, arrest the accused and tell him that I am going to forward him and the file to the county court right away. (*Signs a warrant, hands to the attendants*):

> These ill-gotten gains come first to my hand,
> But I will make a fortune when I get my man! (*Takes silver and exits first.*)

WAI and LAODAN:

> What the right hand has taken in is seized from the other;
> In vain we slaved as cattle[230] for this pestilential judge. (*Exit together.*)

XIAOSHENG (*walks*): We took such pains to get this warrant, but we'll have to use tricks in order to get our hands on any large sums of money.

DAN: This really is a homicide case—don't worry that he won't pay up. We've gone around and turned at corners and here we are. Is Master Qian in?

JING (*enters*):

> Having lost all power and might,
> This dragon's reduced to a snake.
> "Venerable" I'm not hearing again,
> I'm back to just being "Master Qian."

Who is it?

XIAOSHENG: We are *yamen* runners sent by the sheriff. His Honor invites you to come to have a talk with him.

JING: What a disrespectful tone! You did not call me "Master" and had the impudence to address me as "you." How could I, Venerable Master Qian, be addressed as "you"?

DAN: It may be that "you" was not allowed in the past, but now we can use "you."

JING: How so?

XIAOSHENG: Haven't you heard:

>Even relatives of the emperor when they break the law,
>Are punished like common people just the same!
>
>(*Same tune*)
>
>I advise you Not to talk so arrogantly from now on,
>Because no one is frightened by you!
>In years past, seeing the sky from a well,
>The frog[231] felt he really was big.
>But now, Since your "honorable" self has broken the law,
>Your "honorable" name's been knocked down a peg.
>Just term yourself "convicted felon,"
>And hang up your title of "Master!" (*Takes out the warrant.*)

Have a look at this.

JING (*takes a look; turns away*): What? How could they have gone and submitted the complaint even after we had worked it all out so well? I know what to do. (*Turns back.*) I will need the help of all of you for this matter. I have a plan to "borrow flowers to present to the Buddha."[232] If only His Honor is willing to do it, there are a thousand taels of silver there already, and they can be his right away.

DAN: What plan is that?

JING: That woman who has filed the complaint against me has my money chest filled with silver, which was originally a betrothal gift. It is now in her residence, and not one bit of it has been used. She was the one who hounded her daughter to death, which had nothing to do with me. You just need an urgent warrant to impound the silver right away. I will not take a bit of it; I will give it all to His Honor. You two will have twenty taels apiece, which I will give you right now.

> (*Same tune*)
> A profit of a thousand in silver can be had today—
> No need for any torture;
> As long as the case can be kept out of court,
> I will thank you with a gift in due course.
> Even if his superior finds out, it will not matter—,
> This neither bends the law
> Nor was it taken by bluff.
> I, Who gave the bribe, would never confess,
> And no one else will have a thing to say! (*Takes out silver and hands it over.*)

XIAOSHENG and DAN: If this is the way it is, we will go with you to report back to the court and we'll act just according to your plan. (*Walk together.*)

JING:

> A wise man never suffers losses,[233]
> He borrows flowers for the Buddha to get the advantage.

XIAOSHENG:

> Sheep's wool[234] comes from only the body of the sheep,

DAN:

> But you may have to scald the belly to get the bribe. (*They arrive.*)

XIAOSHENG and DAN: You wait outside while we go in and make our report. (*Exit together; at once reenter.*) His Honor understands and has marked the criminal.[235] Please go with us to recover the bribe.

JING: Just as it should be.

> To settle a matter, send the one who made the trouble;

XIAOSHENG and DAN:

To recover the bribe, send the person who reported it. (*Exit together.*)

CHOU (*enters laughing*):

> If you're an official, don't worry if you're low;
> Being a clerk, don't worry about being poor.
> All you need are three days of good fortune—
> And you won't be so poor anymore!

For this matter of Moneybags Qian, I have not exerted even a little effort, but three hundred taels of fine silver have come into my hands, which is really not bad! Who would have expected there would be another thousand taels of silver in that woman's house? I've already dispatched my attendants to fetch it. When they get the silver, I have no fear they will bring it here to the court. What's there to say about such wealth and honor?

(XIAOSHENG and DAN *enter, carrying the money chest and leading* XIAODAN.)

XIAODAN:

> Betrothal gifts are now taken for private bribes,
> And the plaintiff is turned into the accused.

JING:

> I laugh that for having turned on a friend,
> You should receive this fit punishment.

(XIAODAN *kneels in greeting;* JING *stands to one side.* CHOU *enters; he stands and does not sit.*)

XIAOSHENG and DAN: Your Lordship, there was indeed a leather money chest, its original seals left intact. We have brought it here.

XIAODAN: Your Lordship, Impartial Judge: Although my daughter never entered his door, she was forced to die because of him. This betrothal gift should rightly belong to me.

CHOU: Your daughter slipped and fell into the water by accident. What does that have to do with him? Since you have no daughter to give to him in marriage, why should you receive this betrothal gift?

XIAODAN: Please consider this, Your Honor: even if my daughter had slipped and fallen in, can that man have slipped as well?

CHOU: Seeing your daughter fall into the water, he wanted to help rescue her but because he did not have a firm footing, he too slipped into the water. What does that have to do with anyone else?

JING: What an insightful father–mother official![236] Truly, it takes only a few words to settle a lawsuit![237]

CHOU (*salutes* JING *with his hands*): Venerable Sir, please retire to your chambers. Make haste to write a receipt[238] and have your honored assistant come get the silver. Excuse me for not seeing you out.

JING (*makes a bow*): Many thanks, our venerable father–mother official! A written pledge will be delivered to you shortly, in which will be written: I humbly present to you a thousand in silver, to express my insignificant respect. (*Exits first.* XIAODAN *knocks her head on the floor, crying injustice; attendants drive her out.*)

XIAODAN (*sighs*):
> A life has been taken,
> And the money is all lost.
> I wouldn't have done as I did
> If I'd known just what it would cost. (*Exits.*)

(CHOU *opens the money chest, sees the silver, and is delighted.*)

XIAOSHENG and DAN (*kneel*): Congratulations, Your Honor!

CHOU: Why do you congratulate me?

XIAOSHENG and DAN: Congratulations, Your Honor, on striking it rich! This silver,
> (Tune: *Zao luopao*)
> Is not just any ordinary payoff.
> If you use it to buy property,
> You'll enjoy A lifetime of luxury.
> We, now, Deserving none, dare not contest,
> And only ask our kind master to take all!

CHOU (*laughs*): You flunkeys say clever things. If I did not take it all, should I give some share of it to you?

>I am A dab hand at making money,
>And know how to seize the cash;
>Why should I have to rely on Your dog fangs and eagle talons to slash,[239]
>To build up my family property?
>I need no omens for wealth to amass.

Even saying this, I was lucky to have you. I'll give you some as a little reward for your labors. (*Brings out silver.*)

XIAOSHENG and DAN (*aside, happily*): Great! Each of us is certain to get a silver ingot.[240] (CHOU *takes one ingot and bites*[241] *it.*) Be careful of your teeth, Your Honor!

CHOU (*bites two pieces from the edge of the silver ingot and hands them to his attendants*): Here's a piece of silver weighing more than one mace for each of you. Take it to buy tobacco, and you could definitely get drunk on it a couple of hundred times.

XIAOSHENG and DAN: That's too much. We can't accept it, and so we return it to Your Lordship. (*Return the pieces.*)

CHOU: What I gave you this time was a little too heavy. But it was a tough job for you, and I felt sorry; for that reason, I gave you more than I normally would. All right, I will keep one piece and give the other to you as a reward so that you won't hurt your reputation for honesty by accepting, and the giver will not damage his generosity. This is what is known as the virtuous gentleman showing his love for the people.

XIAOSHENG and DAN: We dare not get a payment without deserving it and so return it to Your Lordship. (*Again, they return the piece.*)

CHOU: When you speak of it this way, I cannot force you to accept it. Let me put it back under the original seal and take the money chest inside. (*Picks up the chest and is just about to exit.*)

MO (*enters hurrying, holding an official proclamation*):

> The warrant to question the accused,
> I hurry so that my feet seem to fly;
> If I'm late by even a few minutes,
> I'll be pressed for missing the deadline!
>
> Is the assistant magistrate in?

CHOU: Who is it?

MO: His Lordship the magistrate sent me here because there was a homicide case in this place and said that the petition was in Your Honor's hands. He ordered me to escort under guard both the accused and the bribe money to the county court.[242]

XIAOSHENG and DAN (*aside, happily*): Buddha be praised! This is Heaven's retribution, Heaven's retribution!

CHOU (*alarmed*): His Lordship has gone to the provincial capital. How can he be using Thousand-League-Eyes and Ears-That-Follow-the-Wind?[243]

MO: On his way back from the provincial capital, His Lordship came by this place; he made inquiries and learned of this matter and so sent me to fetch the accused.

CHOU (*turns aside, angrily*): Just as if I'd been stealing food for the dog![244] I was happy for nothing! (*Turns back.*) Then you go ahead to reply. When I have prepared my report, I will submit it under guard along with the thousand taels of silver, to be sure.

MO: More than a thousand. His Lordship instructed me that there are also two smaller packages that were seized by your court; one has two hundred taels in it, and in the other one two packets of fifty each.

CHOU (*sticks out his tongue*): It may really be said that he is "sharp-eyed enough to see 10,000 *li* and wise enough to perceive an autumn hair."[245] When you speak of it this way, even those two little edge pieces of silver must not be left out. Clerk, make haste to write the official report and send it under guard to the county court along with the bribe silver.

CHOU: Senior officials are free to pursue profit,
MO: Which associates are forbidden to do.
XIAOSHENG: What good luck that we were not rewarded!
DAN: I nearly spat out my tobacco, too!

SCENE 18: THE RETURN TO LIFE

MO (*in rush rain cape and broad-rimmed bamboo hat, carrying a fishing net and with a bamboo pole over his shoulder, enters*):
>When master is a noble hermit, his servant is at leisure,
>We call ourselves immortals once removed.
>Than fishermen and woodsmen, I see myself no better:
>We wash our feet[246] and view green hills together.

I am none other than the fishing boy servant of Master Mu. Today suddenly, the wind and waves began to rise out of a clear blue sky. Now it looks as if it were clearing again after a long rain and the river had risen a lot from that spring shower. Perhaps in the muddy water, I can catch some big fish in my net. (*To backstage.*) Wife, heat up some wine; a few bowls will help me pull in the fishing net. (*Response from backstage.*)

MO (*spreads out the fishing net and affixes the rod*):
>(Tune: *Taohong ju*)
>Sitting on Fishing Rock
>To fix The rod onto the net,
>Relying on these great waves
>To drive The fish away from shallows.
>Then I will Cast the net across this turbulent stream,
>Cast the net across this turbulent stream—
>For tonight, Our wine and dainties depend on what I catch!

(*From backstage*): The wine is warm—come and have a drink. (MO *casts the net, exits temporarily.*)

(*Gongs and drums are beaten backstage; shrimp, snail, crab, and turtle each carry banners, and secretly place the paired fish into the net. After a whirling dance, all exit.*)

MO (*enters*):

Having learned to fish, I become too fond of drink;
Fishermen of this world all are heavy drinkers.

Having been gone for a while, there must be some fish in it by now. Let me pull it in and take a look. (*Acts being unable to pull in the net.*) Yikes! Why is it so heavy? Wife, come quickly.

CHOU:
The effects of all that wine are surely strong,
Hearing his call, I can't pretend to be deaf.
I'll go with him to the stream to have some fun,
To paint a landscape painting that's erotic.

Why did you call me? Can it be that the wine is showing its effects?

MO: Don't talk so much. Quick—come help me pull in the net. (*Together pull in the net, see the fish, are happy.*)

Wonderful! Wonderful! Such big fish we've netted—must be a hundredweight[247] or more. Let's carry it ashore and see what kind of fish it is. (*Carry the fish ashore and look.*) It turns out to be a pair of soles, of flatfish.

CHOU: Hee, hee! The two are stuck tight together and playing "that game." You see, they are shaking their heads and wagging their tails together, carrying on their romantic business and doing "that thing" right in front of us. Watching them makes me envious!

(Tune: *Xi nu jiao*)
My envy is hard to bear!
I'm jealous that their bumps and hollows
Coincide so well!

I can't bear to watch them; I just want to pry them apart. (*Tries to separate them with force, but fails.*)

Ah! How can you Stick together side by side all day,
Taking Not even one moment to be apart?

(*Points to the fish and turns to her husband*) You useless bastard, look at the fish!

Embarrassing!

> No one else would Put the Milky Way[248] between us when we're under the quilt,
>
> You even Flee from pleasure and deliberately Turn away from me!

MO: Fish like this are seldom seen. Let's cover them with my rain cape and go ask the master and mistress to come and take a look. (*Takes off the rain cape and covers the fish.*)

TOGETHER:

> So rare to see,
>
> Carefully Cover and shield their rare forms
>
> So they may suffer no injury!

(*Exit together.*)

(*Gongs clash and drums are beaten backstage; shrimp, snail, crab, and turtle, again each holding banners, lead in* SHENG *and* DAN *to exchange them for the paired fish in the net and cover them with the rain cape as before. After a whirling dance, all exit.*)

(XIAOSHENG, LAODAN, MO, *and* CHOU *enter together.*)

XIAOSHENG and LAODAN: Where are they?

MO and CHOU: They're here. (*They remove the rain cape, see* SHENG *and* DAN, *and step back in alarm.*) Ah! Clearly they were a pair of flatfish. How could they have turned into two dead bodies? On top of that, it is a man and a woman hugging each other. It's enough to scare me to death!

XIAOSHENG and LAODAN: How can there be such a strange event?

XIAOSHENG:

> (*Same tune with a different beginning*)
>
> They are startling to see;
>
> They stand my hair on end and chill my heart!
>
> What great wrongs so hard to redress
>
> Would produce such huge waves?

This man and woman must be a husband and wife who were murdered. (*To* SHENG *and* DAN.) You man and woman, if you really have suffered injustice, give me some hints, that I might achieve some redress for you.

> Some response to receiving kindness
> Must be allowed to appear on your youthful faces.

(SHENG and DAN *roll over with a sigh*.)

ALL (*alarmed*): Ah! They have come back to life!

LAODAN:

> Rolling over,
> They breathe and sigh together in unison;
> We can see that Life revives within them
> And their spirits return!
> (*Repeat together*)
> So rare to see,
> Carefully Cover and shield their rare forms
> So they may suffer no injury!

LAODAN: Quickly, get some hot soup to pour down their throats.

(MO *pours soup into* SHENG's *mouth;* CHOU *pours it into* DAN's *mouth*.)

MO and CHOU: Good, good—they have both opened their eyes!

SHENG and DAN: Ah! Who are you? What place is this? The two of us leaped into the water, but why are we out on the bank again?

> (Tune: *Heima xu*)
> We had been drowned in the flowing water—
> Who came to our aid and rescued us
> From the raging waves?

XIAOSHENG: What kind of people are you two? Why did you die together? Stand up and tell us all about it.

SHENG and DAN (*stand up*): We are both actors.

> Because our good match met with ill fortune,
> We suffered many hardships together.
> Encountering an evil man,
> Dear Mother sought connections with his might
> And would compromise my virtue for a price.

TOGETHER:
> Being utterly helpless,
> In order to Keep reputation and integrity intact,
> Both our lives were cut short!

XIAOSHENG: According to your explanation, you are loyal husband and chaste wife, most certainly worthy of respect!

> (*Same tune with a different beginning*)
> May you be praised
> For your righteous courage and loyal sincerity.
> Willing to die as a couple,
> You broke away from all remaining fetters!

LAODAN (*to* DAN): Because you two jumped into water one after the other, you should have died in separate places. How did your two bodies join to become one? Leaving that aside, when we pulled up the fishing net, clearly you were two big fish. But after a while, you suddenly transformed into human shapes. Could it be that you, husband and wife, possess the magic arts of the immortals? Tell me truthfully; do not hold anything back.

> Teach me the ingenious method of hiding yourself;
> Don't conceal this fantastic magic.
> Your alarming return—
> If you were not Immortals of the highest rank,
> How could you Sacrifice your lives without being harmed?
> (*Repeat together*)
> Being utterly helpless,
> In order to Keep reputation and integrity intact,
> Both our lives were cut short!

DAN: Even we ourselves do not know how this came about. As I was dying, I was not necessarily able to wait for him; as he was dying, he was not necessarily able to find me, either. We don't know the means by which we were suddenly together embracing each other. Nor do we know the means by which our two bodies unexpectedly looked like we were originally raised in the water, floating about without experiencing drowning. We don't know when we entered the net or when we came up on the bank. Right now, it's as if we had just awakened from a great dream;[249] even the circumstances of our throwing ourselves into the water we remember just vaguely, as if it didn't really happen to us.

XIAOSHENG: You must have benefited from some deity's protection for it to turn out this way. But I do not know which deity could be so powerful.

SHENG (*nods his head*): Right, right. The plays we staged were for Lord Yan's birthday. Lord Yan is called Pacifier-of-Waves and solely in charge of watery matters. Without a doubt, he must have been the one who manifested his power. The two of us need to bow our thanks toward the Heavens.

SHENG and DAN:

>(Tune: *Jinyi xiang*)
>Entering the Gates of Death,
>We arrived on the Shores of Life,
>He relied on his divine magic
>To carry out this miracle.
>To say nothing of his Rescuing our solitary souls to form a pair
>To patch up our losses and make us whole,
>Even if our Fish bodies had not changed and we had stayed in the billows,
>Forever to be a pair of soles
>Would Surpass joining the immortals!

You two elders, please let this humble husband and wife bow to express our gratitude to you for saving our lives! (*Bow together.*)

>Saving us from suffering and distress,
>Such Loving-kindness is higher than the hills.
>Our humble selves Are not at all ungrateful;

> Respect is engraved on our hearts;
> We will repay your kindness with a thousand in gold—
> How could it be the same as repayment for a meal![250]

XIAOSHENG: But in fact this good deed was not at all my doing. It was my servants, husband and wife, who netted you two.

SHENG and DAN: Then we must also express our thanks to them.

MO: We really don't deserve this; just give me a hand salute and let that be that. (*Both* SHENG *and* MO *salute with hands clasped while* CHOU *and* DAN *each perform a curtsy.*)

XIAOSHENG: Fetch our clothes for the two of them to change into. And also, cook a fish and go buy some wine both to help them get over the shock and for us to celebrate. Go quickly! (MO *and* CHOU *respond.*)

SHENG: We will always be grateful to you for saving our lives—how could we trouble you further?

XIAOSHENG: Think nothing of it. Well, have you two been formally married?

SHENG: Although this is our intention, we have not yet been married.

XIAOSHENG: If that is how it is, let me choose an auspicious day for the two of you, and you can have your wedding right here. If you do not mind our being simple and rude, stay here for the time being while you make plans for the future.

SHENG: Many thanks!

(Tune: *Jiang shui ling*)

XIAOSHENG:
> I'm embarrassed at having but a basket of rice and a ladle of water.

LAODAN:
> I laugh at my rustic looks, disheveled bearing and snow-white hair bun.

XIAOSHENG:
> I have neither meat nor fruit to add to our meal,

LAODAN:
>	Nor do I have cosmetics to keep company with your pretty face!

XIAOSHENG and LAODAN:
>	Don't ridicule
>	Or be fed up with us
>	For not caring enough about etiquette and looks.
>	We'll relax the day long,
>	We'll relax the day long,
>	We'll gaze at the mountains with you;
>	Keep you company for idle talk,
>	Keep you company for idle talk,
>	And put down our fishing rods for you!
>	(*Coda*)

SHENG and DAN:
>	We never thought our pair of souls ever could return again;
>	A moment's contemplation just makes one sweat with fear!

XIAOSHENG and LAODAN:
>	We can only admire that Clever god whose great waves brought you here.

SCENE 19: RUSTIC NUPTIALS

WAI (*enters, costumed as an old woodcutter, carrying firewood*):
>   (Tune: *Lülü jin*)
>   I lay aside my firewood load
>   To celebrate their wedding.
>   I have nothing else to give
>   Besides half a load of kindling.
>   It's enough to heat the nuptial cup
>   While I watch the wedding rites.[251]
>   I'll seize on the occasion to trouble the host,
>   Whose generosity knows no end,
>   Whose generosity knows no end!

JING (*enters, costumed as an old farmer, carrying wine*):
>   (*Same tune*)
>   I cast aside the handles of my plow
>   To celebrate their wedding.
>   I have nothing else to give
>   Besides a jug of wine.
>   It's enough to make the bridegroom drunk
>   While I watch the wedding rites.
>   I'll seize on the occasion to trouble the host,
>   Whose generosity knows no end,
>   Whose generosity knows no end!

FUJING (*enters, costumed as an old gardener, carrying vegetables*)
>   (*Same tune*)
>   I stopped watering all my plots
>   To celebrate their wedding.
>   I have nothing else to give
>   Besides a basket full of celery.
>   It's enough to eat with the new couple's wine

> While I watch the wedding rites.
> I'll seize on the occasion to trouble the host,
> Whose generosity knows no end,
> Whose generosity knows no end!

WAI: I'm just an old woodcutter from deep in the mountains.

JING: I'm just an old farmer from deep in the mountains.

FUJING: I'm just an old gardener from deep in the mountains.

WAI: The three of us have become friends with Old Fisherman Mo, who's a new arrival, and we four mountain village friends have deep attachments for one another. Hearing that he has prepared decorated candles[252] for Tan and his bride's wedding, each of us has brought a gift to congratulate them and to use this as a pretext to get good and drunk. Now we've arrived at the place. Is elder brother Mo at home?

(*From backstage*): Coming!

XIAOSHENG (*enters*):

> (*Same tune*)
> I put down my rod and bait
> To help out with the wedding.
> Food on the plates is all river caught
> But short of mountain delicacies.
> I will urge the bridegroom to drink himself drunk
> So that they can perform the wedding rites.
> I invite my friends over to share the hosting,
> Whose generosity knows no end,
> Whose generosity knows no end!

XIAOSHENG (*greets them*): Ah! I was about to invite you over, but you three have come just at the right time.

WAI, JING, and FUJING: We have heard you netted two big fish that suddenly turned into a man and a woman, and today you have bought the decorated candles for their wedding. Is that all really true?

XIAOSHENG: Yes, it is.

WAI: I'm just a humble woodcutter and have no other wedding gift besides a bundle of pine firewood to serve as a gift. Please accept it.

JING: I'm just a humble farmer and have no other wedding gift besides a jug of thin wine made from the glutinous rice of our own field to serve as a gift. Please accept it.

FUJING: I'm just a humble gardener; I irrigate gardens and have no other wedding gift besides a bundle of celery that I grew myself, just like the old saying that "a rustic presents celery."[253] Please accept it.

XIAOSHENG: How can I, as your humble host, take advantage of the generosity of you all? Since this is the way it is, I can only accept your gifts.

WAI, JING, and FUJING: Is everything ready for the wedding?

XIAOSHENG: It's more or less ready, but there are no musicians or attendants of the bride and bridegroom for this mountain-village wedding, so it feels a little too quiet.

WAI, JING, and FUJING: Getting married is an important matter, so a wedding certainly has to be noisy and lively. Well, we have gongs and drums for offering sacrifices to the gods of the fields.[254] If everybody starts beating them, it will be as good as any musicians. But if there's nobody to take the place of the attendants at the wedding, what can we do?

CHOU (*enters, costumed as a shepherd boy, playing the flute*):

> (*Same tune*)
> I play the short flute
> To celebrate their wedding.
> I have nothing else to give
> Besides my mouth and lips.
> I will set the new couple laughing
> So that they can perform the wedding rites.
> I'll seize on the occasion to go eat off the host,

Whose generosity knows no end,
Whose generosity knows no end!

I am just a shepherd boy from deep in the mountains and have heard that at the Old Fisherman Mo's place, a couple is getting married. The guy who cuts kindling, the one who tills the fields, and the one who waters the gardens have all come to congratulate them, a pretext to cheat him out of some wine. I may be young, but I'm also a native of this village. I have no choice but to barge on in and offer my congratulations to them. How could they throw me out? I'm here already and just have to go right in. (*Enters.*) Uncle Mo, I heard that there's a happy event in your house, so I have come specially to offer my congratulations! (*Greets everyone.*) All of you gentlemen are attending the banquet and did not let me know. How could it be that you are the only ones who get to drink today's wine?

WAI, JING, and FUJING: Let us ask you. As you have come to offer congratulations, you should provide a gift. Although none of us has any silver, one of us gave firewood, one gave wine, and one gave vegetables. We'd like to ask, what did you bring?

CHOU: The thing I give is even a little better than yours, but since I have no gift card, I will just explain it aloud myself. (*Points at his mouth.*) "Allow me to present my 'long life' mouth as a gift with most sincere respect to congratulate the couple. Your student, a shepherd boy, with my respectful kowtow."

WAI, JING, and FUJING: What good is your smelly mouth? How can you provide a mouth to talk nonsense while other people have given things as presents?

CHOU: How can one get a reward without deserving it? There is a situation in which I have use for it. I presume that there are no musicians this deep in the mountains. Let me start playing the flute that I play on the back of the ox to serve as music for the wedding. Now isn't this wedding gift a little better than yours?

WAI, JING, and FUJING: We also know how to play the flute. What's so hard about that? All we lack is an attendant for the bride and bridegroom at the wedding today. Can you be the attendant?

CHOU: What's hard about that? I have learned plays, and serving as master of ceremonies for a singing troupe is my duty as a painted face.[255] I can do it, I can!

WAI, JING, and FUJING: That's fine then. Hurry up and invite the bridegroom to come out.

SHENG (*enters*):

> (Tune: *Juhua xin*)
>
> Having joined our detached souls from the bottom of the river,
>
> We now join once again in matrimony in the mountains.
>
> Our wedding guests being so numerous—
>
> I worry that we'll waste the host's fine vintage!

XIAOSHENG: Mr. Tan, these few rude friends of mine are natives of our village and members of the community. Hearing that you are getting married today, they have all brought rich gifts to congratulate you. Please come over to meet them. (SHENG *greets everyone.*)

WAI, JING, and FUJING: The shepherd boy will act as master of ceremonies. Quick, invite the bride to make her formal bows.

XIAOSHENG: It is still too early to perform the marriage ceremony. I have prepared two meager banquets: one is for the bride, and the other is for the groom. The banquet for the bride is inside, and my consort will keep her company; the banquet for the groom is outside. May I trouble all of you gentlemen to keep him company? Only after the wine is finished will we escort them to the nuptial chamber.

ALL: Right, that's just right.

(MO *enters, bringing wine, and* XIAOSHENG *delivers it to the diners.*)

TOGETHER:

> (Tune: *Gu lun tai*)

> To celebrate the fine match,
> Fisherman, woodcutter, farmer, and gardener offer the best they might,
> Even shepherd boy manages the ceremonies.[256]
> Bracken powder[257] cooked into the rice
> And fish boiled with watershield
> Merely relieve their hunger on this happy night.
> Unworthy of the Soft fragrance and warmth[258]
> Of flowers lovely and willows tender,[259]
> A straw couch will take the place of a fragrant mattress.
> When tonight they drink the nuptial cup,[260]
> It may be hard for the beauty to show her joy:
> Only relying on The mountain scenery to paint her eyebrows,
> The sound of waves to rinse her teeth,
> Pine flowers[261] to decorate her temples,
> Where could she get A golden chamber in a desolate village?
> To express our sincerity,
> We have only Morning breeze and evening moon to serve as breakfast and supper!

ALL: The time is up—please consummate this happy event. (*Rise from the table together.*)

WAI: Mr. Tan, we have a crude custom here. Whenever man and woman get married, everybody must have some fun sending them into the nuptial chamber. We call this "bantering in celebration."[262] For a little while, we'll make mischief, but don't take offense.

SHENG: I would not dare.

XIAOSHENG: We don't need to have fun in any other way: everybody just helps the groom urge the bride to have a few cups of wine. A wedding won't be fun unless you are a bit tipsy.

SHENG (*smiles*): When you explain it this way, it is really not a vulgar custom but a refined affair instead.

ALL: Shepherd boy, as master of ceremonies you must make haste to invite the bride to come out! (ALL *beat drums and gongs and play the flute.* CHOU *acts as the standard master of ceremonies, and* DAN *enters, makes ceremonial bows*[263] *with* SHENG. CHOU *carries a lantern and escorts them into the nuptial chamber.*)

(*Walk together.*)

>(*Same tune with a different beginning*)
>Joyous,
>More than any ordinary wedding:
>We admire the chaste wife and husband true
>For saving their fate and changing their lot,
>Moving ghosts and alarming the gods,
>And almost creating confusion in the blue sea.
>Full of sympathy for your plight,
>Heaven cleared away your gloom,
>Knowing you are not just ordinary folk.
>Honor and splendor are to come:
>Before reaching for the sky you first grew dragons' scales;
>Having shed your fish's body,
>The turtle's head[264] you will occupy.
>The Dragon Gate[265] is close,
>And a favorable turn in life can be foreseen.
>Truly of immortals' stuff,
>For uncouth folk just to know you is a blessing!

Bride, please receive our bows. (*Salute together.*) A fine bride! A fine bride! Indeed pretty and so neat—no wonder that this man took a fancy to her! We all propose a toast! The rules in this mountain village, unlike those in the city, are that we must all be truly dead drunk before you can be properly married. Shepherd boy: you are a child, unlike us. Pour the nuptial cup and go over to urge them to drink. (CHOU *presents them with wine;* SHENG *drinks, but* DAN *does not.*)

WAI (*aside*): She is unwilling to drink. What'll we do? All right, everybody must act rough and offer congratulations by giving the groom a good beating: once he is aching, in her heart she will not be able to stand it and will naturally drink.

ALL: Makes sense, makes sense! (*Turn back.*) If the bride does not drink, it is all because the groom told her not to, which is really unacceptable! We'll each give him twenty punches to replace the wedding wine.

WAI: I'll beat him first. (*Clenches his fists.*)

(Tune: *Bu shi lu*)

My wild nature cannot be tamed,
A woodcutter's hairy fist is as heavy as an ax. (*Grabs* SHENG *and hits him.*)

SHENG (*cries out*): I can't bear this beating; I can't bear it! Wife, just drink it! (DAN *drinks.*)

JING (*shouts loudly*): Now it's my turn!

With my military might,
Surely your Soul will perish at the touch of my poisonous punch! (*Hits* SHENG.)

SHENG: It hurts, it hurts badly! Wife, just drink it! (DAN *drinks.*)

FUJING: You both used your fists, but I will take it upon my humble self to change the rule,[266] and use only my palm. (*Opens wide his hand.*)

I stretch out my palm,
But don't underestimate my palm;
A wave of the whole palm will leave A five-petal plum-blossom print. (*Folds back two fingers.*)
Even Half of my fingers will leave A print of three bamboo leaves!

SHENG (*alarmed*): How can I bear such a big palm? Wife, hurry up and just drink it! (DAN *drinks.*)
CHOU: Now it is your student's turn. You honorable sirs all presented her with small cups, but humble I must present her with a big cup!
WAI, JING, and FUJING: Do you really have a way to make her drink that much?
CHOU: Just saying so is no guarantee; you will see how when I do it. Quick, pour her some wine! (*Pours a big cup and urges* DAN *to drink, but she does not drink.*)

  Ha! You would take advantage of my being young? To be frank with you, even if my hands cannot beat people up, this set of teeth of mine can bite. I would not bite any place else, but I'll give him such a bite on his "important thing" so that you won't be able to become husband and wife tonight! (*Champs his teeth.*)

   I Champ my teeth—,
   I only need to bite off three inches of muscle;
   Surely you will Have no head to go to,
   Have no head[267] to go to!

SHENG: How could this be allowed? Quick, don't let that happen! (DAN *drinks hurriedly, all laugh.* DAN *looks embarrassed and exits to avoid them.*)
ALL: We have made enough mischief, and the best thing in Heaven and on Earth is to make things convenient for people, so let's all go home.
XIAOSHENG (*to* SHENG): Brother Tan, you got married onstage all the time, but you must have followed old-fashioned customs and have never done it this way: the fisherman, woodcutter, farmer, and gardener escort the bride to the wedding hall, while the shepherd boy acts as master of ceremonies. Although it is a bit unrefined, it does have a kind of peculiar charm. Didn't you find it a case of "sights and sounds all fresh and new"?

SHENG: This is not only extremely new but also extremely refined. What did I do to deserve this? A thousand thanks!

TOGETHER:
> (*Coda*)
> So this text's creative,
> To make sights and sounds all new.
> We would echo refined scholars' romantic charm,
> But we didn't want to just Imitate the ways that are tried and true!

SCENE 20: THE SECRET DISPATCH

FUJING (*leads extras onto the stage*):

> (Tune: *Bu changong*)
> Ashamed that I mounted an attack with no sound plan in place
> I rashly lost half my savage fighters.[268]
> Now relying on an adviser
> To work out all kinds of schemes,
> I want to wipe away that earlier disgrace.

Last time when I, Great King of the Mountain, mobilized my troops, I relied entirely on courage and strength and had no general strategy. The enemy ambushed us and launched a fire attack that burned up many of my beasts of prey. I had no choice but to retreat deep in the mountains to hide my vanguard and restrain their vigor. After resting for half a year, I feel they have recovered their energy and strength. Now I have a military adviser who makes plans with miraculous skill, on a par with Chen Ping and Zhuge.[269] Having him direct military operations, I figure there's no way we will not be victorious. And I have another piece of good news: I have heard that Military Defense Circuit Intendant Murong has resigned from his post and has retired into the mountains. Except for this one man, who could be my match? Attendants: quick, summon my military adviser. (*All respond and summon the military adviser.*)

JING (enters):

> (*The beginning of the same tune*)
> A hundred thousand armored troops match the strategy in my breast,
> As Heaven gives me the chance to brew chaos in the world of men!

JING (*greets* FUJING): Great King, today is a propitious date according to the sun's position—just the right time to mobilize the troops.

FUJING: I summoned you here just for this reason. Attendants: quick, bring me my fierce tiger. Once I mount, I'll be ready to lead the troops forward.

(*Attendants lead a tiger[270] onto the stage, and* FUJING *mounts it.* JING *mounts a horse; they walk together.*)

TOGETHER:
>(Tune: *Fan zhuma*)
>The roar of cannons rumbles across the sky;
>When military commands are issued,
>Ten thousand cheer in unison.
>The fierce Tigers boost our remarkable might,
>As they move out ahead of the troops;
>No need to order them into ranks,
>They'd march 100 leagues like a string of fish.
>Observed from a commanding height,
>They seem to form a wall:
>These Soldiers are indeed a marvelous sight!
>Advise the officials who govern these lands—
>Surrender quickly and pledge allegiance.
>Only then you'll keep your heads,
>As the same old place to hang a new hat.[271]
>If you choose to throw away your lives,
>You'll feel Mount Tai crush you like an egg.[272]
>When my sword falls, don't be surprised or sad! (*All exit.*)

SCENE 21: A PARTING GIFT

XIAOSHENG (*enters*):

> (Tune: *Feng ma'er qian*)
> I've helped the young scholar tie the marriage knot,
> But looking to his future,
> All is still unclear.

I, Old Fisherman Mo, rescued Scholar Tan and his wife, and also helped them to get married. This happy event was complete in every way. Even so, although it is pleasant in the mountains, this is not a place for him to stay for a long time, and I still want to find a way forward for him. I see that this young man is graceful in appearance and dignified in bearing, and I surmise that he is no ordinary personage. Yesterday on the writing desk, I saw several new poems that he had written. He is actually a great man of letters and a real scholar; if I tell him to go seek an official rank, winning a distinguished robe[273] will be as easy as picking cress. When he comes out, I can only offer him this advice, prepare some money for his journey, and see him off.

SHENG (*enters*):

> (Tune: *Feng ma'er hou*)
> Our benefactor has raised us from the dead and joined us
>   in marriage.
> But we sit idle all day and simply eat—
> We've used up all his drinking funds.[274] (*Greets*
>   XIAOSHENG.)

XIAOSHENG: Brother Tan, since you are a scholar, you should set your mind on winning an official rank. As the ancient saying puts it, "If you survive a great disaster, your future will definitely be bright." You should take advantage of being in the bloom of youth to go and sit for the imperial examinations. Why are you idling away your time with no concern for your future career? Surely you can't consider the black gauze official's hat you wore on the stage to be the pinnacle of your life's ambition!?

SHENG: My benefactor, let me explain:

> (Tune: *Ji xianbin*)
> I Year after year tied my hair to the rafters, stabbed myself in the thigh,[275]
> Wearing through a bronze peacock inkstone.[276]
> I also know that The roc's path to the clouds[277] is not beyond my reach;
> I Can soar to the blue sky lightly clinging to a cyclone.
> For now I keep my long plumes furled
> Waiting for a favorable wind to head south;[278]
> It's not that I underestimate myself,
> To my shame, I simply lack the travel funds.

XIAOSHENG: Presumably you have no money for the journey? This is not a problem. Although I am a fisherman, I still have some wealth. After buying wine and bartering for millet, I definitely have a few spare coins every day. If you are willing to go back and sit for the examinations, I can meet those traveling expenses for you.

SHENG: If you would do so, my gratitude would know no end! If I make some advancement with this trip, I will not only repay you with silver and silks but even share with you, my benefactor, all my great wealth and high honors.

XIAOSHENG: Don't bother about that.

> (*Same tune*)
> I Eat when I'm hungry, drink water when I thirst, and fall asleep when I'm drunk;
> What use would I have for any more wealth?
> Ashamed to hide valuables[279] in my humble hut,
> I will help you gain wealth and attain high rank.[280]
> I encourage You, noble sir, to be diligent;

> Remember me here in the wilds content with being poor and lowly.
>
> I have no other wish:
>
> May you graciously dispense with all repayment!

Maid, ask Madame Tan and my wife to come out. (*Response from backstage.*)

DAN (*enters*):

> (Tune: *Feng ma'er*)
>
> Happy being with an immortal lady banished from Jasper Pool,[281]
>
> I worry about parting—
>
> Thus I tarry and linger.

LAODAN:

> Having An agreeable chat does not weary my spirits,
>
> But afraid of hindering the newlyweds,
>
> I urge her to bed every night.

XIAOSHENG (*to* LAODAN): Wife, this is the year for the imperial examinations. Because Mr. Tan wants to go back to take the examinations, it would be inappropriate for you and me to delay them long here. Make haste to bring out the travel money I have prepared, and also prepare a jug of thin wine so that we can properly see them on their way. (LAODAN *brings out the silver, and* XIAOSHENG *presents it.* CHOU *enters with wine and presents it,* XIAOSHENG *sees* SHENG *off, and* LAODAN *sees* DAN *off.*)

XIAOSHENG and LAODAN:

> (Tune: *Hupo mao'er zhui*)
>
> To keep you here was not our plan;
>
> Far better to send you back again.
>
> This trip will bring high honor, so much is plain,
>
> But once you reach your goal, put down your whip and then resign.
>
> Leave behind the stench—[282]

>   Make the honors of this world
>   The farthest thing from your mind!

XIAOSHENG: Fishing boy, you carry the luggage and accompany Mr. Tan on the first stage of their journey. (MO *responds and enters with luggage on a carrying pole.*)

SHENG and DAN: Our benefactors, please allow us husband and wife to take leave of you formally with our respectful bows. (*The four all bow together.*)

SHENG and DAN:

> (*Same tune*)
> Our gratitude we will seek ways to repay,
> With our very lives we vow.
> Su Zhang was a second Heaven,[283] they say,
> But only now we believe the ancients' words.
> Our hopes fulfilled—
> The remaining years of our lives
> Are a gift that you have bestowed!
> (*Coda*)

XIAOSHENG (*to* SHENG):

> You should Dedicate all talent and advice to the imperial court.

LAODAN (*to* DAN):

> Don't let your divine beauty[284] distract your young man.

SHENG and DAN:

> We definitely will Win credit and fame to repay our pair of Heavens!

XIAOSHENG: Now your dragon scales are fully grown;

LAODAN: Henceforth in deep pools you'll find no soles in pairs.

SHENG: When I pass to become a dragon, we'll still stay eye to eye,[285]

DAN: I won't allow him by himself to climb those blue-sky stairs.

SCENE 22: A CUNNING PLAN

(FUJING *and* JING *lead extras onto the stage.*)
    (Tune: *Ban jian mei*)
FUJING:
    Our army appeared from nowhere, like an army sent from Heaven.
JING:
    Our strategy can compare with Chen Ping,
    But in cunning we surpass Chen Ping.
FUJING: Since leaving the mountains, we have overrun many cities and killed or wounded innumerable government officials. And yet we do not have enough troops to establish a foothold, and we have not been able to occupy the region. For the time being, we just roam from place to place: first, to scrape up money and treasure to help out with military supplies, and second, to rattle the government soldiers' determination so that they cannot coordinate their actions. There's just one problem: I have heard that when the imperial government learned that I have left the mountains, they want to reinstate that Circuit Intendant Murong. If by any chance this man does return, what stratagems will you use against him?
JING: That's no worry, no worry! It is precisely this man who will assist you, Great King, in conquering all the land under Heaven. I assure you that within a few days, a certain Circuit Intendant Murong will lead his forces here to surrender as soon as he arrives on the battlefield.
    (Tune: *Zao luopao*)
    You need no dagger-ax to aid in this victory;
    We'll defeat the enemy with an ingenious plan.
    Just sit back and watch us succeed.

FUJING: I have heard that Circuit Intendant Murong is a man of ardent loyalty and great courage—and he would not be willing to surrender. Don't be fooled by him!

JING:
>Drinking From the Spring of Avarice[286] can mix the pure with the dross;
>I personally have many Remarkable methods to transform loyalty to doublecross!

FUJING: Could it be that this man has been friends with you in the past?

JING:
>He is in the south, and I in the north;
>When could I be acquainted with Jingzhou's boss?[287]

FUJING: Even though you have never met him, there must have been correspondence between you two.

JING:
>He is Cautious in choosing friends;
>I had no chance to introduce myself.

FUJING: Then when you speak of it this way, in fact you have had absolutely no connection with him. How could you take on such a dangerous thing?

JING:
>It is 90 percent sure, not just a matter of chance.

To tell you the truth, I have a most ingenious plan. Because he is unwilling to serve in office, Circuit Intendant Murong has become a hermit in the mountains. Now the imperial court needs him and has sent local government officials everywhere out to look for him. I, your servant, will institute my plan: we have found a man who looks just like him. I've promised this man a thousand taels of silver for his service. As soon as he arrives, we will send him off to hide himself in the mountains and wait for someone to find him.

Once he leaves the mountains, this imposter is bound to be put in charge of troops, and when he arrives on the battlefield, he will naturally turn his weapons to fight against the government forces. High or low officials in this province all know that Murong is a man of some insight, so hearing he has surrendered, each and every one of them will naturally cross over and pledge allegiance to our side. Then our Great Cause can be settled by simply sending out a general call to arms. Isn't this ingenious plan better than those of Chen Ping and stronger than Zhuge Liang's?

FUJING (*great laughter*): A marvelous plan, a marvelous plan!

> (*Same tune*)
> Your cunning is hard to match, after all;
> Indeed, that Zhuge you wipe away
> And blot out even Chen Ping.
> Making use of his might and relying on his fame,
> We can make thousands respond to a single call.
> To conquer fortified cities and formidable foes,
> We need not do battle ourselves;
> Martial music,[288] songs of triumph,
> We only need to sit back and enjoy!
> One man's wisdom will bring victory to our soldiers all!

Nevertheless, I am still worried about one problem.

JING: What is it?

FUJING: Although some men in this world do look alike, if you look at them carefully, there are after all some differences. If by any chance he is caught out by the local government officials, what's to be done?

JING (*laughs*): We've rattled those local officials so much that they would be only too happy to get a scapegoat to blame. Forget about those who can't tell the difference; even if they do make him out, they will pretend to be deaf and dumb and rely on him to go out to face disaster. Who would want to mount a single objection?

FUJING: What you say does make sense. As soon as he arrives, we will attack their cities to make those local officials anxious so that we can put him forward.

JING: Rightly so.

> The campaign begins only when the stratagem's all in place,
> Unlike the previous time, we were learning how to campaign.
> Of heroes in the world today, you will not find a trace,
> Why worry that we younger folk cannot achieve some fame?

SCENE 23: THE MAKE-BELIEVE HERMIT

CHOU (*costumed as the fake old fisherman, enters, holding a fishing pole in the left hand and carrying a bundle in the right with a black gauze cap and round collar in it*):

> Temporarily trading red headdress for bamboo hat,
> I hide beside the stream and cast my fishing line.
> Hard to meet a true recluse within this world,
> So a bandit in disguise might pass himself off as a hermit!

I am none other than the secret agent of the Great King of the Mountain, who has sent me off to disguise myself as an old fisherman. Even though Circuit Intendant Murong resigned his office and retired into the mountains, the imperial government surely wants to reinstate him. But no matter how much those local officials have searched for him everywhere, they still have not found him. So the Great King of the Mountain's adviser has devised an ingenious plan: seeing that I, my humble self, look just like Murong, he has promised me a payment of a thousand taels of silver for my service. He has hired me to disguise myself as the old fisherman and told me to wait for the local officials to find me. If they ask me to come out of retirement, they are bound to put me in charge of leading the troops, and then I can go into action. Now I wear a rush cape and a bamboo hat and put on the airs of a scholar just like a man of noble character who has withdrawn from the world. I also have a black gauze official hat and round collar with me, so that when people see them they will take me for a retired official. I see someone coming in the distance, so I'd better throw in my line. (*Sits cross-legged, fishing.*)

> (Tune: *San bang gu*)
> If you want people to know your name, pretend to hide your identity;

> This is The true tradition of life as a hermit,
> Called: hiding the body while revealing the shadow.
> This fisherman sings to make himself heard,
> And this sheepskin coat shows off my appearance.
> If you want to Visit me, the "guest star,"[289]
> Just welcome me with pomp and circumstance,
> As I have A black gauze hat here at hand,
> And a blue robe[290] right here at hand.

(WAI and JING *enter, costumed as yamen runners.*)

WAI:
> Recently so much news we have heard,
> But one piece is particularly odd.
> The superior at our office has left his post,
> But we underlings are ordered to have him caught.

We are none other than the runners from the prefecture of Tingzhou[291] sent to search for Circuit Intendant Murong. On recent orders from the imperial edict, every official, high or low, must dispatch people to search for him. Yesterday we heard someone say that an old fisherman who looked like him recently appeared deep in the mountains; that is why we have come here to track him down. There's a man up ahead fishing; that must be him. Let's go take a look. (*They walk closer and steal a glance.*) He's the spitting image of Murong! Let's go over and kowtow to see whether he will accept it. Then we will know.

WAI and JING (*greet the fisherman*): Your Lordship, we prefectural *yamen* attendants kowtow to you.

CHOU (*stays seated without moving*): I am an old fisherman and have no government post. You do not need to show me such respect. Get up and go away.

WAI and JING (*aside*): He sits erect and stays still and also speaks like an official. It must be him, beyond a doubt. Let's search that bundle of his and see what sorts of things are in it. (*They take the bundle, untie it, and look.*) Ah, both a black gauze hat and round collar are here. How could you say you were not His Honor!

CHOU (*pretends to be flustered*): They have found me out! What will I do?

WAI: We have been commissioned by the government to earnestly request Your Lordship to resume your post. We have looked everywhere for you; who would have thought that you were hiding here? Now there is no need to protest any more. Please hurry up and change your clothes and come with us to the *yamen* to assume your official post.

CHOU: I won't return to resume office. Please go report back and let me live on in idleness.

WAI and JING (*pay no attention to him, change his hat and robe for him, and call to backstage*): Where is the local headman? Hurry up and fetch a mountain palanquin and assign several servants to take His Lordship to his headquarters.

(*From backstage*): We have the servants, but this deep in the mountains there is no proper palanquin to be had. All we have is a sedan chair with a soft seat, but I am afraid that the lord won't be used to sitting in it.

WAI: What is a sedan chair with a soft seat?

(*From backstage*): Dry vines are used as a sedan, and the person is tied into the middle of it. Then we pick it up and walk swiftly. This is what is called "a sedan chair with a soft seat."

WAI: If that's what there is, fetch it quickly. (*Two men enter, holding a long rope.*)

CHOU: How can I sit in such a sedan? Oh, all right.

> Although this sedan chair is vicious, the people are nice;
> I'll just have to ride this like a children's hobbyhorse.[292]

(*The men tie him up and carry him.*)

CHOU:

>(Tune: *Dao tuo chuan*)
>Dry vines may be soft but feel hard for a ride,
>Feel hard for a ride;
>It exactly chafes my rod of romance,
>My rod of romance,
>Nearly forfeiting this life of mine.
>Torment me no more—
>Just stop!

(*The men carrying him run fast.*)

CHOU:

>I tell them to stop,
>Yet they march ahead all undeterred.
>Laughing that
>This children's hobbyhorse shows too much affection!

(*They arrive.*)

WAI and JING: Your Honor, please enter the *yamen*. We'll go report to the prefect so that he can come pay his respects. (*Exit.*)

(MO and FUJING, *costumed as subordinate officials, enter hurriedly and pay their respects.*)

CHOU: As circuit intendant, I was extremely loath to serve as an official and so I went into hiding in the mountains. What is the reason that you have asked me to come out of retirement?

MO and FUJING: Because this area has so many troubles, His Majesty insists on enlisting Your Excellency's help; this was not a decision made by us, your humble subordinates.

(*Gongs and drums are beaten, with loud shouts from backstage.*)

ONE MAN (*enters in a hurry*): Disaster! Your Lordship, the mountain bandits are besieging the city. (*Everyone is flustered.*)

CHOU: With me, the circuit intendant, here, you need not be frightened.

(Tune: *Jin shang hua*)
No need to fear the bandits' attack,
No need to fear the bandits' attack,
To protect the surrounding area
I take full responsibility.
With might forge ahead,
With might forge ahead,
To slaughter them one and all!

I will make the first charge, and you will just lead the cavalry and infantry in the rear, waiting to respond.

ALL (*deep bows*): Yes, sir!

CHOU: Dispatch the troops now. (ALL *mount horses and march.*)[293]

TOGETHER:

(*Same tune*)
Just arrived, he mobilizes the army,
Just arrived, he mobilizies the army,
With no need to consult counsel.
Only this can show his talent and ability.
Boldly he assumes command,
Boldly he assumes command,
No wonder he earns such esteem!

(FUJING *leads extras onstage; they attack from all sides.* CHOU *pretends to be defeated.* FUJING *temporarily leads extras off.*)

CHOU: Their momentum is really fierce. I think that we are no match for them; we can only surrender. (*To backstage.*) You government officials, just come along with me to surrender; if you don't, I will turn my cavalry around and kill every last one of you!

(*From backstage*): If even Your Excellency has surrendered, how dare we, your humble subordinates, oppose the enemy? We are also willing to surrender.

(FUJING *leads extras onstage again, comes to a halt.*)

CHOU: There is no need to go on killing, as I am willing to surrender.

FUJING: In that case, order the troops to part and wait for him to come out to meet us. (CHOU *greets* FUJING.)

FUJING: I am deeply obliged to you. From now on, I will temporarily treat you as a distinguished guest and leave all the treasure we've looted in your care; after our conquest is complete, I will in addition award you with a top official position.

CHOU: Thank you for your favor!

FUJING: For the time being, we will return to our camp. (*They march off.*)

>(*Same tune*)
>Victory the moment the cavalry arrived,
>Victory the moment the cavalry arrived!
>Wonderful foresight and superb strategy,
>Extraordinary courage and remarkable skill.
>In the future,
>In the future,
>You will assist a True Ruler to fulfill Heaven's Mandate.[294]

CHOU: Ridiculous that mediocre men lack resourcefulness
And surrender just as soon as a trap is laid;
FUJING: True enough,
But I worry that rumors will reach his mountain valley
And bestir our tough opponent of days past.

SCENE 24: DEPARTING IN GLORY

DAN (*enters, accompanied by* FUJING):

>(Tune: *Xi di jin*)
>
>My husband has viewed flowers[295] while flushed with success,
>
>Allowing me to smooth my worried brows.[296]
>
>The gilded announcement[297] has arrived, yet he is still delayed.
>
>But in my dreams each night, I see his soul return.

I am Fairy Liu. I returned with my darling to his hometown just in time for the autumn examinations.[298] I am delighted that he has reported successes at both the provincial and metropolitan levels; even so, he has not yet been appointed to a government post and is still waiting in the capital to be selected. Over the past few days, I have drawn lots in a temple and divined by the Eight Trigrams, and all the results say that he will fill a regional vacancy and is coming back soon. I think he must have arrived by now.

SHENG (*wearing official hat and belt, leads musicians with drums and horns onstage*):

>(*Same tune*)
>
>In days gone by, when I donned the robe of blue,
>
>I sought only its momentary joys.
>
>Now finally I am acting the play of my life,
>
>And the opening scene is of returning home in glory!

DAN: Ah, my husband has come back.

>Now that you have achieved glory,
>
>This is joy that's worth a million!
>
>Let me congratulate you with a bow.

SHENG: I also want to bow my thanks to you, and for us to greet each other together as husband and wife.

(*They bow to each other.*)

SHENG:
> In those years of drifting, my luck did not come through;
> But your noble eyes perceived me as hero all the same.

DAN:
> Through wind and dust, I got to accompany you to blue clouds[299]
> And feel lucky my beauty did not curse me to a bad fate.[300]
> Plum Fragrance, bring the wine. (FUJING *presents wine.*)

DAN:
> (Tune: *Huamei xu*)
> With this cup of wine, I celebrate your bravely flying high;
> Worth our hardships endured together in days gone by.
> We laugh that our period of playing *sheng* and *dan*
> Became two lifetimes of being husband and wife.
> You abandoned reputation and moral stance for me,
> And I willingly threw away my mortal form for you.
> Now finally, we enjoy glory and high status,
> While we seem still crazy about each other!

Tell me, my lord, what government post did you receive, and where will your office be? When are you setting out? May I go with you?

SHENG: The post of senior officer at the Court of Judicial Review has been conferred on me. I am assigned to the office in Tingzhou and must set out tomorrow. When you and I died in the water, we could not bear to separate and clung tightly to each other. How could I possibly leave to take up my post and not bring you along?

> (*Same tune*)
> Where could we not depend on each other?
> Our paired fish bodies were given by Heaven,
> Strangely sleeping and eating together,

Unable to separate an inch or a step apart.
When poor and lowly, I feared I'd sleep alone;
With wealth and rank, how could I rest without you?
You Deliberately teased me with complaints while
    knowing well my answer.
I laugh: No need have you, my Beauty, for suspicions!

DAN: I had nothing in mind other than to go with you to thank our benefactors on your way to assume office. But I do not know if it is on the way.

SHENG: I have exactly the same thought. Even if it is not on the way, we should still make a detour to go see them.

(Tune: *Shen zhangr*)
Proud and elated,
Proud and elated!
All thanks to The gods and man for their assistance,
That my life might take this wondrous turn.
In gratitude I cannot help myself,
Traveling far to give cattle and brocade,
To bring them baskets of gifts
To repay them for all their aid in our time of need
And thank them for relieving our distress;
To repay them for all their aid in our time of need
And thank them for relieving our distress!

This marriage of ours began with acting in a play. Since it began in a play, it should be brought to a conclusion in a play as well. When we will go to offer sacrifices to Lord Yan, we should put on a religious play. But I fear that we will not be able to find opera actors in that rural area. What can we do?

DAN: The third day of this tenth lunar month will be Lord Yan's birthday again. Now it is already the ninth month, and we have a long way to go, so I am only afraid that we will not get there in time.

Let's just deal with it when we get there. Perhaps Lord Yan is aware of our wish and might keep the actors there until we arrive to fulfill our promise to him.

SHENG: How could that be?!

DAN:

> (Tune: *Di liuzi*)
> This deity,
> This deity,
> Will support us to the end—
> To complete our fine tale,
> To complete our fine tale,
> With a "head" and a "tail."
> He'll detain actors in secret,
> Grant us fair winds
> And hold back countercurrents;
> To reach Prince Teng's Pavilion,[301]
> Our immortal boat will seem to fly!

SHENG: We will have to send someone on ahead to go directly there to make the arrangements for us to redeem our vows to the deity. I will also write a letter about the good news and send it to Old Fisherman Mo; it would be good to let him know beforehand.

DAN: What you said is absolutely right.

> (*Coda*)

SHENG:

> Tonight we will sleep under the mandarin duck duvet.
> People always say The joy of newlyweds is second to
>   reunion after return from far away.

DAN:

> Besides, You have passed the highest examination—
> How can I Not feel joy?

SCENE 25: A PRETEND DEITY

XIAOSHENG (*enters*):

>(Tune: *Juhua xin*)
>Even before the sun has set, I've had three daytime naps,
>I realize here in the mountains that time does slowly pass.

LAODAN (*enters*):

>I think back to the busy days when we had so many tasks:
>We'd even hear the crowing of the cock before we could go to sleep.

XIAOSHENG: Wife, it has already been a year since you and I bid farewell to Scholar Tan and his wife. Having heard that the lists of successful candidates of the provincial and metropolitan examinations have already been published, I wonder whether or not he has passed. I keep thinking about him.

LAODAN: Borrow a *Register of Successful Candidates*[302] to look him up in it, and then we'll know.

XIAOSHENG: It has been said since ancient times, "There are no calendars in the mountains; at the end of winter, you don't know what year it is." Living in the midst of ten thousand mountains, we have no way of even seeing a calendar—where could we go borrow a *Register of Successful Candidates*?

LAODAN: Well, that is right. If he has passed the imperial examinations, he will certainly send us a letter. You and I must just wait patiently.

WAI (*enters, costumed as a servant*):

>(Tune: *Bu shi lu*)
>Amid these vast misty waters,
>The person that I seek lives in this direction.

I am none other than the one who Master Tan sent on ahead. His Lordship has a letter for an old fisherman surnamed Mo. Searching all the way, I have finally arrived here. Is anybody home?

XIAOSHENG:

> I open the gate to look:
>
> Has someone come to collect taxes on farm goods and silk?

WAI: I am Lord Tan's steward and dispatched to deliver a letter. Might you be the greatly esteemed Elder Mo?

XIAOSHENG: Yes, I am.

WAI: Then Your Honor, please allow me to pay my respects to you. (*About to bow*; XIAOSHENG *helps him up.*)

XIAOSHENG:

> Don't be so modest and courteous.
>
> I Have never seen such deep bows,
>
> And your Kneeling can make me feel anxious all over.

May I ask which Lord Tan sent you here?

WAI: It was the man who suffered a disaster and you rescued here last year. Now he is among the top category of successful candidates in the imperial examinations and has been appointed senior officer at the Court of Judicial Review in Tingzhou. He will pass by this place within the next few days and wants to come and express his thanks to you as his benefactors. He sent me ahead to deliver this letter. (*Hands over the letter.*)

XIAOSHENG: So this is how it is. Please have a seat inside and stay for a simple meal.

WAI: I have other business on the way ahead and dare not stay, so I must take my leave.

> I entreat your pardon.
>
> Urgent official assignments cannot be disobeyed.
>
> Respectfully, I decline your food and drink,
>
> Respectfully, I decline your food and drink. (*Exits.*)

XIAOSHENG (*goes inside*): Wife, Scholar Tan has already won an official appointment. On the way to his post in Tingzhou, he will pass by here. He has sent someone ahead to deliver a letter and will arrive soon afterward.

LAODAN: So this is how it is. We did not rescue them in vain! Oh joy, oh joy! But wait a minute: he has been appointed to a position in Tingzhou—that was our former posting. If you have a mind to be a good fellow, you might as well help him to the end. Give him a detailed account of the local customs and conditions of the people as well as the strengths and weaknesses of the local government there so that he can follow your model to be a good official. Wouldn't that be a fine thing to do?!

[XIAO]SHENG (*shakes his head*): I must not do that!

> (Tune: *Jie san cheng*)
> As an official, my loyalty and integrity of days past,
> With him in times to come my experience I'll share;
> But I fear Needlessly stirring up vexations of "blue cloud" problems,
> By following the example of Feng Fu's[303] return to his old trade.
> I wish I could Cleave the mountain to cut off my path to Zhongnan,[304]
> And use an ax to chop away the Earl of Shao's pear[305]
> To dispel public expectation,
> How could I allow myself To choose the shackles of wealth
> Or the fetters of fame!

LAODAN: Are you concerned that if you reveal your background to him, he might urge you to leave the mountains and take up a post? You are right to be worried. But think of this: he may be a man of great talents and abilities, but he is, after all, a scholar who has just passed the imperial civil examinations. Moreover, the bandits in the mountains have never been completely wiped out. If by any chance the bandits make a move after he takes office, he might not only lose his official rank but even his life will be at risk. As I see it, you really should still give him some guidance.

XIAOSHENG: What you say is right, wife.

LAODAN:

(*Same tune*)
Although for yourself, you should cherish lofty goals,
I think you May still have ways to perform good deeds in this world.
When have you ever seen Anyone stop building a stupa at just six stories?[306]
Why not complete this important task despite your fears?
If you let His corpse needlessly be wrapped in the hide of a horse,[307]
It would have been better For him to be stored away in a flood dragon's belly!
Reconsider—
Don't Allow All your previous accomplishments to go to waste
By sitting idly and watching Both sides suffer defeat and injury in due course.

XIAOSHENG: I have an excellent plan, one that will allow me to give him good advice while not revealing any trace of my having been an official. (*Laughs.*) That way should be all right, but I think it a little *too* clever.

LAODAN: What is this excellent plan?

XIAOSHENG: When he first threw himself into the water, that he did not die was entirely thanks to Lord Yan's miraculous power. I mean to use the deity to provide him with instruction. I'll take advantage of the time before he arrives to compose a handbook on the ways of governing the people and suppressing the bandits. I'll add a cover with the four words, "Sealed by Lord

Pacifier-of-Waves," written on it. After he gets here, I will slip it into his luggage on the sly, so that when he suddenly finds the book farther along on his journey, he will just think that Lord Yan has again displayed his divine power to aid him in establishing himself. For that reason, he will have unquestioned faith in it. I had told him that I cannot read a single character, so he will definitely not suspect that it came from me. Don't you think that this plan is ingenious?

LAODAN (*laughs heartily*): Wonderful! Amazing! If this is how it's going to be, you should start on this handbook right away.

XIAOSHENG (*writes*):

(Pastiche: *Luopao ge*)

    (Tune: *Zao luopao*)
    To describe in full the situation in Bingzhou,[308]
    This excellent book of "all that you must know"
    Is certainly out of the ordinary.
    I'll have the Divine duty to assist you,
    And guarantee that no waves will rise on the land.
    Once you enter a state in peril,
    You will transform it into an orderly realm;
    A ravaged land can suddenly change
    Into a magic wonderland.[309]

As the ancient saying makes it: "There is good administration by man but no good administration by law."[310] Even though what I have written is fine as far as it goes, there are still some things I must impress on him: when it is time to make changes as the situation demands, he must make the decisions himself. It will not do for him to rigidly adhere to set rules and fixed standards. (*Writes again.*)

    You will have to deviate slightly from the gourd at hand.[311]
    (*Finishes writing.*)

LAODAN: You and I have racked our brains to use the deity to do good. After the plan has proved itself, he will only know that he should be grateful to Lord Yan. How can he know that the credit should go to us?

XIAOSHENG: Don't talk that way. How can you know that our ideas have not come from the deities? Perhaps He has given us these instructions from the unseen world. Here I might have used the deity as a pretext, and He might have borrowed a human hand—it is all one and the same plan!

LAODAN: Just as you say!

>(Tune: *Pai ge*)
>Relying on each other,
>Mutually sharing the glory,
>Why should not deities and humans work hand in hand?
>People are helping,
>And ghosts assist as well,
>Both are busy on his behalf.

I laugh at my own obsessed mind—no one can compare:
For helping others achieve success, I claim no credit there.
I do have means at hand to buy a bit of fame,
Yet I'd feel ashamed to be ancient angler in the arena of fame.[312]

SCENE 26: PRESENTING THE BOOK

(SHENG *and* DAN *enter, wearing official hats and robes, followed by* JING, *costumed as a servant, and* FUJING *as a maid.*)

SHENG:
>(Tune: *Qingyu an*)
>Our immortal boat happily arrives at where we were restored to life.
>That fishing net
>Was the means of our salvation.

DAN:
>Not only did the old fisherman serve as gracious host,
>But these mountains were companions
>And the river kept us company.

SHENG and DAN:
>Such a joy to be once again united!

SHENG: We have been traveling along our way, and here we are at the boundary of Yanling. Those two figures on the mountain slope ahead are perhaps the revered Mr. Mo and his lady.

DAN: It must be them, beyond doubt.

(XIAOSHENG *and* LAODAN *enter together.*)

(*Same tune with a different beginning*)

XIAOSHENG:
>Mistakenly calling out to others' craft time after time,
>I complained about those boats that would not tarry.

LAODAN:
>The one we've called to this time cannot be wrong—
>From inside the blue-screened window,
>A face has gazed at us for long

XIAOSHENG and LAODAN:
>And he points toward the path beside the stream.

(*Shouting loudly*) Could that really be Master Tan on the incoming boat?

JING: Yes, it is.

(*Extras enter to moor the boat.* JING *and* FUJING *carry gifts and go onto the bank, following* SHENG *and* DAN.)

XIAOSHENG: The path by the stream is wet; it's no place to exchange our bows. Please come and we can greet you in our desolate residence. (*Walk together.*)

>(Tune: *Yi jiang feng*)
>Right past our desolate residence,
>Along grassy paths brings home the celestial carriage;
>Deer and boars observe it in surprise.

LAODAN:

>Here halts the eminent carriage
>At the rustic wicker gate[313]
>Of our narrow and low-lying thatched cottage.
>I just fear your Horses will have no room to turn around.

SHENG and DAN:

>The same humble selves as before,
>Your same noble hut as before,
>How could you think that It is now too small to shelter us?

>(*They arrive.*)

Our two great benefactors, please sit down and allow the two of us, husband and wife, to humbly express our thanks.

XIAOSHENG and LAODAN: You were among the best in the imperial examinations and have been honored with a post in an important prefecture. Let us bow to congratulate you on these two happy events at the same time.

(SHENG, DAN, XIAOSHENG, *and* LAODAN *bow to one another.*)

SHENG:

>(*Same tune*)
>I relied on your support;

> You both saved my wretched life
> And pointed out the way to the blue clouds.

DAN:
> What was withered now has flourished,
> From rotten wood fresh flowers bloom,
> Bleached bones have grown new flesh,
> All thanks to you For rebuilding the foundation for talent!

XIAOSHENG and LAODAN:
> This was all Heaven's design to turn the wheel,
> And the deities' will to perform the spell.
> Don't Wrongly enter us in the book of merits!

SHENG: Considering that I am just now heading off to my first official post and do not have any extra money, I first present you with this trifling gift from my own possessions, until on another occasion I will have the means to repay your kindness properly. Bring over the gifts of local products. (*Extras bring over the gifts.* SHENG *presents to* XIAOSHENG; DAN *presents to* LAODAN.)

XIAOSHENG: Living in mountains and being poor and frugal, we have not prepared a congratulatory gift for you. How can we accept these generous gifts? Many thanks! Plum Fragrance, bring the wine. (CHOU *enters, bringing wine.*)

(XIAOSHENG *presents wine to* SHENG; LAODAN *presents to* DAN. *Each drinks at his or her separate place.*)

(Pastiche: *Liangzhou xinlang*)

> (Tune: *Liangzhou xu*)
> In the low shade of a pine
> And deep under the bean arbor,
> What a delight that we can all be together again.
> Official hat and robe, rush cape and bamboo hat—
> Why not bring them together on occasion!
> Gauze garments can be very charming,
> And gorgeous gowns are attractive,

> All interesting in colors deep or light.
> When Ministers Yi and Lü join the banquet of Chao and You,[314]
> Forests and springs[315] seem even more appealing.

TOGETHER:

> (Tune: *He xinlang*)
> We worry that after parting,
> We may never meet again,
> We lay bare our hearts, holding nothing back,
> Repeatedly we sing
> The words from the "Yang Pass."[316]

DAN (*to* LAODAN): The two of us have agreed that if we have even a little success on this trip, we will share all our glory and splendor with you two. Now as we take up an official post, we want to bring you with us. Please do not decline our invitation.

LAODAN: Many thanks for your boundless hospitality! Considering that the two of us are used to living in leisure, we could not bear the restrictions of *yamen* life. We deeply appreciate your great kindness but we must decline the offer!

> (*Same tune*)
> A mountain fogy of great age,
> And an ignorant woman from the village,
> Can roost in only a humble home with wicker door;
> To go deep within vermilion gates[317]
> Would be like keeping wild cranes in a cage.

SHENG (to XIAOSHENG): Your honorable lady claims that you would be unwilling to go with us. All right, after I arrive at my post, I will send a servant to escort you there. I beg you to stay at my place for a few months and will arrange some means so that you can comfortably live out your lives in retirement.[318] Surely you are at least willing to favor me with a visit?

XIAOSHENG: I rely completely on this fishing rod for a living and would not put my bosom friend to the trouble of supporting me. Moreover, that business of sponging on others is not what I, a recluse, could do. I dare not entertain this suggestion.

> My rush rain cape ragged and tattered,
> And my bamboo hat damaged and torn,
> Are not gear to wear as spongers.
> Only fish soup agrees with an uncouth man,
> And even pork liver could not cure my leanness.
> (*Repeat together*)
> We worry that after parting,
> We may never meet again,
> We lay bare our hearts holding nothing back,
> Repeatedly we sing
> The words from the "Yang Pass."

SHENG: We have drunk too much and thus must say our farewells.

XIAOSHENG: Let me and my wife accompany you a stage of the way; we will take your large boat going and sail back on a small skiff.

SHENG: There is no reason to put you to the trouble of accompanying us far!

DAN: Since they have a small boat to come back in, let us use traveling together as a chance to have a chat.

(XIAOSHENG *whispers to* LAODAN, *who nods in understanding.* LAODAN *picks up the aforementioned handbook and conceals it in her sleeve; all walk together.*)

(Tune: *Jie jie gao*)

LAODAN and DAN:

> Traveling, we're together for the time being,
> Happy and carefree,
> Going on this journey, we regard it as meeting again.
> Time hurries by,

Our paths are winding—
So hard to be together often.
Gibbons and cranes,[319] so full of affection, encourage people to stay;
But the heartless cuckoo[320] urges the visitors away.

TOGETHER:

Many times I've wished to use the Shi-You wind[321]
But worry lest the traveler might miss his appointed time.

(*Arriving; board the boat*)

LAODAN (*to* DAN): They are in the front cabin. Let's you and I go have a seat in the back cabin. (*Takes* DAN *by the hand, exits.*)

XIAOSHENG: Mr. Tan, I think of the many deities in this world, none can compare with Lord Yan in making his divine power felt. You have experienced it. Now that you are on your way to your official post, you might as well pray for his favor and ask this silent benefactor to support you to the end. Pray earnestly for his protection after you take your official post. Perhaps he will provide his protection to the end and may well manifest his power again.

SHENG: This is precisely what I intend to do.

TOGETHER:

(*Same tune*)
In the past, we recovered our lives,
Relying on you for support.
Why should good luck or ill all be predestined;
As long as The deity will support us,
Moved by our faith,
Our fortunes can be changed.
Charcoal in snowy weather[322] was aid from the god,
To add flowers, [323] how would he begrudge assisting again!

(*Repeat together as above.*)

DAN and LAODAN (*reenter*): Having sat for half a day, I do not know where our boat has gotten to.

(XIAOSHENG *secretly asks* LAODAN; LAODAN *nods her head.*)

XIAOSHENG: It's getting dark. We should go back. (*Bids farewell.*)
 Your Honor Tan, listen to me:
>
> (*Coda*)
>
> Heed well the god's instructions in the days to come,
> Fully inform gods and wizards of your concerns.
> Never think that what's unseen is not necessarily there!

SCENE 27: DECIDING ON THE PLAYERS

WAI (*enters*):

    The acts of ghosts and gods are hardest to perceive,
    You may say they are invisible, yet their acts take form to see.
    Consider just the matter here today if you do not believe:
    A plot has been laid to illustrate the deity's divine power.

Why did I, Master Tan's steward, say these few words? Just because my master has dispatched me to come ahead to prepare sacrificial offerings of the three domestic animals and wait for him to come and express his thanks to Lord Yan. The master and the mistress also wish to put on a play to fulfill their obligations. You would have thought that since the birthday of Lord Yan had already passed and the festival plays must be over, we would not be able to hire actors in the countryside and would have to settle for offering silent sacrifices. Who would have thought that Lord Yan would have such power that he could see that the two of them would never make it here in time and so would delay the birthday ceremonies in his honor to wait for them! Wouldn't you call that strange? And how did he do that? Because it had rained heavily for quite a few days during the first ten days of the tenth month and the original stage they put up was open to the elements, theatergoers had no place to stand and so they went together to inform Lord Yan and postponed the show for a month. His birthday will not be celebrated until the third day of the eleventh month. Now those players are all here, but I don't know which troupe they are or whether they have any good players. All I can do is go there and ask around about them. I will pay them a down payment so that there will be no confusion when the time comes. And here I am already. Is there anybody here?

MO and FUJING (*enter together*):

> Nicknamed "hangers-on from Hell,"
> We hang around and serve the gods as well.
> We think of ways to get money from the rest,
> But misers all, we never pay the bill.

Who is it?

WAI: I am the steward of the senior officer at the Court of Judicial Review in Tingzhou. His Lordship is on his way to take up his post; he will pass through your esteemed village and wants to put on a play to redeem his vows to the god. I have heard the two of you are responsible for hiring the players this year and so have come specially to trouble you.

MO: Then in that case, we'll just offer him our services.

WAI: May I ask: What is the troupe of these actors called? How are these actors? Are the plays they put on really worth watching? Before passing the imperial examinations, my master was extremely fond of performing in plays. You could not slip anything past him on any verse or aria.

MO: Hear what I have to say about that:

> (Tune: *Suo nan zhi*)
> The players' title
> Is The Jade Sprouts Troupe,
> Whose good name is known across Wu and Yue.[324]

WAI: Is the performer who plays the *dan* roles a man or a woman? Is she good looking?

MO:

> The *zhengsheng* is
> Also A pretty woman,
> Not only the *fengliu dan*.[325]

WAI: How come even the one playing the *sheng* role is a woman? If that's the case, the play sounds even more interesting.

MO:

> Her voice *and* face
> Are rare in this world;

> But if you want proof,
> Just watch for yourself.

WAI: I have heard that both the *sheng* and *dan* actors of the Jade Sprouts Troupe drowned themselves in a river one day. How can they still be here?

FUJING: Hear what I have to say about that:
> (*Same tune with a different beginning*)
> Ever since they lost their *sheng* and *dan*,
> They rounded up all the former band.
> The only ones replaced were Tan Chuyu and Fairy Liu;
> All the rest are really Just the same—
> All acting in the same roles as before.
> *Dan* and *sheng*,
> Are both Close here at hand;
> If you want A look to check up on their beauty,
> I'll take you in to see.

WAI: If that's so, then where did you find the *sheng* and *dan*?

MO: This *zhengsheng* is the mother of the actress who used to play the *dan* role, called Fallen Angel Liu; the woman now playing the *dan* role is a performer recruited from another place.

WAI: So that's how it is. Here is an ingot of silver. May I trouble the two of you to take it as a down payment? Please tell them that His Lordship will arrive tomorrow and that as soon as he arrives, the play must be put on. I leave this matter in your hands. I now catch a government boat to go reply to His Lordship. (*Exits first.*)

MO and FUJING: You can always depend on organizing plays to bring in pots of money and also get to watch plays. Since it's such an enjoyable job, why not do it? Hurry up and let's go tell them.
> We're hangers-on from Hell
> And now parasites in this world as well.
> When there is plenty of cash around to get
> Nothing from our miserly pockets will be spent.

SCENE 28: A COINCIDENTAL REUNION

SHENG (*enters, wearing official hat and belt*):
>(Tune: *Juhua xin*)
>With fragrant incense today, we thank the god
>To repay blessings past and pray for more to come.

DAN (*enters, wearing ceremonial dress*):
>Today we will pay respects to my mother,
>Yet the meeting will be terribly embarrassing.

SHENG: Madam, the man who set out in advance to make arrangements is back and has reported that the opera for Lord Yan's birthday was postponed for a month and that by chance the performance will be staged today. The actors are those friends of ours from the troupe. All they have changed is that different performers play the male lead and female lead, and the one taking the leading male roles is your mother. Who would have thought there could be such a coincidence in this world!

DAN: This is all thanks to the divine might of Lord Yan! Yet, there is one problem: since my mother is here, as soon as we arrive, we should invite her over to meet us. But after we've seen each other, how could we ask her to perform?

SHENG: When we get there, we should hide our identities from everybody and not let our faces be seen in public. Instead, we will wait while she does what she will do, and when she finishes with her performance we will explain how this all came about. Then we will ask her to meet with us. Only in this way can our reunion scene make a real splash;[326] without it, the end of it would be straightforward and insipid.

DAN (*smiles*): Good idea. If that's the way it will be, we do not need to go ashore even to make our sacrifices for Lord Yan; we can just do obeisance from a distance in our boat.

SHENG: Of course.

(*Drums and horns backstage. The boat is moored.* SHENG *and* DAN *stand side by side stage right.*[327] *In front of them are set up a window frame with hanging screen.*)

WAI (*enters, reports*): All sacrificial offerings of the three domestic animals have been arranged in front of the god. My Lordship and Lady, please announce your offerings.

(SHENG *and* DAN *bow.*)

SHENG and DAN:

>(Tune: *Putian le*)
>We are grateful to the god for Your protection,
>And for intertwining[328] our two souls into one couple.
>Our achieving glory and rank,
>Achieving glory and rank Also sprang from Your divine
> might;
>Your kindness has truly known no limit.
>Ah! We pray,
>That You will help us to the end,
>And not remove Your ladder of support:
>Promptly Lead us away from a wrong path,
>To avert the danger of a fall!

MO (*enters, wearing the clothing for his first role,*[329] *carrying the program*): Here is the list of our plays. May His Lordship select one.

(WAI *passes the program in.*)

SHENG: You tell him that they should perform only selected scenes, not a whole play. The first scene should be "Wang Shipeng Offering a Sacrifice to the River."[330] When that is finished, bring the program back for me to make another selection.

(WAI *passes on the message, and* MO *leaves, carrying the program.*)

DAN: Why did you select this scene?

SHENG: For no other reason than I simply want to test your mother's feelings. You threw yourself into the river while acting in *The Thorn*

Hairpin. Now we can use *The Thorn Hairpin* to test her; we'll see how she responds, whether she is sick at heart when she gets to that scene.

DAN: Yes, good idea.

(*Drums and gongs from backstage.*)

XIAODAN (*enters, wearing official hat and belt*):

>   (Tune: *Xin shui ling*)
>
>   After the examinations, the phoenixes flew apart,
>   Due to an evil scheme, my letter home went astray.
>   Luckily, my mother met no disaster,
>   But sadly, my wife was left lonely and forlorn.
>   Unable to endure harsh insults and mean force,
>   She drowned herself by sinking 'neath the waves.

(*From backstage*): Your Lordship, your mother also wants to come and offer sacrifices.

XIAODAN *as* SHENG (*kneels facing backstage*): Mother, you are of a venerable age, unable to endure such sorrow or ward off torrents of your tears. Please sit in the back for a moment and wait for me, your child, to offer sacrifices on your behalf.

(*From backstage*): If this is how it is, then offer her spirit an extra cup of wine for me.

XIAODAN *as* SHENG: Yes. (*Gets up.*)

(*From backstage, extras speaking together*): We will go up to pour wine and wait on His Lordship as he carries out the memorial sacrifices.

XIAODAN *as* SHENG: A husband holding a memorial ceremony for his wife does not need extra people. None of you needs to come forward. I will pour the wine and offer sacrifices by myself. (*Sticks incense into the burner, bows.*)

>   (Tune: *Zhe gui ling*)
>
>   Burning sandalwood incense puffs from the gold-lion censer,[331]

I make declaration to your soul.
Hear my explanation:
After I attended the banquet at Jasper Pool,[332]
And the palace robe was bestowed on me,
The prime minister forced me to marry into his house.
Because I could not abandon my wife of chaff and husks,
I steadfastly declined a peach and apricot spouse.[333]
Incurring great pressures,
I was reassigned to Chaoyang.[334]
For this reason my date of return was delayed!

(*Sighs.*) Oh, my wife! You threw yourself into the river here, and today I too am here to offer sacrifices. I expect that your soul cannot be far away, even if dim and faint. Your husband is offering sacrificial wine here, imploring you to drink a cup. (*Holds the cup in her left hand; she covers her tears with her right.*) (DAN *also weeps.*)

XIAODAN *as* SHENG:

(Tune: *Yan'er luo*)
In vain, I hold one vessel of wine watered down, watered
    down with tears,
Make a useless display of fragrant, fragrant dainties of
    each kind.
Yearning for your face,
Not seeing you, I pour out my heartfelt grief—
But no reply!
I make another obeisance here and reminisce.[335]
Meet again—
When will we?
I cannot wipe away my streams of tears,
I cannot smooth my furrowed brows!
My late spouse!
It was a divorce letter fabricated by the scheming thief!
My virtuous wife!

If I were not sincere,

Heaven would certainly know.

Oh, my wife! For me, you kept your reputation and chastity intact, and buried yourself beneath the waves. Now as your husband, I have nothing else to requite you with but this cup of wine, and I beg you to drink a bit more. (*Holds up the cup, offers the sacrifice.*)

(Tune: *Shou Jiangnan*)

Ah! Had I known that we would be separated like this,

How could I have gone off to the spring examinations?

What value is there in gold waist ornaments and a purple robe to wear?

Much better to remain a commoner,

Better to remain a commoner, indeed!

What can I do but weep,

Alone in my despair!

(*Cries loudly while burning sacrificial paper money.*) Oh, Fairy my child! Your mother burns money for you! Come quickly to accept it! (*Wails bitterly;* DAN *also weeps.*)

(*Shout from backstage*): You are sacrificing for Qian Yulian—why do you start crying about Fairy?

XIAODAN: Ah! The scene makes me sick at heart, and unconsciously I thought of the daughter I have lost. I was crying for the wrong person.

(Tune: *Gu meijiu*)

Paper money floats away,

Like butterflies in flight;

Paper money floats away,

Like butterflies in flight.

Dyed with tears of blood,

The cuckoos cry aloud![336]

This sad scene makes me yet more sick at heart.

> Soul, you know full well,
> I am not a faithless man,
> The faithless will expire like a lamp.
> Flowers that wither will be fragrant once again,
> The waning moon will again be full for reunions.
> I, oh—
> Whether I rise early or go to sleep late,
> In vain longing for you, thinking of you:
> To meet, only if in dreams,
> We could be married once again!

(*Weeping, she falls over.*)

DAN (*rolls up the screen and shouts loudly*): Mother, get up! Your daughter did not die—I am here right now!

XIAODAN (*stands up, alarmed, to look*): Help, help! Both of their souls have appeared! Quick, come help—I have to get away! (*Exits hurriedly.*)

(*From backstage*): It can't be good when living people see ghosts! Everyone, leave! (*Uproar.*)

WAI (*enters, shouts loudly at front center stage*): Calm down! Those people sitting in the boat are not ghosts; they are His Lordship Tan and the Lady his wife in the flesh! They were rescued from the river, and so did not die. Now he has won top honors at the imperial examinations and is on his way to take up his post. If you do not believe me, come up close and see for yourselves.

(*From backstage*): I do not believe there could be such a strange thing!

SHENG: Attendants, put up the handrail so that we can go ashore.

(*Drums and horns backstage.*)

(*Two people enter, holding blue umbrellas; one shades* SHENG, *and one shades* DAN. *They come up the bank together.*)

SHENG and DAN:

> (Tune: *Putian le*)
> We reveal our true appearance and do not hide away,

To dispel the people's doubts and alleviate their fears.
Husband and wife,
As husband and wife, we Join our jade white hands,
Far better than before when pretending the husband sang and the wife followed.
Ah! Look,
This vast river
Still makes us miserable at heart;
Hard to believe: It may flow north or may ebb south,
But it brings us all together once again!

(*From backstage*): Oh! Sure enough—that's them in the flesh. There is no need to be scared anymore. Let's go out and meet them. (MO, LAODAN, FUJING, *and* XIAODAN *enter together*.)

MO and LAODAN: Ah? Elder brother Tan and elder sister Liu, you never died after all, and now you even wear a real gauze hat and a real phoenix coronet! Congratulations! This is truly rare! (*Greet one another*.)

DAN (*meets* FUJING *and* XIAODAN): Dad and Mother, please sit down and allow me to thank you for your kindness in raising me.

MO and LAODAN: There is no need to thank them for their kindness of bringing you up, but you should be thankful for the kindness of saving your life.

FUJING and XIAODAN: We are so ashamed! (SHENG *and* DAN *bow*.)

FUJING and XIAODAN:

(*Same tune*)
A shamefaced expression is hard to hide,
Ridiculed, we have no excuse to make.
Ashamed of in those days,
Ashamed of in those days Being short-sighted, of narrow mind,
We mistook simurgh and phoenix for mere pheasants.
Ah! We hope
To mitigate our shame—

Let's stop bringing up mistakes of days ago.
We would be lucky to rely on The favor of the pepper
   apartment[337]
To grant us her sunset glow![338]

XIAODAN: My child, tell me in detail how you were saved after you leaped into the water.

DAN: The whole story would take as much time to tell as would putting on a whole play. In a few moments when we go aboard, I will tell you all about it. But there is just one problem: since your son-in-law has become an official, it is inappropriate for you to act onstage anymore. Disband the troupe quickly and come along with us to his post.

FUJING: Certainly we would like to go, but we would be mortified to face anyone.

MO and LAODAN: That's not a problem! Just take two masks out of the costume trunk, one for each of you. You could be called the "ox-headed father-in-law" and "ghost-faced mother-in-law."[339] There's no reason you should not go along!

   (*Same tune*)
   Don't just hum and haw and feel ashamed;
   As an official's relatives, you'll share glory and rank.
   With a truly excellent son-in-law—
   Of this truly excellent son-in-law You'll feel proud and
      elated,
   As he brings glory to us all the same.
   Ah! Admire how,
   Both chicken head and phoenix tail,[340]
   When the time comes, may suddenly fly away.
   Only now do we believe Those with many gifts were born
      with luck
   And will not suffer losses after all!

WAI (*enters hurriedly, holding a handbook*):
   Several bits of news were just reported,

And two strange events have come to view.

Your Lordship, the runner who went ahead to make contacts has arrived and says that mountain bandits have taken over Tingzhou and are running wild. Happily, they did not occupy the city but only looted money and silks and abducted some boys and girls. Now they have gone somewhere else.

SHENG (*alarmed*): Ah! If this is the situation, then Tingzhou is actually a perilous place! Since I have received the favor of the state, I cannot decline to go even at the risk of having my body smashed to pieces and my bones ground to powder. But because that place is in chaos, it is unsuitable to bring my family along. I have a proposition. (*To* DAN) Madam, you must go to Old Fisherman Mo's place to stay temporarily. Once peace is restored in Tingzhou region, I will send someone for you. (*To* WAI) What is that official document you are holding?

WAI: This official document came in an astonishing way. I unexpectedly found it inside your traveling case, and on the cover were inscribed the words "Sealed by Lord Pacifier-of-Waves." Therefore, I dared not open it without authorization and so bring it here to Your Lordship.

ALL (*alarmed*): Ah, speaking of it that way, Lord Yan must be making his sagely presence felt again!

SHENG (*opens the wrapper and looks at it*): How can such a strange thing be? It is none other than a *Handbook of Essential Knowledge*: it has the conditions of the people and malpractices of the officials in the prefecture of Tingzhou as well as the actual situation inside the enemy camp all written out clearly. It tells me to act according to the handbook as soon as I get to that place, which will ensure that both my life and my reputation are secure and that as a consequence I will receive exceptional promotions. This means that Lord Yan does indeed wish to support me to the end. Madam, you and I must immediately bow our thanks! (*They bow together.*)

(*Same tune*)
We express our deep gratitude for the favor of instruction,
Clarifying my confusions and enlightening me from ignorance.
I am accorded your earnest advice—
I am accorded your earnest advice And dare not fail to follow it.
While pursuing your instructions I rely on your divine might.
Ah! With
The divine mentor's support,
We will have few disasters and dangers from now on.
Prepare To mount an image and mold a statue,[341]
That we may revere throughout our lives.

Father-in-law and mother-in-law, just remain here for the time being. When it is the time for me to receive your honorable daughter, you will be invited to come with her to my post. But there is trouble in Tingzhou, and I cannot delay. I take my leave.

Steward: Hire a small boat and escort Madam back.

WAI: Yes, sir!

SHENG and DAN: His Heavenly plan is so subtle that we are all amazed,
Having formed our perfect match he manifests his might again.

ALL: Though both bestow brilliance and illustriousness,
He does not prevent a bit of sin like God Erlang.[342]

SCENE 29: GRABBING THE CART SHAFTS

WAI (*costumed as a venerable old man, enters, leaning on a staff*):
>It's hard to find an upright official anywhere on Earth,
>And our loving mothers cannot be allowed to endure a perilous war.
>We grab the official's cart shafts and lie down before his marching army,[343]
>To express a bit of our heartfelt love and esteem.

I am none other than an elderly man employed in the city of Tingzhou Prefecture. Since the mountain troops began harassing Tingzhou, our rich and prosperous region has been reduced to a world of desolation. Luckily, a government official in charge of penal affairs has taken up his position here. He is not much over twenty years old, and yet he seems like an old magistrate with many years' experience. It's been less than three months since he arrived at this post, but he has already brought great benefit to this place; by loving the people as much as his children and being totally incorruptible, he really is the father and mother of the people. But there is just one problem: relying on his exceptional ability, he not only is unwilling to avoid his own duties, but even takes burdens upon himself that others cannot shoulder. Watching the mountain bandits move back and forth destroying the area, leaving the local people without a quiet day, he has gone so far as to submit a petition to every *yamen* and wants to lead troops out to exterminate the bandits. Do you think these mountain bandits could really be exterminated? You should be grateful if they do not come to harass you—and you want to go harass them?! Therefore, the common people of the whole prefecture have put me forward to be their head as we go together to earnestly admonish him to stop. We agreed to assemble in front of the prefecture office today. Why haven't they arrived yet?

MO, FUJING, and CHOU (*all costumed as venerable old men, enter*):
>We do this good deed with one heart,
>And admonish the upright official with our common effort.
>If we manage to keep him here with us,
>All our houses will be safe and sound.

Ah! Our leader got here before us. Pardon, but do you know if the court is in session to hear cases yet?

WAI: The watchman's clappers have struck the second time, and court will open in just a moment.

MO, FUJING, and CHOU: Then get our petition ready. As soon as he opens the session, everybody will just walk in on our knees and speak.

(*The watchman's clappers strike the third time from backstage, with a call that the court is in session. All kneel together.*)

SHENG (*from backstage*): Who are you people kneeling before my bench? This court is busy with the matter of dispatching troops and will not accept any written complaint from the people without exception. Tell them to go home.

ELDERLY MEN: We, the elders of the whole prefecture, have an official matter to report to His Lordship.

SHENG (*from backstage*): What is the official matter? Just tell me.

ELDERLY MEN:
>(Tune: *Zhu ma ting*)
>We elderly men present our plea:
>We have heard that dispatching the troops is at hand.
>Just because that The demonic aura is rampant,
>Its mayhem will be hard to prevent.
>Therefore We worry that the sky might start to fall:[344]
>We cannot expose our mothers to the beacon fire!

> To delay you we offer blind devotion.
> We wish to forestall the armies' march:
> Like Gong and Huang,[345] just sit and bring peace by moral power!

SHENG (*from backstage*): You do not want me to take risks, which shows your good intentions, but if the mountain bandits are not exterminated, eventually they will become a hidden threat to the imperial government itself, and even you common people will have no peace. Tingzhou can rely on my ability to suppress any attack; nothing unexpected can possibly occur. You just set your minds at ease.

ELDERLY MEN:

> (*Same tune*)
> Putting down attacks is hard to predict,
> And a cart has overturned up ahead.[346]
> Also just because he was Impatient to take credit for goals achieved,
> And worried little about possible defeat,
> He was resolute in predicting victory.
> Mobilizing troops, he hoped to return with songs of triumph;
> Who could know that his expected success would not appear!
> Once before The one who aspired for a Lingyan portrait,[347]
> Turned round and shot Tianshan arrows[348] at *our* side!

SHENG (*from backstage*): The command has already been issued, and our forces are ready to move out. You need say no more. You are all to leave.

(*Backstage beating of drums, calls to seal the gates.*)

ELDERLY MEN (*rise from their knees and sigh*):

> Since he will not heed us elders,
> He will surely shed sad and anxious tears.

It is a pity that this good official is walking straight into the hands of the mountain bandits! Let's all just go home.

It seemed that this place had good fortune;
Who'd have known that we'd still have no luck?
This deployment bodes more ill than well;
We will weep for our "clear sky"[349] official.

SCENE 30: WINNING THE BATTLE

CHOU (*enters, wearing official hat and belt, and carrying clothes and a cap*):

    How could a sheep pretend to have a tiger's might?[350]
    Only because I gained an advantage through outward resemblance.
    Even though deceiving all contemporaries' eyes,
    When was Yang Hu ever Confucius?[351]

I am none other than the one who at first disguised myself as an old fisherman and later pretended to be the circuit intendant. Ever since the day I rendered him meritorious service, the Great King of the Mountain has bestowed great favor on me. He has left all the looted wealth in my care and does not ask me to command military forces or take risks, which makes me extremely happy. There's just one problem: I originally took on this job only to get that thousand taels of silver he offered; that payment is in my hands now, and my worries are over. Now even to hope for riches and rank, one cannot be a simpleton. I must prepare several different escape routes while I watch how their campaign turns out. If they continue to win victories, I expect that my meritorious service will not be erased. But if by any chance they are defeated, I need an escape plan. Recently, I have heard a government official in charge of penal affairs has newly come to the prefecture of Tingzhou, a man of some real ability. He's the one who is leading troops into battle today. I now have the clothes and cap with me that could save me from calamity. If I get wind of bad news, I'll just change clothes and go away. Indeed:

    A wily hare often employs the ruse of three burrows,[352]
    A clever man is used to straddling two boats.[353] (*Exits.*)

SHENG (*enters, costumed in martial attire, and leads extras on stage*):

(Tune: *Queqiao xian*)
Songs with strings had just begun,[354]
Now army drums boom forth;[355]
Ritual and music, weapons and arms all employed together.
Stratagems put to use the power of spirits and ghosts;
Look—our forces form a remarkable column.

Ever since I arrived at my post, I am delighted that the people have been living in peace, that the officials are restrained, and that holding this post even affords some leisure. Only the mountain bandits have yet to be eliminated, and consequently I cannot rest in peace. Some time ago, Lord Yan manifested his wisdom by creating a handbook containing strategies for administration of the people and for the suppression of bandits; this he presented to me as a gift. From the first, I applied his tactics for governing the people and tested his methods of suppressing bandits. Who would have thought not a single word would be mistaken and everything would turn out as predicted. Since the previous achievements are like this, later outcomes can be known. Therefore, I went to each *yamen* to petition them to combine their strengths to suppress the bandits with a punitive expedition. My superior has approved my petition and put all the troops and horses, money and food grains under my command. In addition, because he was concerned that in my low official position I might not be able to bring the troops under my control, he has temporarily appointed me circuit intendant so as to facilitate my command of the military, because a Circuit Intendant Murong had surrendered to the bandits in battle before I arrived. If I succeed in wiping out the bandits, the emperor will approve his memorial to appoint me to this official position. Since today is an auspicious day for mobilizing troops, I must command the generals and field officers to head out with the campaign. Tell the generals of every encampment to assemble all their cavalry and infantry here to receive my commands. (ALL *respond and transmit orders.*)

WAI (*enters, in a suit of armor*):

> (Tune: *Fan busuan*)
> Our chief commander uses a superb strategy,
> Like a thunderclap, he rouses our military might.

MO (*enters, in a suit of armor*):

> Buckling on armor with weapons in hand, I go to the government office,
> And ask to try out my leaden blade.[356]

WAI and MO (*meet* SHENG): We two generals of the left and of the right salute you.

SHENG: Today I will direct our operations, unlike my predecessor, who acted rashly. Our wise strategy will certainly prevail, and our plan is perfectly safe. I presume that our forces will wipe out those petty bandits hands down. There is just one problem: once they are defeated, we must guard against their retreating back into the mountains as before. If they get back into their lair, we will have to waste a great deal of effort to exterminate them. General of the left encampment, lead a column of men and horse to guard the strategic road into the mountains so that they will have no way in. General of the right encampment, first lead a column of men and horse into the mountains and destroy their lair by fire so that they will have no base to return to. Slaying the bandits and capturing their king will hinge on this one action. Obey orders carefully, and let there be no disobedience.

WAI and MO: Your Lordship, we have some questions. There are very many ways into the mountains: How do we know which one to guard? There are several separate lairs: How do we know which one to burn out? We request Master to point out the place names, to avoid our bungling matters.

SHENG: Strategic points are indeed not few, and I must not say much; moreover, secret military plans should not be fully revealed. There are two notes with instructions here. Each of you gets one, which you will read carefully once you get under way. Just proceed according to those plans. (*Hands to each.*) Move out your troops now. (*They march together.*)

TOGETHER:

(Pastiche: *Qing bei Yu furong*)

(Tune: *Qing bei xu*)

Brilliant planning and mighty courage,
We anticipate many surprising moves.
We'll lay a trap to catch the king,
Beasts will scatter and humans flee;
We'll set the fires throughout the lair,
Leaving land burned brown and the mountains bare.

(Tune: *Yu furong*)

Even An immortal could not find his maze cave again,
Even a phoenix can be tricked into entering the clever cage,
Let alone Such petty monsters as these—
How could it be hard to bring them under control!
Even returning in triumph,
We would feel embarrassed any great merit to claim!

(FUJING *leads a group onstage, fights them a round, and exits greatly defeated.*)

SHENG: Tell all units, big or small: the brigands have been defeated and will undoubtedly flee into the mountains. Let everyone fight bravely to be the first in pursuing the enemy together. Except for their leaders, slay any brigand you meet; there is no need to take live captives. Only one important brigand criminal must be caught and presented as a military sacrifice; he is not to be punished or killed on your own authority.

EXTRAS: Your Lordship, please tell us which brigand criminal it is.

SHENG: It is the traitor who pretended to be a recluse in mountains and surrendered in battle. The charges against him are even greater than those against the bandit chief. Let everyone pursue him diligently and capture him; don't let that chief culprit get away. (EXTRAS *respond, all sing again the three lines of "Such petty monsters as these," exit.*)

FUJING (*leads* the group *onstage*):

> (Tune: *Shuidi yur*)
>
> All our plans have come to naught;
> Our mountain might has suddenly collapsed.
> I hasten on my homeward road,
> Where I'll seal the gate fast!

This little plague came on fiercely—none of you should provoke him. Withdraw our troops right away, and make a quick retreat into the mountains. (*Sounding of gongs, beating of drums, and cheering from backstage.*) There are men and horse ahead and pursuing troops behind. We can neither advance nor retreat! What can we do?

(Medley: *Dui yuhuan* with *Qingjiang yin*)[357]

> (Tune: *Dui yuhuan*)
>
> Disguising their shadows and concealing their tracks,
> In pursuit they give us no respite.
> Restraining our vigor and hiding our vanguard,
> We still worry about a pincer attack.
> Our counselor's stratagem is fruitless,
> My commanders have exhausted their strength.
> My fate's unlucky, the times are all against me,[358]
> And all voices blame me, their leader!

BRIGANDS (*looking backstage, alarmed*): Ah! Great King, look: deep in the mountains, leaping flames light up the sky. It must be that government troops have gone into the mountains and are burning out our lair. Even if we can flee back there, we will have no place to roost. What can we do? (*Cheering backstage again.*)

FUJING: Attacked from all sides, I think we cannot get out. Let's toughen our heads and get ready for them to be chopped off!

> (Tune: *Qingjiang yin*)
> Neither Heaven nor Earth has a crack in which to hide,[359]
> And we are certain to give away our heads.
> We risk our lives to suffer a five-inch wound,
> And bear a little momentary pain
> To form a Bowl-sized scar that will not swell.

(WAI *and* MO *from left,* SHENG *and* EXTRAS *from right, fight onto the stage together and capture them.*)

SHENG: Which one is the head of the brigands?

ALL (*point to* FUJING): This one is.

SHENG: Which one is the traitor who surrendered in battle?

ALL: He left a while ago.

SHENG: Let's withdraw troops for the time being. I will send an official dispatch to all the administrative offices with a drawing of his likeness. We must seize this traitor and then offer him as captive sacrifice at the Imperial Ancestral Temple.[360] Any one of you generals who can secretly make inquiries and capture him to send him to me under guard will earn first-class merit and also be awarded promotion.

WAI: Your Lordship, I have a friend who came back from Zhejiang the day before yesterday and said he had met a man in the mountains who clearly looked like the traitor. I request that Your Lordship grant me a warrant so that I can disguise myself as a constable and go apprehend him. If that is indeed the traitor, I only need to arrange with the local government to bring him here.

SHENG: If this is the case, as soon as I go back to my office, I will depute you to go catch him. (*Marches.*)

TOGETHER:
>
> (Tune: *Zhu nu'er fan*)
>
> We've rooted out the people's scourge, the demons are no more,
>
> With loyalty and indignation, we've wiped out mutinous brigands,
>
> Unwilling to let the imperial house have a rebel lie concealed!
>
> Abusing the law,
>
> Leaving a turncoat at large—
>
> This crime surpasses that of the rebels' head!
>
> Eating the emperor's food and tramping his land,[361]
>
> The common man[362] should offer loyal service;
>
> Even more, for those receiving royal favor—
>
> We cannot claim a victory until that traitor is arrested!

SHENG:
>
> (*Coda*)
>
> Happily we have secured the sovereign's lands today.
>
> All think I Acted on my own without a counselor in play.
>
> Who knows there was A silent military adviser behind the scenes!

SCENE 31: MISTAKEN ARREST

XIAOSHENG (*enters*):

>(Tune: *Ye xing chuan*)
>Heading home, weary from fishing even though it is still early,
>With nothing else to do, I take a walk in highland woods.
>Listening to the water in a leisurely mood,
>Looking at the mountains, I feast my eyes,
>Everything around me is just what I enjoy!

Without my realizing it, half a year has gone by since I, Old Fisherman Mo, parted from Scholar Tan. He sent his wife here and asked me to look after her for him because Tingzhou was in turmoil and it was unsuitable to bring his family along. More happily, she and my wife find each other most congenial, just like sisters. But for my part, I feel somewhat awkward just sitting at home. That is why in my leisure after fishing, I saunter around outside. Today I've already caught enough fish to have with some wine, and so why not take a stroll through the mountains? (*Walks.*)

>(Tune: *Feng ru song*)
>A man in a painting crosses the painting's bridge,
>Along the path exploring quiet and repose.
>The old fisherman no longer seeks material for verse;
>It brushes past him with the wind where'er he goes.

Having walked for a while, I realize that I've become a bit fatigued. I will just take a little nap here in the shade of this pine tree.

>Do not say that Planning national affairs unsettles one's soul as well as his dream;
>Even Commenting on the hills and streams involves some mental work. (*Sleeps.*)

WAI (*leads* TWO SOLDIERS *onstage, disguised as constables, concealing an iron chain and handcuffs*):

>For now, I've resigned my rank as a general
>To serve temporarily as constable.
>I go into the mountains to seize the traitor
>And bring the tools of justice in advance.

    I am none other than a subordinate general serving under the Zhangnan General Surveillance Circuit. Because an acquaintance of mine passed through here and saw Circuit Intendant Murong hiding in the mountains, I reported to Lord Tan, who then issued an unrestricted arrest warrant.[363] I disguised myself as a government constable and came to make an investigation. Here I am at the border of Yanling; I must be cautious as I track him down. (*To the* TWO SOLDIERS.) We all need to keep our eyes peeled; we must not let him slip away from us.

TWO SOLDIERS: Yes, sir. Someone is sleeping under that pine tree over there. We should go wake him up and ask him for information in advance. How about that?

WAI: Right you are.

>(Tune: *Ji san qiang*)
>First from this Local person's mouth,
>We'll get a piece of
>Concrete information;
>And then We'll go look for his tracks
>And catch that traitor official.

TWO SOLDIERS: This man is sleeping so at ease. Let's scare him awake! (*Shake him.*) Sleeper, wake up! There's a tiger up ahead of us!

XIAOSHENG (*wakes up*):

>(*Same tune*)
>Who called out
>And startled me awake
>From my deer-and-firewood dream?[364]

Just let me Rub my sleepy eyes
And take a look at him. (*Stands up, greets* WAI.)

WAI (*alarmed, aside*): This is him! Why should we go to look for him anywhere else? See if you recognize him, too.

TWO SOLDIERS (*scrutinize him carefully, aside to* WAI): Needless to say more; quick, get out the tools!

WAI (*to* XIAOSHENG): Lord Murong, I haven't seen you for a while. Do you still recognize us?

XIAOSHENG (*alarmed*): Ah! I am just a rustic from the deep mountains and have no acquaintances at all. I am absolutely not familiar with you gentlemen's faces. Surely you've made a mistake!

WAI: No mistake at all! You formerly held the post on the Zhangnan General Surveillance Circuit, and I was a general under your command. How could I not recognize you? Quick, don't decline; just come along with me back to our former place.

XIAOSHENG (*aside*): He recognizes me! What shall I do? Perhaps the imperial court is asking for me, and local officials sent him to look for me. I might as well tell the truth and beg him to let me go. (*Turns back.*) Now that you recognize me, I need not try to deceive you anymore. But I absolutely will not come out of the mountains.[365] Please report to your superior that you have let me go!

WAI (*to the* TWO SOLDIERS): Make your move quickly, and don't be careless.

(SOLDIERS *grab him, affix chain and cuffs.*)

XIAOSHENG (*greatly alarmed*): What is the reason for this? If you want me to go, you have to cordially invite me to leave retirement. How could you arrest me like a common criminal? Such nonsense—which official sent you here?

WAI: By military order of Acting Circuit Intendant Tan of the Office of Punishments in Tingzhou, I have come specially to apprehend you. I have the warrant here. See for yourself.

XIAOSHENG (*reads the warrant, greatly alarmed*): Ah! It really is his! Let me explain: that chief official of yours and I are on intimate terms and have built a profound friendship. Before he rose to power and position, I saved both his life and that of his wife. Why does he requite kindness with enmity and go so far as to accuse me with the two words "traitorous criminal"?

WAI: In your heart, you know all about it. Why ask me? Soldiers, take him away, and pay no attention to what he says. (*They take him away with them.*)

XIAOSHENG: In this case, just wait until we pass my house. His wife is there now. If you do not believe me, just go ask her.

WAI: Where is your house?

XIAOSHENG: Just there, by the path.

WAI: In that case, we will pass right by it on the way.

XIAOSHENG: Here we are. Wife, quick, ask Mrs. Tan to come out!

DAN and LAODAN (*enter together*):

> Why are our springtime hours
> Disrupted by such urgent sounds?
> Quickly we go out of doors,
> To investigate what's come around.

Ah! What's all this about? What kind of people are the three of them? Why have they chained you up without cause or reason? Tell us quickly!

LAODAN: I understand:

> (Tune: *Feng ru song*)
> These Gangsters must be greenwood bandits
> Who harass people here in the mountains.
> Taking advantage of our Inability to appeal because Heaven's
>   high and the emperor far away,[366]
> They use illegal means to carry out torture.
> How can he endure this outrageous calamity?

Now I have no choice but to Risk my life in kneeling to beg for mercy.

(*Kneels to them.*) Great King, my husband is a fisherman; he wears a rush rain cape and lives here in this thatched cottage of a few rooms. We have no gold, pearls, treasures, or jewels. I beg you to display your great compassion and let him go!

GROUP: We have come on official commission to capture him, and we are not bandits. How could you call us "great kings"?

DAN: Who sent you on this official mission? It has been said since ancient times: "Although it may be sharp, a steel sword does not behead an innocent person." Why do you arrest him?

XIAOSHENG: It was none other than that loving and loyal husband of yours who could not be more grateful to me and sent them to pay his debt of gratitude! Well, many thanks!

DAN (*greatly alarmed*): How could this be!

XIAOSHENG: They have an official arrest warrant inscribed in his own hand. (*To* WAI.) Show it to her. (WAI *hands over the document.* DAN *and* LAODAN *read it together.*)

DAN: Ah! It is really his handwriting! If he has really done this, he is not even human! (*To* ALL.) With me here, do not worry about how vicious he can be! Set free the fisherman quickly, and let me go speak to him about this.

WAI: Humph! See how important you are! If you are his wife, why didn't you go along with him to office instead of living here in the house of a traitor? Even if you really are his wife, there is no way that the wife could release a bandit that His Lordship has captured. Let's get going; there's no need to waste any more time here talking.

(Tune: *Ji san qiang*)
Even though you
Monopolize your husband's favor
And you are his lawful first wife,

> Don't imagine that it's possible To interfere with the laws of the state
>
> By begging for mercy for another.

DAN: How could the words "husband and wife" be fake? Since you do not believe me, just take me there so that we can be interrogated together.

WAI: What you say seems quite reasonable. In that case, we'll hire a larger boat. We will sit in the front cabin with the prisoner; you and his wife will stay in the stern cabin, and we will all go along together.

DAN: Then that's what we'll do.

LAODAN (*to* DAN): Sister Tan, it must be that my man was unguarded in his speech and may have offended His Honor Tan. Maybe His Honor Tan has thought out a way to do him harm by avenging personal wrongs in the name of official interests. It seems that we husband and wife must rely on you to make things right, for our lives are in your hands.

DAN: No such things ever happened. Aunt, there is no need to be overly concerned.

LAODAN:

> (*Same tune*)
>
> It all depends on you
>
> To pardon us from crime,
>
> To bestow favors and justice.
>
> Go forth To contain the thunder and lightning
>
> And to still the wind and waves!

DAN: He is a man with heart, and he would never do heartless things. I have thought this over carefully: there must be some reason after all!

> (Tune: *Feng ru song*)
>
> These circumstances seem so strange,
>
> So hard to comprehend, this breaks my tender heart.

It may be his plan to pay a debt of gratitude. Knowing that your husband is noble-minded and unwilling to leave retirement to become an official, perhaps he wants to emulate Duke Wen of Jin's way of repaying a kindness: he has set mountains on fire expecting Jie Zhitui to come out.[367] Nevertheless,

> Even if you want to Imitate the ancients to pay a debt of gratitude,
> You must guard against bringing fire down on his head.[368]
> (*To* XIAOSHENG.) I hope you Avoid the fire for the time being: do not embrace a tree;
> But wait for him To use rank and stipend to reward your service instead!

XIAOSHENG: If that is how it is, go quickly and arrange a vessel so that we can set out at once. We will see what official law will be used to punish me when we get there. (*Sighs.*)

XIAOSHENG: Having saved a tiger, who expects that the tiger will eat him?

LAODAN: I urge you, Lord, to bestow resentment and not to bestow kindness.

DAN: How do we know this isn't just a plan for a reward? An unexpected disaster is but the gateway to good fortune.

SCENE 32: A SHOCKING REUNION

SHENG (*in official hat and belt, leads generals and field officers and executioners onstage*):

> (Tune: *Southern Fendier*)
> We've beheaded all the mighty whales,[369]
> Relying on our shields and city wall on our south.[370]
> Steps to disorder became a ladder to Heaven instead:
> Receiving imperial kindness
> Along with extraordinary favor,
> I was immediately promoted to a position of honor.
> I am grateful to the deity for indeed Supporting me to the end!

I volunteered[371] to destroy the bandits and succeeded by good fortune. The emperor bestowed his favor and broke precedent to promote me: now I have the post of circuit intendant for military defense in Zhangnan. He also said that there was no need to offer the apprehended bandit chief at the Imperial Ancestral Temple; instead, we should wait until the traitor is captured and then decapitate them both and impale their heads. Yesterday the subordinate general of the left encampment reported that the traitor had already been captured and that my wife was at his place. That means it was Old Fisherman Mo. I do not believe that man of noble character could be willing to do such an evil deed. Perhaps the constable arrested him by mistake. I've considered it carefully: if in fact he was really arrested by mistake, then all would be well. But if by any chance it is him, how should I deal with him? If I execute him according to the law, I will betray my benefactor; if I pay my personal debt of gratitude, I will obstruct the law. This case presents really grave difficulties. I will just wait for him to be sent here under guard and interrogate him carefully.

WAI (*enters*):
> My original mission was to capture and bring back the traitor;
> Who would have thought I'd bring along His Lordship's spouse?
> His wife and the imperial criminal are both here,
> I escort them together into his own office.
>
> Your Lordship, the traitor has been captured.

SHENG: Where did you catch him? What business does he do? How many people are there in his family? Have you made corroborating inquiries to be certain that you did not capture an innocent man by mistake?

WAI: He lives in the Yanling area and is a fisherman by trade. They were husband and his wife with a man servant and a serving maid in the household. His looks not only correspond; with his own mouth, he confessed that he had in fact been an official here.

SHENG: Who else was there besides?

WAI: There was also a woman who said she is Your Lordship's spouse. Since I am unable to tell the true from the false on this, I had no alternative but to invite her to come with us. Now she is outside and wants to come in to appeal for redress on his behalf.

SHENG (*aside*): When he speaks of it this way, then the traitor is Mo, beyond doubt. In this court of law, how could I follow my personal feelings? I have a plan. (*Turns back.*) That woman is indeed my wife. At the time I left her at his place, I had no inkling that this man was a traitor. Now that he has been exposed, he is punishable by law. Not only can this criminal not be helped out of personal considerations, but that woman also falls under suspicion as well. Tell the surveillance officers to have a residence cleaned and help her settle in for the time being. I will not meet with her until I have dealt with the traitor and presented a memorial to the imperial court to lay bare my true motives. (WAI *responds, exits.*)

A COUPLE OF SOLES

DAN (*shouts from backstage*): Old Fisherman Mo definitely did not commit any offense at all. How can you arbitrarily punish him? There must be injustice in this! Let me in to offer an explanation for him.

SHENG (*in a great rage*): Attendants: quick, go out and give her these instructions. Ask her who she is and what place this is. Outside a court of law, how can a family member's shouts be tolerated! If she does not withdraw at once, even she could be implicated when I investigate this case. (MO *gives instructions to backstage.*)

SHENG: Bring the traitor in. (MO *transmits the order.* WAI *binds* XIAOSHENG's *hands; they enter.*)

XIAOSHENG:

> (Tune: *Northern Zui hua yin*)
> Mistakes of the past I cannot bear to repent:
> Having helped that Ungrateful person for no reason.
> This time forfeiting my old head,
> I'll let him burn beanstalks to cook beans[372] as he pleases.
> Now that he wants to fry me,[373] I do not mind his haste.
> It will save me from Suffering humiliation,
> And Bearing restraints.
> I will become a Hate-filled ghost who will drive him mad
> in the daytime to get my revenge! (*Greets* SHENG.)

SHENG: Huh! It turns out that the person who brought disaster to the people and endangered the realm, deceiving the world while seeking undeserved fame, is you? As you received high government pay, you should have offered your loyalty with utmost moral integrity; even if you were exhausted and in dire straits, you should have died at the frontiers enacting the tale of Zhang Xun and Xu Yuan![374] Why did you lead the army to surrender to the enemy first? What was the reason? Tell the whole truth!

> (Tune: *Southern Huamei xu*)
> Write out your statement of confession

> So as to save me Many interrogations and you from torture.
> Don't even mention the four words,
> "Show mercy, be lenient."
> To aid a friend, I'd readily sacrifice my life;
> But to uphold the state's laws, I cannot take your place.
> My black gauze cap requires turning my back on my feelings,
> Solely because the laws cannot be opposed.

XIAOSHENG (*furious*): Bah! You are not demented; you are not mad—why do you speak such nonsense in broad daylight? When did I ever surrender to some bandit?

SHENG: How is it that you reprove me instead? This is extremely strange!

XIAOSHENG:

> (Tune: *Northern Xi qian ying*)
> Why are you barking at me in an angry voice?
> For what reason do you implicate me in a case of treason?
> It leaves me Fierce browed, with glaring eyes,
> My hair lifts my cap[375] and splits my scalp to pieces!
> You want to imitate Qin Gui's killing of Yue Fei,[376]
> By leveling a Groundless charge against me!
> Try asking: When I erected that flag of surrender,
> Who was there and saw my face?
> When I plotted that rebellion,
> Which men followed along?

SHENG: Humph! Are you saying there were no witnesses? All you *yamen* runners: come over.

EXTRAS (*kneel*): Here!

SHENG: You all go to take a careful look at him. Three years ago, was he the official at this post? We do not want to make a false arrest.

EXTRAS (*get close to examine him carefully*): Your Lordship, he does not differ by a hair. He is our former master, and we used to serve him all day. How could we not recognize him?

XIAOSHENG (*to* SHENG): When did I ever say that I was not an official? I only ask who witnessed my surrender to the enemy. Why didn't you ask what you should instead of asking what you should not?

SHENG: What you say is correct. Generals, you come over.

WAI, MO, JING, and CHOU: Here!

SHENG: Is it true or false that he surrendered to the enemy? Did you see it with your own eyes? You must all speak the truth and not accuse him falsely.

WAI, MO, JING, and CHOU: We saw it with our own eyes, and he is definitely not falsely accused.

SHENG (*to* XIAOSHENG): How about this? What else do you have to say?

> (Tune: *Southern Diliu zi*)
> In a court of law,
> In a court of law,
> When a thousand speak with one voice,
> It is not that they Harbor personal resentment,
> Harbor personal resentment
> And therefore slander you.
> It's impossible to shield you for personal reasons,
> I ask you to commit suicide and make our final farewells!
> I wish to pay my personal debt of gratitude
> But I fear offending the might of the state.

XIAOSHENG: These generals and *yamen* runners are all your underlings. If you are ungrateful, how dare they not go along with you? It is you who taught them all these cunning words.

SHENG: You committed a towering crime against Heavenly laws! How can you slander me instead?

XIAOSHENG: Humph! I know your malicious intent.

> (Tune: *Northern Chu dui zi*)
> It is not that you unwittingly
> Happen to betray your benefactor;
> There's an Evil intention quite carefully concealed.

> Fearing I Might reveal the truth, you kill me to prevent me from doing so.
>
> Therefore, You've put on a painted face and offended your own conscience!

All right! I will become a Mr. Tian Guang[377] and silence myself for you.

> I will be like Tian Guang silencing himself never to leak the secret!

SHENG: Humph! Do you think these generals and *yamen* runners—all of them in this command—are not to be believed? All right! Attendants: go choose a few of the local common people and summon them to come in.

ATTENDANTS: Aye! (*Call backstage.*)

(FUJING *and* LAODAN, *costumed as elderly people,* DAN *and* XIAODAN *as children, enter together and greet* SHENG.)

SHENG: You all go take a close look at him and see if he is really the man who surrendered to the enemy.

ELDERLY PEOPLE and CHILDREN (*look carefully*): There's no mistake. There's just one problem: at first, while serving in office, he was a good official; only he should not have become a turncoat when he came back later. We beg Your Lordship to let his good deeds atone for his crime and pardon him.

XIAOSHENG (*alarmed*): Hmmm! How could this idea come from the mouths of the common people as well?

SHENG: Other offenses are pardonable. But how could the crimes of plotting a rebellion and treason be pardonable? You may leave.

(ELDERLY PEOPLE and CHILDREN *respond, all exit.*)

SHENG (*to* XIAOSHENG): I expect that now, you have nothing more to say. Since my wife and I are indebted to you for saving our lives we are duty bound to repay our debt of gratitude. But in this court of law, feelings cannot be allowed to prevail. Attendants: untie him for the moment, and bring out a jug of wine. I will present him respectfully with three cups and then carry out the supreme punishment. It accords with two lines of an old saying: Today we drink wine because of private feelings, but tomorrow we apply punishment in accordance with the law.[378] (EXTRAS *respond, untie* XIAOSHENG.)

SHENG (*takes up the wine, offers it*): Mr. Murong, I have absolutely no alternative in this matter today; it is not that I do it intentionally. You are a scholar who understands moral standards and will certainly forgive me. I entreat you to drink this cup of wine.

> (Tune: *Southern Di di jin*)
> Just before execution, I offer wine to requite your kindness
>   and friendship,
> Contrary to neither the laws of the state nor personal
>   feelings.
> (*Hides his tears.*)
> It makes me Secretly shed sad tears on the edge of the
>   blade,
> For apparently I must Turn my dear benefactor into a
>   resentful ghost!

"Although I did not kill Boren,[379] he died because of me." These two lines are precisely the accusation I face.

> Committing the crime as a person in the know,
> If you Would examine the situation and put yourself in my
>   position,
> Perhaps you, too, Would rather be a detestable leader
> Than violate the law!

XIAOSHENG (*throws down the cup in great anger*): You set all these snares to cover up past errors. Who would believe you? When first you threw yourself into the river, I was the one who saved your life; when you went to take the examinations, I was the one who provided money for the journey. None of these acts of kindnesses need to be mentioned; let's talk about only your rendering meritorious service and taking high position. To whom do you owe thanks? Could this be solely the product of your own abilities? If I had not used a secret stratagem to provide you with a point-by-point plan for administration of the people and suppression of the bandits, not only could you not have succeeded, I am afraid even your dog's head could not have been preserved to today—you'd have lost it in battle!

SHENG: The credit for the first is yours. But what has my suppression of the bandits got to do with you? You are laying a false claim to it. When did you ever provide me with any stratagems? What is the basis for your claim?

XIAOSHENG: Oh! You still don't know? Let me just ask who created that *Handbook of Essential Knowledge* you found on your way to your post.

SHENG (*alarmed, aside*): Ah! That book was bestowed on me by the deity. How does he know about it? There's something strange about this!

XIAOSHENG:

> (Tune: *Northern Gua di feng*)
> I speak the truth and yet feel so wretched—
> You should not Talk big to trot out your own heroic might.
> If he had known beforehand ruthless Peng Meng with cruel treachery would kill him,
> How would Hou Yi have agreed To teach him the methods of archery?[380]
> You thought that miraculous "Divine talisman" was Heaven's gift, not the work of man,[381]
> As the title inscribed on the cover now proclaims.
> How could you know I Assumed the revered Master Yuan's[382] name
> To transmit the art of the sword
> While instructing in subtle strategies?

> You can see that each of those issues Has now been made totally clear,
> Thanks to me also, The former prefect, by exerting great mental effort again,
> The former prefect, by exerting great mental effort again!
> Who'd have thought that Trying to set things right would bring down this calamity?

SHENG: From what you say, that handbook actually was written by you. If that is the way it was, why didn't you use your own name rather than write the divine name of Lord Pacifier-of-Waves?

XIAOSHENG: I meticulously strove to avoid drawing attention to myself and was unwilling to reveal any clue that I had been an official. That's why. In the first place, I wished to eliminate all threats to the imperial court; and second, I wanted to help you become a good official. Who would have thought that after making a reputation for meritorious service for yourself, you would think of a way to do me harm?

SHENG: Ah! From what you say, you have been an official loyal to the state after all. Then why were you willing to plot the rebellion?

XIAOSHENG: When did I ever plot a rebellion? I think you must be imagining things!

SHENG: After you went into the mountains, because it was impossible to suppress the bandits the emperor reinstated you in your former office. Local officials looked for you everywhere to bring you out of the remote mountains, hoping that you would again exert yourself for the imperial court as you did before. Who could have expected that you would become a turncoat! All this uproar is because of this mortal sin. How could it be that you don't fully understand this in your heart?

XIAOSHENG (*alarmed*): Ah! When you explain it all this way, it is clearly not you who would purposely do me harm. Perhaps when the local officials were looking for me in such haste, somebody deliberately came out to plot rebellion under my name. I entreat you to make a thorough investigation; otherwise, my life may be a minor matter, but how could I bear an eternal reputation for infamy! At first, I was unwilling to go down on my knees, but now I have no choice but to resign myself to being a criminal and to kneel in this court of law to await your investigation. (*Kneels.*)

SHENG: If this is the case, let me summon the brigand head for thorough interrogation on your behalf; if the case is really as you said, then I can set you free. Just one question: When he is brought here, you must resign yourself to being the person who surrendered to the bandits and just say you conspired and worked together with him. I have some clever ways to interrogate him. One try should be enough to determine what is true and what is not. Attendants: bring the prisoner out. (EXTRAS *respond, exit.*)

SHENG (*aside*): Heaven, Heaven! I only hope that this is really true! Then I would not have to be such an ingrate. I beg you to protect and support us!

ATTENDANTS (*bring* FUJING *onstage*): Your Lordship, we've brought the bandit leader.

SHENG: The imperial edict has been issued, which says I do not need to offer you as sacrifice at the Imperial Ancestral Temple and that when the traitor has been arrested I should decapitate you both and impale your heads. Now the traitor has been captured and should be executed together with you. But there is just one question: When I interrogated him a moment ago, he said that he was not a real traitor but that you paid him to assume the name of someone else; for that reason, it was a pardonable crime and not one punishable by death. In my heart, I want to release him; therefore, I have summoned you to ask for clarification. Is this matter of assuming another's name really true?

FUJING: Oh, it is true enough, but this person is very treacherous, and I cannot hate him enough. If you want to kill me, kill him with me. I beg Your Lordship not to let him go!

XIAOSHENG: You and I worked together. Why do you hate me like this?

FUJING: Even before you came out of the mountains, you got from me a thousand in silver as an invitation gift; later you pretended to be the circuit intendant and surrendered in battle. I kept you in the army and left you in charge of all the looted wealth. You should have stuck with me through life or death and gone through thick and thin together. When you saw the wind about to shift, you floated away taking all the booty with you. How could it be that in all I did as a bandit chief, I was only working for you? If I die, we'll die together—I would never let you off!

SHENG: There are many people under Heaven. Which one of them would not impersonate someone? Why did you want to hire only him?

FUJING: It was all because he looks exactly like Circuit Intendant Murong that I invited him to come out with a thousand in silver as an invitation gift.

SHENG (*laughs heartily*): So that is what happened! Now that you explain the situation, this man is not your personal enemy. Your personal enemy has not yet been captured. When he is captured, he will be executed with you, and that will be that.

FUJING: It's him without a doubt. Why say it's not?

SHENG: This is Circuit Intendant Murong himself. After resigning from his office, he never left the mountains again. If you do not believe me, just take a close look at him.

FUJING (*gets close to look carefully*): Ah! He's really not the one. So don't wrong him. From the beginning I was worthy of death and shouldn't have ruined your reputation with a proxy. My apologies for giving offense!

SHENG: Attendants, take the bandit chief back to prison as before, and send out an official dispatch to every *yamen*: search for the traitor who impersonated Circuit Intendant Murong, and bring him here for skinning and stuffing with rice straw[383] to avenge the wrong done your former superior. (EXTRAS *respond and take* FUJING *away.*)

SHENG: Please come into the inner quarters of the *yamen*. Attendants, bring out clothes for Master Murong to change into; and second, go ask the two ladies to meet us in the inner quarters. (EXTRAS *respond, exit.* XIAOSHENG *changes clothing, greets* SHENG.)

SHENG: I was too muddle-headed and ignorant to perceive the truth, which caused me to implicate my great benefactor with this false charge. I have offended you deeply!

XIAOSHENG: If you were not a clear mirror hung on high[384] to redress the wrong done me, I would not only meet my death on this day but also leave a name that would stink to eternity. When my wife arrives, we will express our thanks together!

LAODAN and DAN (*enter*):

>The quick redress of this strange injustice is a matter for great joy;
>The reunion of old friends truly brings delight.

EXTRAS: Your Lordship, the two ladies are here. (LAODAN *and* DAN *come in.*)

SHENG (*to* DAN): My lady, my achievements in suppressing the bandits were also thanks to Mr. Murong's guidance. Come quickly, let us express our thanks to our benefactor!

XIAOSHENG (*to* LAODAN): Wife, I am exonerated from the strange and unjust charge of surrendering to the enemy, all thanks to Mr. Tan. Come quickly, let us express our thanks to our benefactor! (*The four bow together.*)

TOGETHER:

>(Tune: *Southern Bao lao cui*)
>Two acts of merit equally outstanding—
>Like lofty mountains neither of them is small.
>You first saved him, and then he saves you.
>The Way of Heaven is to make recompense,

> Retribution is made evident,
> And conscience is assuaged.
> Good deeds are never without benefit:
> Adding it up, you've earned more than 30 percent interest:
> Although that still seems small, it does multiply.

XIAOSHENG: I have always aspired to be loyal and upright, and yet I was suddenly ascribed the reputation of an outlaw. Although my conscience is clear, I feel ashamed about my movements and expression. Now what I expect from my bosom friend is that he must not only save my life but also cleanse my reputation: I am just afraid that you cannot avoid both submitting a memorial of explanation to the emperor and circulating explicit instructions several times.

SHENG: I will not only report the facts to the emperor and circulate explicit explanations among the army and the people but also recommend you in a special memorial to the Throne—you will definitely be invited to come back out of retirement and take up an official post.

XIAOSHENG (*faintly smiles*): Please don't do so. Listen to me:

> (Tune: *Northern Si men zi*)
> You ask me To prepare sacrificial meat and wine, hurriedly laying fishing rod aside
> To ready myself again for meetings of wind and clouds.[385]
> How could you know my Obsession with springs and rocks has attacked my vitals,
> And I have a chronic infection of mists and clouds?[386]
> Even An entire fierce army could not peel my iron rain cape away!
> What's so fearful about War carriages urging eastward
> And cavalry urging west?
> The relentless bow and banner are better than the prisoner's escort.[387]

> I entreat you to Persist no more in pressing me,
> But petition the emperor on my behalf,
> To let this idler grow old and die on Fishing Rock!

SHENG: You are so adamant in your lofty ideals! In that case, I dare not pressure you further.

XIAOSHENG: I insist on this. I not only have no intention to come out of retirement and take up an official post—I also have some thoughts about inviting you to withdraw from officialdom. Although these words might come unwelcome to the ear, I wish that you would hear them. Whenever a person is enjoying success, one should anticipate a time of frustration. Take the theater as an example: drums and gongs do not beat forever, and costumes get worn out. Where there are *sheng* and *dan*, there are *jing* and *chou*; excitement alternates with desolation. *Jing* and *chou* are the opposites of *sheng* and *dan*; desolation is the consequence of excitement. Among career officials, *jing* and *chou* regularly appear; so in the sea of officialdom, it is easy to end up desolate. The sensible man must put away the drums and gongs in scenes of excitement and never wait until he reaches the state of desolation to take off his official hat and belt. Be sure to remember in your hearts these words that are so unwelcome to the ear. (SHENG *and* DAN *nod their heads.*)

SHENG: These words are actually a blow to the head with a shout[388] and the bell that awakens me from dream—hearing them has made me sweat all over! When you go back this time, sir, please construct for us a thatched cottage with several rooms beside your residence. At the expiration of this term of office, I will resign my post at once and move to the mountains to live in seclusion with you.

(Tune: *Southern Shuang sheng zi*)

SHENG and DAN:
> To enlighten our ignorance,
> To enlighten our ignorance,

The earnest advice is finally offered;
To guard against collapse,
To guard against collapse,
Shake off the burden of fame and gain before it is too late!
Accomplish our high aspirations,
Accomplish our high aspirations;
Renew old friendships,
Renew old friendships.
See: Men in rush rain capes, women in bamboo hats
Stick together in loyal pairs.[389]
(Tune: *Northern Shuixian zi*)

XIAOSHENG and LAODAN:

Strange—for no reason,
We trod on disaster and danger,
Strange—for no reason,
We trod on disaster and danger!
This is indeed That blessings and immortals attract peeping ghosts.[390]
Go, go, go—
Evade cool breezes,
Avoid the bright moon;[391]
Shirk pleasures,
And repent your former errors.
Cut, cut, cut—
Cut down on simple food,
Discard your plain clothing.
Wear, wear, wear—
Wear out your bamboo hats
That merely cover your head.
Fish, fish, fish—
Using your fishing rod,
But don't drop a line near the road.

Fear, fear, fear—
Fear people who are not concerned
And tail you into the Peach Blossom Land.[392]
Choose, choose, choose—
Choose some other
Quiet and secluded fishing rock!
(*Northern coda*)
Arias of this new play have been filled in[393] to the end,
Weaving together all my endless schemes.
Now pass it on to that Handsome Master Zhou[394] for him to appreciate the tunes
And impartially
Favor me with his critique.

"Integrity" and "righteous deeds" of late seem a bit absurd,
And all would blame the theater for promoting what is lewd.
I hoped to use the stage to uphold integrity and righteous deeds,
So that the one who tied the bell on shows the way to take it off.[395]

Appendix

THE PLAYWRIGHT AND HIS ART

JING SHEN

A VERSATILE MAN

A creative writer, dramatist, drama theorist, musician, theater manager, editor, publisher, and gardening connoisseur, Li Yu 李漁 (Li Liweng, 1610–1680) stood out for his versatile talents on the literary and artistic scenes of the Ming–Qing dynastic transition period.[1] His many gifts lent him unique perspectives from his diverse fields of expertise when discussing literature and art, as shown in the informal essays collected in *Random Repository of Idle Thoughts* (*Xianqing ouji* 閒情偶寄, 1671), which includes his treatise on drama. That disquisition synthesizes previous achievements in Chinese drama theory and, in reference to his own theatrical creation and practice, brings them to full development. Being versed in every sector of theater—theorizing, composing and staging plays, as well as training actors—makes Li Yu peerless in late imperial China. Further, none of his contemporaries had tried as many types of writing as he did in stories, novels, essays, poetry, plays, drama treatise, and the rewriting of classics and of his own fiction.[2]

Of all the genres, what has contributed most to his fame are his ten existing *chuanqi* 傳奇 (romance) plays, of sixteen mentioned in *Random Repository of Idle Thoughts*:³ "Liweng's plays enjoyed a great reputation in the early Qing. When his ten plays were first printed [ca. 1670], the price of paper rose for a period of time."⁴ Such comments indicate that his dramas were very popular in his own day. The collection *Liweng's Ten Plays* (*Liweng shizhong qu*) has been reprinted repeatedly since then.⁵ These plays were introduced to Japan during Li Yu's own lifetime. According to the Japanese Sinologist Aoki Masaru (1887–1964), "Since Li Yu's works are plain enough to be easily read, printed editions of his ten plays could be found in all the bookshops, and lots of them even spread into Japan. When people of the Tokugawa period (1603–1867) talked about Chinese drama, without exception all were referring to Hushang Liweng [Li Yu]."⁶

Unfortunately, the popularity of his works drove him away from his beloved Hangzhou:

> I have moved to Moling [Nanjing] solely because my imprints provoked the unscrupulous to produce many [unauthorized] reprints. Hence, although I hated to leave my native land, I decided to migrate and seek my livelihood here. Unexpectedly, as soon as my new imprint appeared, avaricious merchants in Wumen [Suzhou] coveted reprinting it. Fortunately, I got wind of it extremely early and tried all I could to request the Suzhou-Songjiang circuit intendant, the honorable Mr. Sun, to put up a notice to prohibit it. Only then was their scheme foiled. The disputes in Wumen had barely died down when a letter from home suddenly arrived saying that people in Hangzhou already completed the reprinting and the new books would be on sale soon.⁷

As a professional writer who made a living from publishing his own work, Li Yu took very seriously his ownership of the books and notepapers produced by his bookshop. If anybody infringed his copyright, he "would lodge complaints with local authorities to which that person belongs and hope the authorities would uphold justice. As for those who rely on their wealth and power to reprint Liweng's books, I can't tell how many there are in the world. I plow, and they eat. How can I contain my outrage? I swear I will fight them to the death," he declared.[8] To sell his books, Li Yu managed very successful bookshops in Nanjing, including Yishengtang 翼聖堂 and Jieziyuan 芥子園, which enjoyed a great reputation for a long time.[9]

A CONTROVERSIAL FIGURE

Li Yu had a contradictory and controversial reputation, however, as "an extraordinary person" 異人 and "an oddball" 怪物.[10] Li's son-in-law Shen Yinbo 沈因伯 describes his oddity with the following observation: "All his life, my father-in-law said what other people could not say or dared not say; this is widely known nowadays. However, what is less widely known is that he said what others were unwilling to say or disdained to say.... Nevertheless, whatever others were unwilling to say and disdained to say is what he is extremely willing to do and did not disdain to do."[11] Li Yu's "An Impromptu Poem on a Birthday" (Shengri kouhao 生日口號) is an example of his unrestrained words, in which he does not conceal his pragmatic outlook on life:

> All hope to live for a hundred years,
> But more years means more worry.
> It would be better to accept the life you're allotted
> And indulge in pleasures to avoid wasting time.

人皆願百歲,
歲多愁亦多.
不如聽修短,
行樂戒蹉跎.[12]

Li Yu's controversial reputation can be seen through an anecdote recorded in Liu Tingji's 劉廷璣 (b. ca. 1654) collection of comments on his contemporaries, *Zaiyuan's Random Notes* (*Zaiyuan zazhi* 在園雜誌):

> Li Liweng (Yu) is a skilled literary man of our time. His numerous works include a collection of ten *chuanqi* plays, *Random Repository of Idle Thoughts*, [the short-story collection] *Silent Operas*, and [the novel] *The Carnal Prayer Mat*. Both his conception and his diction are extremely original and unique. Mr. Shen Quan has commented: "His cleverness outstrips his learning," which is truly an insightful remark.[13] However, every place he goes, he carries a set of hardwood clappers to select ladies from Qin and beauties from Wu,[14] and he is a bit too wild and unrestrained in speech and behavior. In the past, he resided in the capital and inscribed on the tablet of his inn "Residence of the Humble." Some busybody teasingly inscribed on the place opposite his "Residence of the Respectable."[15] Liweng's inscription was originally self-effacing, but the teaser deliberately misrepresented his meaning to ridicule him for this practice. Nevertheless, the poetry he compiled is quite good; the poetry, historical judgments, and other comments recorded in his *One Man's Words* also show an original perspective and technique.[16]

These comments by scholar-officials of Li Yu's time affirm that he was a prolific and creative writer, but his unconventional lifestyle as a theater professional incurred criticism. The anecdote about the mocking inscription also reveals the low social status of actors. Li Yu's biographical sketch in the eighteenth-century reference book *An Encyclopedia of Plays* (*Quhai zongmu tiyao* 曲海總目提要) indicates how people regarded his profession: "[Li] Yu was originally from a family of government clerks and scribes. He was an intelligent child. He could write songs and fiction, and he kept company with members of the lower classes. People regarded him as an entertainer."[17] Although he received the education of a man of letters, he was reduced to making a living from the theater. His reputation for gaining money by artifice further deprived him of the virtuous reputation that a Confucian scholar was expected to achieve. Jiang Ruizao 蔣瑞藻 (1891–1929) remarks: "Yet the way he conducted himself was really frivolous and shameless. He was also good at speculation and often collected others' money by clever means."[18]

Li Yu indeed made no secret of his need for money when in straitened circumstances and explicitly begged men of high position for financial support in writing.[19] Among his writings on his poverty, it is of interest to note that drama composition helped him escape the reality of his fiscal situation:

> I was born amid hardship and live in dire straits. From childhood to adulthood and from adulthood to old age, I've never been able to have peace of mind for a moment, except for a little while when I write songs and compose lyrics to a tune. This not only chases away my gloom and dispels my resentment but also often allows me to assume the title of the happiest man on Earth. At times like that, I feel that the benefits of glory, splendor, wealth, and rank can be no greater than this. Nothing that one wishes to do in paradise can exceed this: if I want to be an official, then glory and rank are mine; if I want to resign from an official post, I can enter a mountain forest in the twinkling of

an eye. If I want to be one of the most talented scholars in the world, I become a reincarnation of Du Fu or Li Bai;[20] if I want to marry a woman of exquisite beauty, I will create a match for Wang Qiang and Xi Shi.[21] If I want to become an immortal or a Buddha, the Western Paradise and the Isle of Penglai will be no farther than my inkstone and brush holder;[22] if I want to display my filial piety and express my loyalty, then our monarch's times of peace and the age of my parents will be even better than those of Yao, Shun, and Peng Zu.[23]

Li Yu's description of his artistic dreamland lays bare the motifs of *chuanqi* drama. Despite living through the world-shaking dynastic transition that witnessed the collapse of the last Han Chinese empire and the takeover by Manchu forces, he inherited the late Ming fashion to write romantic comedies, plays that lacked the historical depth and social concerns seen in the works of his contemporary literati or professional playwrights. For this, his plays were criticized.[24] His were popularized transformations of the late Ming dramatic tradition that emphasized the power of emotions. Yet they lack the vigor and individualistic spirit of the Ming literati, with attention redirected to the secular world.[25]

Li's comedies do not address political, historical, and sensitive issues directly, but depict local customs and satirize social evils of the seventeenth century.[26] His "Editorial Principles" (Fanli 凡例) to *Random Repository of Idle Thoughts* may explain his choice of subject matter and style: "[P]eople nowadays are fond of light reading and are afraid of hearing serious talk" 然近日人情喜讀閒書，畏聽莊論.[27] Thus he claims to combine moral exhortations with recreation, and the title *Random Repository of Idle Thoughts* was intended to draw readers to the book by this means. His apologetic tone reveals his accommodation to popular taste.

AN INNOVATOR IN STYLISTIC COMPROMISE

Li Yu's lifestyle and creative work were both products of the period of political transition, displaying an eclectic style. Being a poor, failed scholar with no prospects for wealth and rank through administrative appointments, he still yearned for a life of pleasure—the vogue during the late Ming, which can be seen through the variety of subjects covered in *Random Repository of Idle Thoughts*: drama, performance, voice and appearance of women, elegant housing, food and drink, and keeping physically fit.[28] Gardens were an important aspect of late Ming elite culture, which was related to one of the two "consummate skills" 絕技 that Li Yu claimed to possess: "One is to distinguish and evaluate music; the other is to construct gardens and their pavilions" 一則辨審音樂, 一則置造園亭.[29] (Not surprisingly, he uses architectural terms to discuss drama in his treatise.) Li Yu had his first garden, Yiyuan 伊園, built in the hills at his hometown Lanxi 兰溪 of Jinhua as a haven during the war: "I recollect that after the Ming dynasty [1368–1644] fell and before the Great Qing Empire [1644–1912] took control, I had given up all thought of empty fame and was unconcerned with any meager official's salary. Dwelling in mountains as a refuge from the chaos, I took pride in having nothing to do."[30] Yet this haven cut off from the world was not sustainable, as he had to rely on business opportunities in town to support his family. He moved first to Hangzhou (1650) and then to Nanjing (ca. 1661), where he published the last four of his ten *chuanqi* plays. Unable to afford an idyllic rural life, he had the Jieziyuan 芥子園 garden constructed in Nanjing and later the Cengyuan 層園 garden in Hangzhou to create a reclusive space within the cities.[31] While seeking refined enjoyment beyond his economic means, Li Yu encouraged frugality with regard to construction: "Building must avoid all extravagance and waste. Not only households of the common people should advocate thrift and simplicity; even the nobility and high officials should also value this practice."[32] In his opinion, a novel and original building surpasses a magnificent one in taste.

Nonetheless, when it came to novelty, his ideas of embellishing a garden sometimes reveal a contradictory attitude toward frugality. Although he and his family were often so poor that they were forced to live in rented space, Li Yu scrimped on food and clothes in order to adorn his gardens tastefully: "I have a natural liking for striped bamboo, but I cannot afford to purchase it. So I must let my wife and children go hungry for a few days or endure cold for a winter to economize on food and clothing in order to please the senses. Other people laugh at me, and yet I feel the glow of satisfaction."[33] Bamboo stood for refinement to men of letters, and this was a novel species.

Conversely, he advises impoverished men to tailor their gardens to fit their straitened circumstances:

> A poor scholar's family that is fond of rocks but lacks the means does not have to build a rockery. A small stone can by itself satisfy the obsession to have a spring and rockery, provided that it is arranged in an appealing way and he often sits or lies by its side. If even a small stone must cost money, this thing can also have an important use for people. How could it be set up merely for viewing?[34]

The stone can serve practical purposes, Li Yu argues, such as a chair, couch, banister, tea table, and clothes-beating block for laundry. Why does he earnestly admonish people to include a rock in their gardens? He contends that, like bamboo, it can treat the illness of vulgarity. Thus a rock, a symbol of excellent taste, suggests an affinity with refined literati gardens even in a poor scholar's garden, where aesthetic designs have to compromise with practical uses.

Just as destitution did not provide the ease and comfort he sought, Li Yu's occupations blended social strata that were traditionally separate: the scholar-merchant and scholar-actor. Literati were supposed to be engaged in writing, calligraphy, and painting purely for aesthetic enjoyment and self-cultivation, whereas openly exploiting this learning for profit, as did Li Yu—despite being commonplace—was considered beneath the dignity of the scholar.[35] What is worse, he freely associated with actors, the lowest profession, considered interchangeable with prostitutes. Scholar-officials might own theatrical troupes, but their household ensembles performed for only their own families or literati gatherings. Li Yu also put together a private troupe; however, it was later reduced to performing for money in the houses of the rich, blurring the distinction between literati household troupes and professional companies.

Likewise, Li Yu's plays show his ability to adapt to his times in terms of theme and style. In response to the expression of romantic feelings unrestricted by ethics in the late Ming and to the importance attached to moral principles in the early Qing as well, Li Yu advocated "romantic morality" that harmonized romantic talent with moral ethics, as expounded at the beginning of his *chuanqi* play *Be Careful About Love* (*Shen luanjiao* 慎鸞交, 1667).[36] A similar attempt to reconcile conflicting expectations is shown in his ideal style of drama: refined and popular tastes do not usually go together, but as a writer of popular drama, Li Yu pursued a refined style free from vulgarity. His simple popular writing incurred criticism from some Qing literati. Li Diaoyuan 李調元 (1734–1803), who loved *A Couple of Soles* and had his household troupe perform it, disapproved of the farcical style of Li Yu's work but affirmed its popularity: "Li Yu is skilled at melodies and structure, and recently his *Ten Plays by Liweng* have been very popular."[37] Yang Enshou 楊恩壽 (1834–post 1888) says: "Liweng's ten plays are vulgar and lacking in literary grace; they are frank, simple, and funny. His intention was to popularize his plays, so he strove to be plain in the theme and wording. This is why they spread in the theater world, and the reason why he was a laughingstock among the refined."[38] Li Yu did intend his drama to be plain so that it could arouse broad interest: "*Chuanqi* are unlike formal literary works. Literary works are intended for scholars, so their abstruseness is not surprising; plays are intended for both scholars and non-scholars as well as uneducated women and children, so they are valued for simplicity, not for being abstruse."[39] Meanwhile, Li Yu emphasizes the importance of refined taste, regardless of whether in drama or in other art.[40] His comment on garden rocks is an example. Li Yu's ability to accommodate conflicting expectations in his writing indicates his recognition of the conflicting philosophical and social trends that coexisted during that time of dramatic political change. But his efforts to cater to diverse tastes also stemmed from his fluid identity and his desire to achieve an elite lifestyle despite being a poor scholar-commoner.[41]

A RECLUSE AND OFFICIALDOM

One of Li Yu's short lyrics, "An Extemporaneous Verse on Living in the Mountains" (Shanju man xing 山居漫興) to the *Yi wangsun* 憶王孫 tune, written at Yiyuan, hints at the meaning of his literary name Liweng (Old Man in a Broad Bamboo Hat):[42]

> I did not expect that here in the mountains,
> I would practice living as Liweng,

And rely on fishing to learn quiet sitting.
Since I let the fish go,
There is no harm coming up empty nine times out of ten.

不期今日此山中,
實踐其名住笠翁.
聊借垂竿學坐功.
放魚松,
十釣何妨九釣空.[43]

Angling with pole 垂竿 or fishing line 垂綸 implies living in seclusion.

Among Li Yu's ten poems on the advantages of living in Yiyuan (Yiyuan shi bian 伊園十便), "Yin bian" 吟便, about acquiring ideas for poetry, is reminiscent of the *Feng ru song* 風入松 aria in *A Couple of Soles* (scene 31, "Mistaken Arrest"):

The door unintentionally opens to the mountains;
I go not to seek poetry, but poetry comes of itself.
Don't wonder at abundant poems from empty pockets,
It's all because I live in a fairyland like Penglai.

兩扉無意對山隈,
不去尋詩詩自來.
莫怪囊慳題咏富,
只因家住小蓬萊.[44]

Similarly, the *Feng ru song* aria describes the beautiful scenery from which Murong Jie can easily draw inspiration for poetry while taking a walk in the mountains after fishing:

The man in a painting crosses the painting's bridge,
Along the path exploring quiet and repose.

The old fisherman no longer seeks material for verse;
It brushes past him with the wind where'er he goes.[45]

Murong Jie's choice of Yanling for his retirement not only suits his new means of supporting himself—fishing—but also alludes to Yan Ziling 嚴子陵, a noble recluse whom Li Yu admired.[46] Yan Ziling (39 B.C.E.–41 C.E.) became a hermit in the Fuchun Mountains (or Yanling) after retiring from political life, and the rock on which he sat when fishing is called Yan Ziling's Fishing Terrace. In scene 12 ("Luxuriant Escape") of *A Couple of Soles*, when Murong travels to Yanling, he decides to set up his hermitage there, the place where his ancient "true friend" used to reside.[47] He is clearly compared with Yan Ziling in Lord Yan's description of him: "When they get to Yanling, there will be a man of noble character who has resigned from his official post and become a hermit among fishermen and woodcutters."[48] Li Yu's poems and lyrics suggest that he feels unworthy of the ideal exemplified by Yan Ziling. His poems, "Accounts of Yanling" (Yanling jishi 嚴陵紀事), express his thoughts about taking his sons to Yanling for the imperial examinations at the county level. The eighth poem says: "Ziling was not concerned about his posterity;/Going back, I do not have the face to pass his Fishing Terrace" 子陵不為兒孫計, 歸去何顏過釣台.[49] The lines in his lyric "Passing Ziling's Fishing Terrace" (Guo Ziling Diaotai 過子陵釣台) reveal similar soul-searching:

> Holding the same fishing rod,
> Both wearing rush rain cape and broad bamboo hat,
> Why do you, sir, have great reputation and I am slighted?
> Having overrated my abilities
> To match myself with this noble-minded person,
> I then understand and respect him.

A world of difference between us:
You, sir, declined high government pay,
And I fish for an empty reputation.

同執綸竿,
共披蓑笠,
君名何重我何輕?
不自量,
將身高比,
才識敬先生.
相去遠,
君辭厚祿,
我釣虛名.⁵⁰

By comparing himself with Yan Ziling, Li Yu critically examines his own pursuit of the reclusive life and sees its inadequacy in substance due to his worldly attachment. The criticism of superficial reclusion in *A Couple of Soles* is suggested through portrayal of the fake fisherman in scene 23 ("The Make-Believe Hermit") and allusions to dubious historical hermits such as Lu Cangyong in scene 25 ("Pretend Deity").⁵¹ But Murong Jie's determination to make his resignation final and become a genuine recluse, especially as seen in scene 12, is intended to follow the ideal of Yan Ziling. The envoi of scene 25 reinforces Murong's sincere indifference to fame: "I do have means at hand to buy a bit of fame, /Yet I'd feel ashamed to be ancient angler in the arena of fame."⁵² This echoes the self-consciousness revealed in Li Yu's poem "Passing Ziling's Fishing Terrace." In the end, however, Murong and his wife still show repentance for not having secluded themselves deep enough in the mountains, which has caused them unexpected troubles from the government's continuing demands.

The theme of seclusion carries increasing weight in the second half of *A Couple of Soles* as Murong Jie's retirement moves to the foreground and plays an important role in further developing the plot and generating drama after Tan Chuyu and Fairy Liu's romance reaches a climax by scene 16 ("Divine Protection").[53] What best attests to the significance of this theme is that the play concludes with a serious conversation about seclusion. Enlightened by Murong's wisdom, Tan plans to end his official career early and follow in Murong's footsteps by becoming a recluse in the mountains. This conclusion is distinct from the conventional *chuanqi* closure, which celebrates official titles and honors. Two of the six illustrations in early Qing period editions focus on Murong's retirement, highlighting the theme as well. One depicts the moment he throws his official cap into the river while his wife discards her phoenix coronet to transition into rustics in scene 12 (see figure 2).[54] The other illustration gives a view of Murong's leisurely life with his wife in the mountains, as depicted at the beginning of scene 25, that contrasts the leisure of retirement with the strenuous government service of the past (see figure 4).

A factor justifying retirement from public life, as implied in *A Couple of Soles*, is corrupt officialdom. Scenes 11 ("The Fox's Might") and 17 ("Scrambling for Profit") ridicule corrupt officials and the channels that aspirants must utilize for an official career, although Li Yu emphasizes in *Random Repository of Idle Thoughts* that playwrights should avoid personal satire in their *chuanqi* drama.[55] Li Yu's other plays occasionally sneer at incompetent and depraved government officials, but this kind of description, which is also meant to provoke laughter, is not a prominent subject in his plays.[56] Exposure of corrupt practices among local officials, however, stands out in *A Couple of Soles* through the portrayal of the retired official Moneybags Qian and county officers. Qian's crooked ways of obtaining a government post through wealth and of using his connections with the district magistrate to fleece the people add a strong dimension of political satire to the romantic drama. The lawsuit against him for causing the death of Fairy Liu and Tan Chuyu occasions the ugly practices of county magistrate and assistant magistrate: they abuse justice and intrigue against each other to monopolize Qian's bribes in the lengthy scene 17—a scene that gives full play to the role of *chou*.[57] Qian's misdeeds can be regarded as an allusion to the venal practices of rural gentry during Li Yu's own time. The policies established by the founding emperor of the Ming, Zhu Yuanzhang (1328–1398), placed respected elder landlords as local leaders in rural governance. As urbanization spread, however, some landowners migrated to cities, investing little in their rural communities and evading levies— even if they were not as ruthless as Qian in exploiting peasants.[58] Moneybags Qian's meeting with local heads of household units in scene 11 furnishes a dramatic twist of that variation: Qian, who claims to be a country gentleman having retired from his career in the city, bosses and bullies the hapless local heads; these so-called community leaders lack wealth or power to protect their village, whereas the landed gentleman does not concern himself with the welfare of villagers at all. As exemplars at opposite poles of morality and public service, the characters Moneybags Qian and Murong Jie broaden the depiction of society in the world of *A Couple of Soles* and deeply engage with the play's concern with the morality of officialdom.[59]

REWRITING A STORY FOR THE STAGE

An examination of the story "Tan Chuyu Declares His Love in a Play; Liu Miaogu Dies for Honor's Sake After Her Aria," from which *A Couple of Soles* (1661) was adapted, can shed more light on the significance of the play.⁶⁰ Li Yu originally published this story in *Silent Operas, Second Collection* (*Wusheng xi er ji* 無聲戲二集 [no copy extant]), although it is not the first piece in that compendium.⁶¹ Zhang Jinyan 張縉彥 (1599–1670), provincial administration commissioner of Zhejiang (1654–1658), who was minister of the Board of War during the Ming dynasty, helped publish the collection and wrote a preface in which he allegedly called himself a "hero who did not die" 不死英雄, whitewashing his surrender to the bandit leader Li Zicheng (1606–1645) as an attempted suicide when Li's rebel band entered Beijing. This information is mentioned in the impeachment proceedings against him, conducted in 1660.⁶² Li Yu recompiled the collection as *The Combined Volume of Silent Operas* (*Wusheng xi he ji* 無聲戲合集, ca. 1658), replaced Zhang Jinyan's preface, and moved the story about Tan Chuyu and Fairy Liu to the very beginning. The book's subsequent republication as *Precious Jade* (*Liancheng bi* 連城璧) maintains the same order of the stories.⁶³ As the exact publication year of *The Combined Volume of Silent Operas* is uncertain, it is hard to determine whether Li Yu made the change directly because of concern about the case of Zhang Jinyan. Nevertheless, the fact that the Tan Chuyu story heads the list of the tales sets a moral tone for the combined edition and gives prominence to this story, which was favored by the author himself and highly acclaimed by a commentator.⁶⁴ *A Couple of Soles*, published a year after Zhang was removed from office and banished, can be read in light of this incident.⁶⁵ The ethical language that permeates the play surpasses the virtuous image of the lovers portrayed in the story and underscores Li Yu's ostensible effort to foster social morals in his works. Transforming Old Fisherman Mo from the story into the retired-official-turned-fisherman Murong Jie adds to the issue of public service in the romantic play; the episodes involving Murong Jie largely do not exist in the original story. Murong Jie represents an upright and dedicated official, yet could his concern about the vicissitudes of an official career and his desire to resign from office, starting from his first appearance, stem from the author's personal feelings for his own former patron's political lot? Some characters' comments on officialdom are especially reminiscent of Zhang's removal. Murong's wife exhorts him to retire early in scene 5 ("Punishing Bandits"): "If at some point you are impeached and convicted, will you still be able to just float away?"[66] In scene 11, Moneybags Qian boasts of his status as a rich country gentleman: "I have also heard that it is certainly dangerous to hold a high government post, so that's not as good as my separate path of advancement: I'll never be a very high official, but you have never seen a memorial to the emperor specially impeaching a local functionary for scraping the fat off the land."[67]

"Fiction provides the blueprint for *chuanqi* drama" 稗官為傳奇藍本.[68] This voices Li Yu's emphasis on the close connection between fiction and drama. His plays that drew their material from fiction, however, were composed in the later stage of the approximate twenty-year span of his career as a dramatist.[69] This supports the view that the Zhang Jinyan case and other literary inquisitions around that time made Li Yu turn away from real-life sources to existing fiction for dramatic material that would shelter him from suspicion of references to sensitive political and historical events while extending the sale of his works.[70]

Li Yu's deliberate practice to adapt his own fiction was unprecedented.[71] He rewrote four of his stories as *chuanqi* plays, among them *A Couple of Soles*.[72] The only illustration of the Tan Chuyu story that demonstrates its central theme on the devoted lovers foreshadows a dramatic re-creation representing the symbolic image of paired fish (see frontispiece).[73] Its inscription, which is an elegy on the double suicide in the story, betokens the presentation of the lovers plunging into the river and being transformed into a pair of soles in the play:

> They swore to die before they'd break their vow.
> Why call them mad? They'd promises to keep.
> As one, they leapt into the raging flood,
> And turned to sole (soul) mates in the wat'ry deep.[74]

Scenes 16 ("Divine Protection") and 18 ("The Return to Life") fully explore the visual potential of that episode in the water. Meanwhile, the play expands and dramatizes the relationship between the two couples—Tan Chuyu and Fairy Liu, Old Fisherman Mo and his wife—that is depicted in the illustration, by changing the background of Mo, who appears in only the lesser second half of the story. The illustration suggests the theatrical adaptability of the story. Equally intriguing was that other writers recomposed four of Li Yu's *chuanqi* plays, including *A Couple of Soles*, as novellas.[75] With its vulgarity, the novella *A Couple of Soles* differs from the original play and appeals to less sophisticated readers.[76] If Li Yu rewrote his fiction as drama to "double the profits" 雙重獲利 on his original story material,[77] the novella writer recycled and vulgarized the play to exploit further its commercial potential. The development of the story material has really come full circle, in that Li Yu re-created it from fiction to drama and it was later adapted to a novella!

PRACTICE AND THEORY

Li Yu's ability to compose drama suitable for staging is generally recognized. Yang Enshou accurately points out the strength of his plays: "Not only can contemporary worthies rarely match his skill of arrangement and role types, his ingenuity of structural development and closure and plot, and marvelous tact of actions and spoken parts and gags; even playwrights of the Yuan and Ming are not as good. No wonder he enjoys such a great reputation."[78] These elements are essential if a play is to be successfully presented on stage, especially comedy. Wu Mei (1884–1939), a theorist of classical Chinese drama, ranks Li Yu first among the dramatists of the Qing dynasty for his expertise in arranging scenes and plot to create theatricality onstage.[79]

Through his influential treatise on drama in *Random Repository of Idle Thoughts*,[80] Li Yu summarizes his experience in this respect as a playwright and theater manager,[81] which can be illuminated in the light of his *chuanqi* play *A Couple of Soles*. The beginning of "On Performance" (Yanxi bu 演習部) in *Random Repository* states: "A play is written solely for performance on stage" 填詞之設, 專為登場.[82] Li Yu had performance in mind when composing drama; he had little interest in the *antou ju* 案頭劇 (desktop plays) or closet dramas popular for reading during his time. He was the first Chinese dramatist who put the topic of structure in first place in his drama theory.[83] To ensure that a play will be performed onstage, he advises that before starting to write, the author should devise a primary story line about one individual as a *zhunao* 主腦 (control center) and the plot's overall structure as well.[84] The development of other characters and plots should be connected to the control center throughout, and the presentation must be clear enough for the audience to follow. This is the wise remark of an experienced dramatist who knew full well that lengthy *chuanqi* plays were prone to "having many main threads" 頭緒繁多, which would produce a "beamless house" 無梁之屋.[85] Li Yu regards *The Thorn Hairpin* (*Jingchai ji*), one of the four great *nanxi* 南戲 (Southern drama; the predecessor of *chuanqi*) classics, as an exemplar of tight structure with a single narrative thread.[86]

The story of *A Couple of Soles* is complicated, but its main thread is clearly stated in the prologue and is consistently followed through to the end:[87] To demonstrate her devotion to Tan Chuyu, in defiance of a match arranged by her greedy mother, Fairy Liu drowns herself while performing *The Thorn Hairpin*. Tan follows her into the water. This central incident sets off a series of dramatic episodes with numerous surprises. The aim of the play is to raise the reputation of the acting profession through an ingenious portrayal of actor-lovers. All the major characters enter early, in accordance with the principle expounded in *Random Repository of Idle Thoughts*:[88] Tan Chuyu appears in scene 2 ("Burning Ears") and Fairy Liu (whose parents come along), in scene 3 ("Organizing a Troupe"). The government official Murong Jie (extra male lead), along with his wife, appears in scene 5 because he plays an important role in Tan's life and career, especially in the second half of the play, and because he adds a significant dimension to the moral message. To follow the major plot, audience members familiar with this rule would pay special attention to characters who enter in the beginning scenes.

Novelty of subject matter is also underscored in *Random Repository of Idle Thoughts*, the essay "On Being Unconventional" (Tuo kejiu 脫窠臼):

> The ancients called drama *chuanqi* (literally, "transmitting marvels") because it tells very curious stories that have never been seen before. This is how it got this name. Evidently, only the marvelous can be transmitted. The new is another name of the marvelous. If a plot has already been performed on stage, thousands and thousands of people will have seen it. Then it is not marvelous in the least, and what need is there to transmit it?[89]

For marvelous plots, Li Yu advocates fresh material. Nine of his ten existing plays depict stories of his original creation, deviating from the convention of traditional Chinese drama that often adapted historical events or existing stories. The prologue to *A Couple of Souls* states that this play distinguishes itself in featuring actors as devoted lovers and their profession, regarding which Qinhuai zuihou 秦淮醉侯 (Drunkard from the Nanjing Pleasure Quarters; Du Jun) comments: "Instead of imitating the ancients, *sheng* and *dan* act this and portray directly their own profession. How could they be careless?" 生旦演此，非優孟古人，直是我與我周旋，那得草草。[90]

Even if a playwright reworks an old play, Li Yu also insists in his treatise, it must be done in an original way.[91] The integration of the classic *The Thorn Hairpin* into *A Couple of Soles* exemplifies an ingenious way to renew an old play, although it serves more of his purpose in making *A Couple of Soles* a novel play rather than exhibit criticism of the earlier one. *The Thorn Hairpin* was very popular during Li Yu's time and after; it was also a favorite in the collections of selected scenes or arias.[92]

An early Qing period illustration of scene 15 ("Together in Death") depicts the dynamics on- and offstage in reaction to Fairy Liu's "falling" into the river. Viewers are aghast, and then further alarmed at Tan's jumping off the stage (see figure 3). The illustration for scene 28 ("A Coincidental Reunion") shows three parties watching Fallen Angel Liu's impersonation of Wang Shipeng on a stage that is only slightly above the waterline: one man backstage, part of the audience on shore, and Tan and Fairy Liu in a boat on the water (see figure 6). This illustration depicts a typical venue for performing a play as a sacrifice to gods in the lower Yangzi region during late imperial times.[93] The fact that two of the six illustrations for *A Couple of Soles* describe the performance of *The Thorn Hairpin* indicates that the play within the play is central to *A Couple of Soles*, or at least the illustrator thought that this feature was most worth depicting—as a new twist to *chuanqi*. The re-creation of *The Thorn Hairpin* in scene 15 also brings about the involvement of water deity Lord Yan in Tan and Fairy Liu's life, and he continues to play an important role in the second half of *A Couple of Soles*. The supernatural element not only adds theatricality to its presentation but also complicates the plot development. Li Yu takes pride in his re-presentation of the classic piece, as conveyed in the choral song of scene 15: "This version of *The Thorn Hairpin*/will be even more widely known."[94]

Even Li Yu's sternest critics speak approvingly of *A Couple of Soles*. Literary historian Zheng Zhenduo (1898–1958), not an admirer of Li Yu's style in general, makes the following favorable comments on the play: "Of Liweng's ten plays, the least affected and the most natural would be *A Couple of Soles*. In its scenes such as 'Plunging into the River,' I could hardly tell whether the presentation is a play within the play or a real situation before my eyes; true feelings are gushing, by which no one remains unmoved."[95] This play within the play leads to a climax of *A Couple of Soles*. As Li Yu points out, "The last scene of the first half temporarily summarizes the action where gong and drum are briefly put away in suspense, which is called 'a small ending.' It should be tense and avoid relaxation, should be active and avoid cooling off" 上半部之末出, 暫攝情形, 略收鑼鼓, 名為小收煞. 宜緊忌寬, 宜熱忌冷.[96] Scene 16 is such "a small ending," a scene of bustle and excitement.[97] To celebrate Lord Yan's birthday, there are memorial ceremonies at his temples everywhere. On this festive occasion, the first two temples that Lord Yan visits are vibrant with the sound of drums, horns, and gongs as well as with song and dance. On his inspection tour of the third one, he learns about the double suicide following Fairy Liu's performance for his birthday and decides to rescue her and Tan Chuyu. The deity's magic transformation of the lovers' inseparable bodies into a pair of flatfish, to be caught by the servant of the retired-official-turned-fisherman Murong Jie, is quite a spectacle. The audience is kept in suspense, in accordance with Li Yu's requirement of "a small ending," as to how Murong will bring about the lovers' marriage, riches, and honor in the later development of the story. This is a visually lively scene that involves many role types portraying characters in colorful costumes and makeup, such as water deity Lord Yan; a judge from the Underworld; the village gods; shrimp, snail, crab, and turtle generals; priests; and temple patrons in addition to Tan Chuyu and Fairy Liu.[98] It forms a corresponding contrast to scene 8 ("The Bandits Set Out"), in which the government troops led by Murong battle the mountain bandits, who have a vanguard of tigers, bears, rhinoceroses, and elephants. Those beasts in action, including the bandit chief with the face of a tiger, can visually and aurally enliven the performance of *A Couple of Soles* as much as the magic water animals.[99]

The final climax, the *da shousha* 大收煞 (big ending), should also be unpredictable to make a lasting impression on the audience, in Li Yu's opinion:

> Where the streams and hills end [at the resolution of the dramatic plot],[100] it is most suitable for great waves to suddenly appear: perhaps as a surprise first and delight afterward, or begin with doubt and end with confidence, or turn the height of delight and belief into surprise and bewilderment. Be sure to have all the seven human emotions in the one scene. Only when the writing is exciting to the end with increasing skill throughout, can this be called a truly fascinating conclusion.[101]

The last scene of *A Couple of Soles* resorts to all these devices. In accordance with *chuanqi* conventions, all the major characters get together again in this scene, but their happy reunion does not happen until the very final moment, after being postponed by shock and doubts. This makes scene 32 ("A Shocking Reunion") unusually long. The dramatic confrontation between Tan Chuyu and Murong Jie is a surprise, since Tan Chuyu and Fairy Liu have already happily revisited Murong and his wife; they have expressed their gratitude in scene 26 ("Presenting the Book") after Tan becomes an official with Murong's aid. Yet, from scene 22 ("A Cunning Plan"), when bandits scheme to have a man resembling Murong lead government troops in surrendering to them, the story starts to foreshadow that later development, and the misunderstanding is aggravated in scene 25 by Murong's plan to give Tan instructions on how to suppress bandits in the name of Lord Yan without claiming credit for himself. Thus although the tense confrontation in court is unexpected, the conditions are ripe for the major characters to reassemble in this dramatic manner, as Li Yu suggests: "Where the water flows, a channel is formed" 水到渠成.[102]

Li Yu's talent is also seen in creating amusing scenes. No drama critics have attached as much importance to comic gestures and remarks (*kehun* 科諢) in *chuanqi* drama as Li Yu, who discusses the topic in one essay of *Random Repository of Idle Thoughts*. Considering the structure of a lengthy *chuanqi* play, he holds that comic gestures and remarks can keep audiences from falling asleep, especially in the play's second half:

> Comic gestures and remarks are a trifling skill in writing a play, but to make the play suit both refined and popular tastes and appeal to both the intelligent and the ignorant, you must pay close attention to this matter. If writing is fine and the plot is fine, yet the comic gestures and remarks are not fine, not only will a vulgar person not be able to bear watching the play, but even a refined scholar would also feel drowsy during the performance.[103]

These comic elements were intended to help *chuanqi* drama reach broad audiences.

Li Yu's innovation in this regard lies in his portrayal of romantic leads in a comic light:

> These two words—making gags—are worked out not only for the painted-face role [*jing*]; they are indispensable for all role types. There are comic gestures and remarks characteristic of *sheng* (the young male lead) and *dan* (the young female lead), and those characteristic of *wai* (older male role) and *mo* (supporting male role). It is the job of the *jing* (painted face) and *chou* (clown) to make impromptu comic gestures and remarks. However, *jing* and *chou*'s gags are easy to make, whereas it is hard to create gags for *sheng*, *dan*, *wai*, and *mo*. Refinement can contain some vulgarity, while refinement is shown in vulgarity.[104]

This blending of refinement and vulgarity, which makes Li Yu's drama popular, is a delicate task. His advice is to identify a point "bordering on vulgarity" 近俗 without overdoing it.[105] Although comic elements normally appear in *chuanqi* drama, they are rarely associated with the romantic hero and heroine. Scene 19 ("Rustic Nuptials") furnishes a rare instance of placing romantic lovers in a farcical situation. To heighten the celebratory atmosphere, a woodcutter, a farmer, a vegetable gardener, and a shepherd boy from the mountain village bring rustic gifts to their wedding and banter and embarrass the newlyweds at their nuptial chamber in vulgar ways. Regarding the boorish and naughty ways they make fun of the newlyweds, scholar Tan comments: "[I]t is really not a vulgar custom but a refined affair instead" and "This is not only extremely new but also extremely refined."[106] These unconventional nuptials for a *sheng* and a *dan* do display a unique style for *chuanqi*. An original idea, even if it may be realized in a rustic farce, is ironically promoted as refinement by Li Yu.

Another new practice advocated by Li Yu was to increase the weight of spoken parts in his plays. He observes: "From the beginning, *chuanqi* writers have laid stress only on composing arias and regarded spoken parts as a minor device" 自來作傳奇者, 止重填詞, 視賓白為末着.¹⁰⁷ The spoken parts were largely left for actors to develop on their own. Li Yu protests: "Hence, I know that the art of the spoken parts ought to be put on an equal footing with arias. If there are most satisfactory arias, then there should be most satisfactory spoken parts" 故知賓白一道, 當與曲文等視, 有最得意之曲文, 即當有最得意之賓白.¹⁰⁸ What motivated him to expand the spoken parts is consideration for performance:

> Elaboration of spoken parts in *chuanqi* actually began with me, for which there are the same numbers of people who understand me and who blame me throughout the country. Those who understand me say: Spoken parts have always been looked upon as speaking, and you can just blurt out whatever comes into your head; Liweng treats spoken parts as literary writing and weighs each word. It has always been that as long as spoken parts are clear on paper, whether their tones are in perfect harmony is ignored. Oftentimes, a block-printed edition looks coherent, and yet it sounds confusing when performed onstage. Can there be any difference between a person's eyes and ears, one sensitive and the other deaf? It is because the author just wields his writing brush and does not put himself in somebody else's position to both speak for actors and listen as audience. He does not tie up his heart with his mouth to ask whether it is easy to say and pleasant to the ear. That is the reason why the play is markedly different as reading and as performance. Liweng may hold a writing brush in his hand, but he speaks as if he were coming on

stage, completely substituting himself for the theater. Again, with his mind moving around, he studies the key plot and tries out its voices. If it is good, he will write vigorously; if it is bad, he will stop writing. This is why his plays are suitable for both watching and listening.[109]

Well-known classics such as *The Thorn Hairpin* can be comprehensible to audiences even if they get to enjoy only the sound of arias from the performance of the plays, yet spoken parts are essential to a new play for expounding its story. This is especially true for Li Yu's plays, which are based mostly on original story material.[110] Li Yu also encourages the author to "put himself in somebody else's position" while writing spoken parts, for the purpose of characterization: "Portraying each person, you must speak like each person without making them sound identical or superficial, as *Outlaws of the Marsh* tells its stories and Wu Daozi sketches from life. Thus it is called the consummate skill of this art."[111]

As he himself noted, Li Yu also incurred criticism for elaborating spoken parts to the extent that that modification altered the conventional ratio between singing arias and speaking. An example from *A Couple of Soles* that has been debated, as indicated by the marginal comment, is the long dialogue in scene 10 ("Becoming Leading Man"). This is the disciples' (ludicrous) performances when their drama instructor checks up on their memorization of scripts as well as their fight after he leaves. Each character acts according to the expectation of his or her role type: *sheng* and *dan* prove themselves to be brilliant students, the work of *wai* and *mo* is passable, but *jing* and *chou* accomplish nothing and they cheat. Consequently, the most hilarious buffoonery is attributed to *jing* and *chou*, especially the latter, who incites his fellow students to attack *sheng*. This farcical dispute involving the students in all the six roles gives an idea of what Li Yu means by comic gestures and remarks appropriate to *sheng* and *dan*, *wai* and *mo*, and *jing* and *chou*, respectively. Although the disciples are tested on singing selected arias, this long scene is presented primarily through spoken parts with stage directions. Perhaps responding to criticism of this practice, Qinhuai zuihou defends Li Yu in the notes and commentary at the top of that page:

> Seeing this scene has too many spoken parts and very few arias, people say it has the defect of numerous branches and a weak trunk. They do not know that the section on reciting scripts in this scene fills in old tunes with new words and that singers just suffer from too many arias. If new tunes were added, that would cause the defect of numerous trunks and weak branches. Viewers will inevitably be aware of this.[112]

It seems that the balance of spoken parts and arias is meant to regulate the workload for actors on stage.

All the passages quoted from *Random Repository of Idle Thoughts* stem from Li Yu's consideration for the performability of a play onstage and its effect on its viewers. As a professional playwright who made a living from selling his work, Li Yu understood the importance of entertaining broad audiences. This popularized his drama but also made him the target of criticism because literati generally wrote plays primarily to express their own sentiments, regardless of their audiences.[113]

MORE ABOUT MUSIC

The arrangement of tunes in *A Couple of Soles* shows how Li Yu creatively followed the prosodic rules to compose a readable and performable text. *Chuanqi* dramatists could utilize pastiches (*jiqu* 集曲) to make arias more expressive of different emotions, a device in which phrases extracted from several tunes in the same mode are fused to form a new tune. In *A Couple of Soles*, the use of pastiches also enabled Li Yu to underscore the play's theme through the selection of tunes and creation of new tune titles. *Shuangyu bimu you chunshui* (A Couple of Soles Swim in the Spring Stream), which is a pastiche in scene 1 ("Making a Start"), synthesizes three tunes—*Yujia ao* (Fisherman's Pride), *Mo yu'er* (Groping for Fish), and *Yu you chunshui* (Fish Swim in the Spring Stream)—to summarize the romantic story; the combination of the tune titles ingeniously touches on the major themes of the play. Additionally, to give full expression to arias, Li Yu employed the form of medleys (*daiguoqu* 帶過曲), which refer to when a tune matrix is strongly linked in performance with a following matrix in the same mode to form a musically relatively fixed unit. *Dui yuhuan* with *Qingjiang yin* in scene 30 ("Winning the Battle") is such a cluster that binds together the tune matrixes *Dui yuhuan* and *Qingjiang yin*, as indicated by the word *dai* (with).

Chuanqi drama is sung to mostly Southern tunes (*nanqu*), but this dramatic genre can also borrow Northern tunes and alternate arias in the Northern and Southern styles to create a mixed suite. Northern tunes are conducive to solemn and stirring songs, but only one primary singing voice is heard throughout the Northern tunes of one scene, whereas every role may sing a solo, a chorus, or an antiphony in Southern tunes despite the distinction of primary and secondary roles. In scene 16, Lord Yan on his inspection tour learns about Tan Chuyu and Fairy Liu's double suicide in the river and decides to rescue them. The *wai* actor who plays Lord Yan sings all the eight arias in Northern tunes. Scene 32, however, alternates Northern (*bei*) and Southern (*nan*) tunes, in which *xiaosheng* (Murong Jie) and *sheng* (Tan Chuyu) sing the arias alternately when Tan interrogates Murong, who has been framed for treason. Toward the end, *dan* (Fairy) and *laodan* (Murong's wife) join in chorus after the whole truth has been revealed. This arrangement heightens the excitement of the finale.[114]

LI YU ON THE MODERN STAGE

Kunqu 崑曲, or the Kunshan musical style (the oldest Chinese living operatic form), was favored by literati for *chuanqi* drama, and all of Li Yu's plays were performed in that musical style in his time.[115] Along with the decline of Kunqu opera during the late eighteenth century, *A Couple of Soles* seems to have faded away from the Kunqu stage. Two of its tunes are included in fascicles 9 and 25 of *Jiu gong dacheng nan bei ci gongpu* 九宮大成南北詞宮譜 (1746), which indicates that it had indeed been performed, but no collections of *qu* tunes 曲譜 since then took it in.[116] The 1950s saw the revival of Kunqu, with the support of the Chinese government. After the interruption of the Cultural Revolution (1966–1976), Kunqu was revitalized. As the result of Kunqu artists' efforts, this opera tradition was recognized as an important cultural legacy under the protection of the state in the 1980s, and in 2001, UNESCO proclaimed Kunqu as one of the "Masterpieces of the Oral and Intangible Heritage of Humanity."[117] After a hiatus of more than two centuries, *A Couple of Soles* was staged again as Kunqu in June 2009 in Suzhou. At the Fourth Chinese Kunqu Opera Art Festival, the Hunan Provincial Kunqu Troupe 湖南省昆劇團 performed it. Director Cong Zhaohuan 叢兆桓 (b. 1931) points out the meaning of the production to Kunqu artists today: this play featuring actors "is intended to add luster to our acting profession" 要為我輩梨園生色, as stated in scene 1.[118] *A Couple of Soles* has been adapted to *Jingju* 京劇 (Beijing opera), *Chuanju* 川劇 (Sichuan opera), *Wuju* 婺劇 (Wu or Zhejiang opera), and other regional theatrical forms.[119]

In 2010, the quatercentenary of Li Yu's birth, students at the National Academy of Chinese Theatre Arts 中國戲曲學院 presented the Beijing opera *Li Yu chuanqi* 李漁傳奇, composed of a prologue and seven scenes written by Xie Boliang 謝柏梁 (b. 1958).[120] In scene 5, Li Yu and his household troupe rehearse the episode of *A Couple of Soles* that integrates the *Thorn Hairpin* highlight, "Clasping a Rock and Plunging into the River," a prelude to Fairy Liu's and Tan Chuyu's suicidal acts. *A Couple of Soles* was also reproduced on the modern *huaju* 話劇 (spoken drama) stage. In 2000, the renowned Beijing People's Art Theatre 北京人民藝術劇院 put on the play *Boundless Romance* (*Fengyue wubian* 風月無邊) in five acts, featuring Li Yu's life with his household troupe; his troupe performs *A Couple of Soles*.[121] The production was quite a hit in Beijing and other parts of the country. The prominent director Lin Zhaohua 林兆華 (b. 1936), famous for his remarkable experimental and avant-garde drama in China and abroad since the 1980s, always seeks to break down boundaries between theatrical genres. In *Boundless Romance*, he applies the style of traditional Chinese theater to the modern spoken play. It incorporates the Kunqu performance of *A Couple of Soles* into the story, particularly the scene from *The Thorn Hairpin* in which Fairy Liu jumps into the river, and that constitutes the climax of *Boundless Romance*. This play within the play and the blending of Kunqu and *huaju* deserve further study.

Both biographical plays depict Li Yu, a writer of comedy, as a tragic figure oppressed by corrupt officials, in contrast with his reputation of making up to powerful men for a profit. A note by Lin Zhaohua may account for the spoken play's appeal to contemporary audiences: Li Yu is portrayed as a character who "lives according to his own mode of life" 按自己的方式生活.[122] That perspective agrees with the spirit of modern times. Li Yu's individualistic consciousness and seemingly postmodern attitude give new life to his works to attract modern-day audiences.

NOTES

INTRODUCTION

1. The story title also exists in a single-line version: "An Actress Scorns Wealth and Honor to Preserve Her Chastity" (Qing fugui nüdan quan zhen 輕富貴女旦全貞). An excellent translation of this story can be found in Li Yu, *Silent Operas*, trans. Patrick Hanan (Hong Kong: Chinese University Press, 1990), 160–201.
2. On the relationship between *nanxi* and *chuanqi*, see William Dolby, "Yuan Drama," and John Hu, "Ming Dynasty Drama," both in *Chinese Theater: From Its Origins to the Present Day*, ed. Colin Mackerras (Honolulu: University of Hawai'i Press, 1983), 32–33, 62–69.
3. For an insightful exploration of the conventions of performance and how audiences responded, see Cyril Birch, *Scenes for Mandarins: The Elite Theater of the Ming* (New York: Columbia University Press, 1995), and introduction to Meng Chengshun, *Mistress and Maid (Jiaohongji)*, trans. and ed. Cyril Birch (New York: Columbia University Press, 2001), ix–xxi. Other useful background information can be found in William Dolby, *A History of Chinese Drama* (New York: Barnes and Noble, 1976); and Tina Lu, "Drama," and Wai-Yee Li, "Early Qing to 1723," both in *The Cambridge History of Chinese Literature*, ed. Kang-I Sun Chang and Stephen Owen, vol. 2, *From 1375* (Cambridge: Cambridge University Press, 2010), 127–148, 152–244. For a study of theater architecture and performance practices during Li Yu's lifetime, see Sophie Volpp, *Worldly Stage: Theatricality in Seventeenth-Century China* (Cambridge, Mass.: Harvard University Asia Center, 2011).
4. Birch, *Scenes for Mandarins*, 3; Hu, "Ming Dynasty Drama," 66.

5. For tune titles, see James I. Crump, *Song-Poems from Xanadu* (Ann Arbor: Center for Chinese Studies, University of Michigan, 1993), 15, 18.
6. For an extended analysis of role types, see Jing Shen, "Role Types in *The Paired Fish*, a *Chuanqi* Play," *Asian Theatre Journal* 20, no. 2 (2003): 226–236.
7. Patrick Hanan, *The Invention of Li Yu* (Cambridge, Mass.: Harvard University Press, 1988), 88.
8. Eric Henry, *Chinese Amusement: The Lively Plays of Li Yü* (Hamden, Conn.: Archon, 1980), 41.
9. Henry, *Chinese Amusement*, 51.
10. Henry, *Chinese Amusement*, 19, 39.
11. Henry, *Chinese Amusement*, 33–38, 57.
12. Henry, *Chinese Amusement*, 55–56.
13. Cai Dongmin sees most of Li Yu's *chuanqi* plays as satirical or light comedies, only *Bimuyu* as a "serious play imbued with tragic components" ("Li Yu xiqu bianju yanjiu" [Ph.D. diss., Shanghai Xiju Xueyuan, 2013], 34–35).
14. Wang Shipeng (the male protagonist in *The Thorn Hairpin*), who refuses to accept the prime minister's marriage proposal after winning the imperial examination, is distinguished from the ungrateful husbands in other old *nanxi* plays. See Cyril Birch, "Tragedy and Melodrama in Early *ch'uan-ch'i* Plays: 'Lute Song' and 'Thorn Hairpin' Compared," *Bulletin of the School of Oriental and African Studies* 36, no. 2 (1973): 228–247; and Zhao Shanlin, "Shi lun *Jingchai ji* de chuanbo jieshou," *Yishu bai jia* 1 (2011): 142–143.
15. For a study of the staging of scenes from *The Thorn Hairpin* in *A Couple of Soles* and a comparison of the characters in the two plays, see Jing Shen, *Playwrights and Literary Games in Seventeenth-Century China: Plays by Tang Xianzu, Mei Dingzuo, Wu Bing, Li Yu, and Kong Shangren* (Lanham, Md.: Lexington Books, 2010), 178–179, 183–201.
16. The female poet Huang Yuanjie (黃媛介, fl. 1645–1655) wrote a preface for and comments on Li Yu's play *The Destined Marriage* (*Mingzhong yuan* 命中緣).
17. Chun-shu Chang and Shelley Hsueh-lun Chang, *Crisis and Transformation in Seventeenth-Century China: Society, Culture, and Modernity in Li Yü's World* (Ann Arbor: University of Michigan Press, 1992), 68–69.
18. For biographies of Wang Duanshu, see Ellen Widmer, "Wang Duanshu," in *The Indiana Companion to Traditional Chinese Literature*, ed. William H. Nienhauser Jr. (Bloomington: Indiana University Press, 1998), 2:185–187; and Dorothy Ko, *Teachers of the Inner Chambers: Women*

and Culture in Seventeenth-Century China (Stanford, Calif.: Stanford University Press, 1994), 129–136.
19. Birch discusses the significance of feeling as portrayed in *The Peony Pavilion* and its influence on later drama in *Scenes for Mandarins*, 14–15, and in Meng Chengshun, *Mistress and Maid*, xiii–xiv. For a full-length study of Tang Xianzu's masterpiece, see Catherine Swatek, *"Peony Pavilion" Onstage: Four Centuries in the Career of a Chinese Drama* (Ann Arbor: Center for Chinese Studies, University of Michigan, 2002).
20. Dolby, "Yuan Drama," 47; Hu, "Ming Dynasty Drama," 79.
21. Hu, "Ming Dynasty Drama," 81.
22. On the publishing of plays, see Katherine Carlitz, "Printing as Performance: Literati Playwright-Publishers of the Late Ming," in *Printing and Book Culture in Late Imperial China*, ed. Cynthia J. Brokaw and Kai-Wing Chow (Berkeley: University of California Press, 2005), 267–303. For studies on illustrations for theatrical publications, see Michela Bussotti, *Gravures de Hui: Étude du livre illustré chinois de la fin du XVIe siècle à la première moitié du XVIIe siècle* (Paris: Ecole française d'Extrême-Orient, 2001); and Li-ling Hsiao, *The Eternal Present of the Past: Illustration, Theater, and Reading in the Wanli Period, 1573–1619* (Leiden: Brill, 2007).
23. Hanan, *Invention of Li Yu*, 9–13; Henry, *Chinese Amusement*, xiii–xvi; Chang and Chang, *Crisis and Transformation*, 2–3, 326–330, 344–349; Nathan K. Mao and Liu Ts'un-yan, *Li Yü* (Boston: Twayne, 1977), 14–30, 135–138; Patricia Sieber, *Theaters of Desire: Authors, Readers, and the Reproduction of Early Chinese Song-Drama, 1300–2000* (New York: Palgrave Macmillan, 2003), 173–174.

PREFACE

1. This quotation is based on "Xugua" 序卦 of *Yijing* 易經 (that is, *Yi* [*The Book of Changes*]), which states that the union of man and woman came into existence following closely the birth of Heaven and Earth and all things on Earth.
2. "Human ties" (*yi* 義): generally, moral standards.
3. *Daodejing* 道德經 12. In D. C. Lau's translation, it reads, "Hence the sage/is for the belly/not for the eye" (Lao Tzu, *Tao Te Ching* [Harmondsworth: Penguin, 1963], 69).
4. This is a somewhat shortened quotation from *Zuo zhuan* 左傳 (*Zuo Commentary*), Duke Huan, 1.5. See Stephen W. Durrant, Wai-yee Li, and David Schaberg, trans., *Zuo Tradition/ Zuozhuan: Commentary on*

the *"Spring and Autumn Annals"* (Seattle: University of Washington Press, 2016), 1:72–73. *Zuo zhuan* is the earliest historical narrative about the Spring and Autumn period (770–476 B.C.E.).

5. This allusion comes from "Zhou yu shang" 周語上 of *Guo yu* 國語 (*Discourses of the States*), a history about eight states of the Spring and Autumn period written during the Warring States time (475–221 B.C.E.).

6. *Zhuangzi* 莊子 17. See Chuang Tzu, *The Complete Works of Chuang Tzu*, trans. Burton Watson (New York: Columbia University Press, 1968), 188–189.

7. These two sentences are quoted from the Daoist work *Hua shu* 化書 (*The Book of Transformations*), pt. 1, sec. 3, "Lao feng" 老楓 (Old Sweetgum). It continues: all things have feelings and basic nature; all are spiritual in essence.

8. This adapts a section of Mencius 5A.2 as an example of a deception. See *Mencius*, trans D. C. Lau (Harmondsworth: Penguin, 1979), 140.

9. Hexagram 61 from *The Book of Changes*. It means that when sincerity can touch even foolish and ignorant pigs and fish, it certainly brings good luck. Thus Tan and Fairy drown themselves for love and come back to life as the result of their complete sincerity.

10. "Orchids" (Yilan 漪蘭): name of an ancient zither song attributed to Confucius, in which the singer laments his unfulfilled aspirations for public service and compares his noble and unsullied qualities to hidden orchids.

11. "Dian Mo Xun Gao" 典謨訓誥 (model and admonition): originally, the combined title of chapters from *Shang shu* 尚書 (*The Book of Documents*), a collection of prose texts: "Yao dian" 堯典 (The Canon of Yao), "Shun dian" 舜典 (The Canon of Shun), "Da Yu mo" 大禹謨 (The Counsels of Yu the Great), "Yi xun" 伊訓 (The Instructions of Yi), and "Tang gao" 湯誥 (The Announcement of Tang). Later, it came to mean "to give instructions and admonition using classics." *The Book of Changes* and *The Book of Documents* are among the canonical Confucian classics.

12. Xu Wenchang: the courtesy name of Xu Wei 徐渭 (1521–1593), a well-known dramatist, poet, calligrapher, painter, and essayist from Shanyin (modern Shaoxing, Zhejiang Province). *The Four Cries of a Gibbon* (*Sisheng yuan* 四聲猿), a collection of his four plays, was an important representative work of *zaju* (Northern drama) from the Ming dynasty (1368–1644). Xu's *Nanci xulu* 南詞叙錄 (*A Review of Southern Drama*) is a major contribution to the study of Southern drama. See Colin Mackerras, "Hsü Wei," in *The Indiana Companion to Traditional Chinese Literature*, ed. William H. Nienhauser Jr. (Bloomington: Indiana University Press,

1986), 1:436–437; and Shiamin Kwa, *Strange Eventful Histories: Identity, Performance, and Xu Wei's "Four Cries of a Gibbon"* (Cambridge, Mass.: Harvard University Asia Center, 2013).

13. Wang Duanshu 王端淑 (1620/1621–ca. 1701) was also known by her literary name, Yingranzi 映然子. This is the preface as found in *Li Yu quanji* (1991; rpt., Hangzhou: Zhejiang guji chubanshe, 2010), 5:107.

A COUPLE OF SOLES

1. *Mo* plays the part of a prologue speaker in *chuanqi* drama and can also act the head of a theatrical troupe, such as in scenes 27 and 28. By convention for introductory sections of plays, here he speaks for the dramatist.
2. A pastiche, which is in common use in Southern arias, synthesizes two or more tunes. For more information on musical pastiches, see the appendix.
3. The "Rainbow Skirts" (*nishang* 霓裳) dance was made famous by Yang Guifei 楊貴妃 (719–756), the favorite consort of the Tang emperor Minghuang (685–762). She performed it to his great satisfaction. Referring to the skirt conjures images of dancing in many later plays and poems.
4. Seed of passion (*qingzhong* 情種): a man of strong emotions or a lovesick suitor.
5. *The Thorn Hairpin* (*Jingchai ji* 荊釵記): a classic of *nanxi* 南戲 (Southern drama). For a synopsis and a discussion of its relevance to this play, see the introduction.
6. The marginal commentary at this point reads: "I would pay a thousand to anyone who could improve even a single word here!"
7. Going straight (*congliang* 從良): reference to the legal removal of a female entertainer from the official registry of those classified as demeaned so that she could make a proper marriage. Prostitutes and actors and their offspring were not allowed to compete in the civil service examinations.
8. Pinglang Hou 平浪侯 (Marquis Pacifier-of-Waves) was a title given to Yan Shuzi 晏戍仔, a native of Jiangxi. Known for his heavy features and abhorrence of evil, Yan was appointed to an official position in the capital toward the end of the Yuan dynasty (1271–1368). He suddenly passed away while boarding a boat to return home. After that, his spirit often manifested itself to safeguard vessels sailing on rivers, lakes, and the sea. Zhu Yuanzhang, the founding emperor of the Ming dynasty (1368–1644), conferred on him the title Manifest Marquis Pacifier-of-Waves

顯應平浪侯. Temples were built to offer sacrifices to Lord Yan as the god of waters.

9. Immortal (Bu *xian* 逋仙): Lin Bu 林逋 (967–1028), a poet, lived in seclusion at West Lake in Hangzhou and amused himself by growing plum trees and keeping cranes. Unmarried, he claimed to take the plum trees as his wife and the cranes as his son. He was called Bu *xian* (Immortal Bu) by later generations.

10. *Hua tang chun* 畫堂春: name of a tune indicating that this *ci* lyric is chanted rather than sung as an aria.

11. Given name (*hui* 諱): literally, "tabooed name," which normally would be his given name. It is presumptuous for Tan to refer to his *own* given name with this term. Chuyu must be his courtesy name or style name (*zi* 字), which conventionally was given at the age of twenty. Scholars might also take on a literary name (*hao* 號).

12. The historian Sima Qian 司馬遷 (145–90 B.C.E.) was well read, roamed famous mountains, traveled great rivers, and associated with all social strata. Those experiences were important to writing *Shiji* 史記 (*Records of the Grand Historian*).

13. Wu–Yue 吳越: names of two kingdoms during the Spring and Autumn period (770–476 B.C.E.). They later were used to refer to the area in which they were located, covering parts of present-day Jiangsu and Zhejiang south of the Yangzi.

14. Already come of age (*nian yi ruoguan* 年已弱冠): he is twenty years old.

15. Real stunners (*youwu* 尤物): more literally, "extraordinary items," a term regularly used in Chinese romantic literature to describe beautiful women, who perhaps were dangerous because their beauty might cast a spell over an ordinary man.

16. Humble reed (*jianjia* 蒹葭): metaphor for humble origin.

17. Branch of fine jade (*qiongzhi* 瓊枝): metaphor for a man of great capability.

18. When a marriage pledge was made between the families of a young man and a young woman, the families exchanged betrothal gifts, starting with a ribbon as the simplest and going all the way to very expensive objects.

19. According to Ren Fang 任昉 (460–508) in *Shu yi ji* 述異記 (*Tales of Anomalies*), Wang Zhi 王質 of the Jin dynasty (265–420) was cutting wood in Shishi Mountain 石室山, or Mount [Lan]ke [爛]柯山 (Mount Rotted Axhandle), in Quzhou 衢州, Zhejiang, where some boys were playing chess and singing. He sat down to listen, and they gave him something like the pit of a date; holding it in his mouth, he no longer felt hungry.

After a while, the boys said to Wang Zhi: "Why don't you leave?" He then realized that so much time had passed that even the handle (*ke* 柯) of his ax had rotted (*lan* 爛) to pieces. After he returned home, he could not find anybody from his own time still living. Nine Dragons 九龍 Lake is south of Mount Ke, and Sanqu 三衢 is present-day Quzhou in Zhejiang.

20. *Taixi* 台戲: name for opera styles other than the Kunshan style and Yiyang style in the Yangzhou area during the Qing dynasty (1644–1912). Here, it means "local opera."

21. *Bi sheng hua* 筆生花: allusion to imaginative power and a brilliant style of writing. According to "Meng bitou sheng hua" 夢筆頭生花, in *Kaiyuan Tianbao yishi* 開元天寶遺事 (*Events of the High Tang*) by Wang Renyu 王仁裕 of the Five Dynasties (907–960), when the famous poet Li Bai 李白 was young, he dreamed that flowers grew on the tip of his writing brush. Later, he became famous for his writing.

22. In the age of foot binding for women, shoes were regarded as intimate apparel. See Dorothy Ko, *Every Step a Lotus: Shoes for Bound Feet* (Berkeley: University of California Press, 2001). For a monk to have a woman's shoe would be quite unacceptable in religious terms.

23. Bald donkey (*tulü* 禿驢): disparaging term for Buddhist monks.

24. Facing the wall (*mianbi* 面壁): sitting in meditation while facing a wall. According to legend, the Central Asian monk Bodhidharma 達摩 (d. 536), founder of Chinese Chan Buddhism, sat facing a wall in meditation for nine years at the Shaolin Temple. Return to the Western Paradise with a single shoe (*zhi lü Xi gui* 只履西歸): Bodhidharma later returned to the Western Paradise carrying one shoe in his hand, having left the other in his coffin after he apparently died.

25. The old frontiersman who gained a horse (*saiweng de ma* 塞翁得馬): allusion to the parable of an old man on the frontier whose mare ran away. Others came to comfort him, but he said: "How do you know it was not a blessing in disguise?" Ultimately, the lost mare came back with a fine stallion.

26. Circles the rafters (*rao liang* 繞樑): reference to the idiom *yuyin raoliang* 餘音繞樑 (the music lingering around the beams), which describes a voice so impressive that it seems to linger in the theater after the song is over.

27. Talk flowers out of the sky (*zhui tianhua* 墜天花): description of the effect when the Buddhist priest Yunguang 雲光, in the reign of Emperor Wu of Liang 梁武帝 (464–549), expounded Buddhist teachings so powerfully that Heaven sent flowers cascading from the sky.

28. The original line plays on the words *huayan* 花眼 (presbyopia) and *huarong* 花容 (the flower's looks [a great beauty]), which share the character *hua* 花.
29. Finest rewards (*chantou* 纏頭): reference first to colored silk put on singers' and dancers' heads as a reward and later to money and other presents given to female entertainers.
30. Even greater charm (*zhuang po yan lou* 撞破煙樓): literally, "to break up a stovepipe," metaphor for a son surpassing his father and later generations being better than their forebears.
31. Erlang shen 二郎神: one of the deities once revered as the patron god of Chinese actors.
32. *Sui* 歲 (year of age): Chinese babies traditionally were considered to be one year old at birth and became two at the next Lunar New Year. Fairy Liu is fourteen *sui*, or probably thirteen years of age. Tan Chuyu is twenty *sui*, or about nineteen.
33. Invite seduction (*huiyin* 誨淫): the much-loved Yuan period romantic play *The Story of the Western Wing* (*Xixiang ji* 西廂記) often was castigated for encouraging seduction. See note 35.
34. This line plays on the words *mian hou* 面厚 (thick-skinned, meaning "shameless") and *jia hou* 家厚 (well-off family).
35. These two lines parody the archetypal love story between Student Zhang 張生 (given name, Gong 珙) and Cui Yingying 崔鶯鶯 in the Yuan period play *The Story of the Western Wing*. Fallen Angel Liu suggests that even if a patron is as infatuated with the actress as Zhang Gong was with Cui Yingying, the actress herself need not be as sentimentally attached as Cui Yingying was to Zhang.
36. Shattered jade (*sui yu* 碎玉): metaphor for fallen flowers. The two metaphors in this line refer to the true damage that such actions would do to her, despite physically keeping her chastity. The marginal commentary at this point reads: "Every word in [Li] Liweng's writings is a remonstration [with frequenters of brothels]."
37. Hearsay (*feng ying* 風影): may derive from the idiom *bufeng zhuoying* 捕風捉影 (chase the wind and clutch at shadows), which means "to speak or act on hearsay evidence."
38. For the role types of *da* (*hua*)*mian* 大(花)面 (first painted face; often dignified and sedate figures) and *xiao huamian* 小花面 (third painted face; generally, clowns), see Jing Shen, "Role Types in *The Paired Fish*, a Chuanqi Play," *Asian Theatre Journal* 20, no. 2 (2003): 227–228. *Da huamian* is also known as *zhengjing* 正淨, which is called *dajing* 大淨 (major *jing*) in scene 10.

39. In this play, the young male lead is called *zhengsheng* 正生 or simply *sheng*.
40. *Yusun ban* 玉筍班 (jade sprouts group): originally, a reference to a galaxy of talented men in the imperial government.
41. Jing 涇 and Wei 渭: names of rivers. The Jing rises in Ningxia and flows into central Shaanxi, where it empties into the Wei. The water of the Jing is muddy, whereas that of the Wei is clear. This metaphor signifies the clear separation between a clumsy, vulgar male actor and herself that she hopes to maintain.
42. A voice that circles the rafters (*rao liang yin* 繞樑音): reference to memorable singing. See note 26.
43. Zither (*qin* 琴): a seven-stringed plucked instrument. Playing the zither is most often identified as a scholarly accomplishment, along with mastering chess, calligraphy, and painting.
44. Stages were covered by a large rug, on which the performances took place.
45. Pan Yue 潘岳 (247–300) of the Jin dynasty, whose childhood name was Tannu 檀奴, was very good looking and admired by women. Hence Tanlang 檀郎 or Tannu is a synonym for a handsome man or a laudatory name (such as "my darling") that a woman might call the man whom she adores, her husband or lover.
46. *Chuitiao* 垂髫 (a child's short drooping hair): reference to an unmarried girl. *Tianxiang guose* 天香國色 (ethereal color and celestial fragrance): said of the peony, which is a metaphor for a beautiful woman.
47. Insightful friend (*zhiyin* 知音): literally, "one who knows the sound," referring to an old parable about friendship: only a true friend can recognize the deep meaning in one's music or one's voice.
48. Fullest flower (*deqi* 得氣): to succeed in reaching *qi*. This medical term refers to bringing about the desired sensation in acupuncture treatment.
49. Melon's been cracked (*pogua* 破瓜): loss of virginity.
50. This reference is to "Zuiweng ting ji" 醉翁亭記 (The Drunken Old Man's Pavilion), an essay by Ouyang Xiu 歐陽修 (1007–1072)—who called himself the Drunken Old Man—in which he reveals that his enjoyment of a drinking party is not in partaking of the drink but in watching his guests enjoy themselves among the mountains and waters. See Ouyang Hsiu, "A Record of the Pavilion of an Intoxicated Old Man," trans. Robert E. Hegel, in *The Columbia Anthology of Traditional Chinese Literature*, ed. Victor H. Mair (New York: Columbia University Press, 1994), 590–591. Later, the allusion came to mean "to have other things in mind." Here, Tan Chuyu suggests that he is not as excited

about the play because he stays through the performance just in order to follow Fairy afterward and find out where she lives.

51. Little darling (A Jiao 阿嬌): from *jin wu cang jiao* 金屋藏嬌 (hide away a mistress in a golden room). According to *Han Wu gushi* 漢武故事, when Emperor Wu of Han (156–87 B.C.E.) was a child, he was fond of his cousin A Jiao and wished to build a golden house for her if she became his wife. The name became an idiom for a favorite wife or concubine.

52. The first line refers to his desire for retirement from public life, in that "tall woods and luxuriant grass" (*chang lin feng cao* 長林豐草) alludes to living in seclusion, whereas the second line says that he is still an official and holds a high position, as indicated in his *zao gai* 皂蓋 (black canopy for officials) and *huaxuan* 华軒 (formal carriage).

53. *Guchen* 孤臣: an estranged official in an isolated post. A source of the allusion is Jiang Yan's 江淹 (444–505) "Hen fu" 恨賦 (Rhapsody on Regret): "或有孤臣危涕, 孽子墜心. 遷客海上, 流戍隴陰 . . ." (There are also an official in disgrace weeping in his grief and the son of a concubine overcome by fear. A degraded official at sea and an officer banished to the frontier at Longyin . . .). The phrase *guchen niezi* 孤臣孽子 (a minister in disgrace and the son of a concubine out of favor) appeared first in *Mengzi* 孟子 (*Mencius*) 7A.18, to signify a supporter of a doomed dynasty or a lost cause. Here, *guchen* refers to an official of personal integrity who does not seek fame and gain or to curry favor with the powerful.

54. Mountain forest (*shanlin* 山林): circles of recluses.

55. Candidates in the Ming–Qing period who succeeded in the examination presided over by the emperor were honored as *jinshi* 進士 (metropolitan graduate), holders of a degree that was further divided into three grades. The second grade was regular metropolitan graduate (*jinshi chushen* 進士出身). His home in Xichuan (present-day Sichuan) was far from his post in Zhangnan (in modern-day Fujian).

56. Have no worldly desire and can be firm (*wuyu neng gang* 無欲能剛): derived from *Lunyu* 論語 (*Analects*) 5.11, indicating that a person free from worldly desire can be upright and above flattery.

57. Pedantic scholar (*yuru* 迂儒): a negative label often used to denigrate staunch Confucians.

58 Aroused the disapproval of my peers (*fan shilin zhi ji* 犯士林之忌): seems to indicate his persistent desire to cling to impractical rules as a socially unsophisticated man.

59. *Shengchen* 生辰 (birthday): may mean *shengchen bazi* 生辰八字 (Eight Characters of one's birth), pairs of symbols indicating the year, month,

day, and hour of a person's birth, each pair consisting of one Heavenly Stem 天干 and one Earthly Branch 地支, used in fortune-telling.
60. *Yamen* (衙門): government office in premodern China that included the residence of the official and his family.
61. Gate of the Deer (Lumen 鹿門): allusion to the *Hou Hanshu* 後漢書. Noble-minded Pang De 龐德 (d. 219) of the Eastern Han dynasty (25–220) lived south of Xian Mountain 峴山 in Xiangyang 襄陽 (in present-day Hubei) and never participated in government; he and his wife treated each other with respect. Later, Liu Biao 劉表 (142–208), the governor of Jingzhou 荊州, invited him to serve as an official several times, but he declined firmly and then went to the Lumen Mountains (in Xiangyang) with his wife to pick medicinal herbs, never to return. Thus Lumen refers to where a recluse lives.
62. Plum Fragrance (Meixiang 梅香): often used as a maid's name and became a synonym for "servant girl."
63. The role type *sheng* noted here in the Chinese texts is obviously wrong, so it is emended in translation.
64. Fill . . . with stones (*xia shi* 下石): from the phrase *luo jing xia shi* 落井下石 (drop stones on someone who has fallen into a well), which means "hitting a person when he's down."
65. Gods of earth and grain (*sheji* 社稷): the state; the country. In ancient times, each state had its own altars to the gods of earth and grain, and a state remained independent only as long as its ruler was able to maintain these altars.
66. This line refers to the rhapsody (*fu*) written by the Han imperial court official Zhang Heng 張衡 (78–139), *Guitian fu* 歸田賦 (*On Returning to the Fields*), in *Wenxuan* 文選, chap. 15.
67. *Lingjian* 令箭: arrow-shaped token of authority used in the army in ancient China.
68. *Tuntian* 屯田: to have garrison troops or peasants open up wasteland and grow grains to provide the troops with provisions (a policy pursued by rulers since the Han dynasty [206 B.C.E.–220 C.E.]). *Futian* 福田: Buddhist term. Buddhists believe that accumulating merit by good works will be rewarded with good fortune, just as sowing seeds in the field will bear fruit in the future.
69. Putting it away (*guaguan* 掛冠): to hang up the hat, or resign from office.
70. These two lines allude to the story "Pei Hang" 裴航 in Pei Xing's 裴鉶 late-ninth-century collection of miraculous stories *Chuanqi* 傳奇: After Pei Hang failed in the imperial examination, he admired Lady Fan 樊夫人, who was traveling in the same boat. Her poem to Pei Hang read:

"One taste of agate nectar arouses a multitude of feelings;/Yunying will appear after mystic frost is pounded./Lanqiao is an immortal cave;/no need take the tortuous path to Jade Pure Heaven" 飲瓊漿百感生, 玄霜搗盡見雲英。藍橋便是神仙窟, 何必崎嶇上玉清. Later, Pei Hang really did meet the maiden Yunying when he passed the Lanqiao post station 藍橋驛. He was so thirsty that he asked for a drink, and she offered him something that tasted as sweet as jade-like wine. He took a fancy to her, but her grandmother demanded that he find a jade mortar and pestle to pound the immortal medicine called mystic frost before he would be allowed to marry her. He did find the mortar and pestle and eventually married Yunying; both became immortals. Hence Lanqiao (Lan Bridge), on Lanxi 藍溪 (Lan Stream) in Lantian 藍田 County of Shaanxi, came to symbolize a lovers' rendezvous. *Lanqiao xianjing* 藍橋仙境 can mean "fairy abode."

71. *Yun zhong quanfei* 雲中犬吠: According to "Daoxu pian" 道虛篇, in *Lun heng* 論衡 7 by Wang Chong 王充 (27–97), Liu An 劉安 (164–122 B.C.E.), the Viscount of Huainan, sought immortality and attained the Dao. Then his whole family ascended to Heaven, and even his dogs and chickens that ate the leftover elixir crumbs went with him. Consequently, cocks crowed and dogs barked in the clouds. The aphorism *yi ren dedao, ji quan shengtian* 一人得道, 雞犬升天 (when a man attains the Dao, even his pets ascend to Heaven) comes from this story.

72. Exceptional beauty (*youwu* 尤物): here, Tan uses precisely the same term that he used when describing his ideal mate in scene 2. See note 15.

73. Hide her safely away (*yundu er cang* 韞櫝而藏): phrase adopted from *Lunyu* 9.13: "Zigong said, 'If you had a piece of beautiful jade here, would you put it away safely in a box or would you try to sell it for a good price?' The Master said, 'Of course I would sell it. Of course I would sell it. All I am waiting for is the right offer'" (Confucius, *The Analects*, trans. D. C. Lau [Harmondsworth: Penguin, 1979], 98).

74. *Yima xin pian jiang* 意馬信偏韁: from the idioms *Xinyuan yima* 心猿意馬 (restless and whimsical; a heart like a capering monkey and a mind like a galloping horse) and *xinma youjiang* 信馬由韁 (ride a horse without holding the reins; stroll about aimlessly; act or do as one pleases). The phrase means "one's thoughts are scattered and confused."

75. *Mo zhang* 魔障 (barrier set by a demon; an evil influence): Buddhist term that came to be used for twists and turns or accidents that interfere with reaching a goal.

76. This allusion in this line comes from the biography of Qiu Lan 仇覽 in *Hou Hanshu* 後漢書: "Bitter orange and brambles are not where simurghs

and phoenixes [men of outstanding worth and talent] perch" 枳棘非鸞鳳所栖. *Zhiji* 枳棘 (bitter orange and brambles) is a metaphor for a difficult and perilous environment.

77. "The Powerful" (Jian xi 簡兮); poem 38 in the ancient anthology *Shijing* 詩經 (*The Odes* or *The Book of Songs*). According to its later preface, this poem "criticizes not making proper use of a worthy person, as people of outstanding worth in the state of Wei became official musicians" 刺不用賢也, 衛之賢者仕於伶官. *Jian xi* came to mean that a worthy person who cannot achieve his ambition may turn to music. See Arthur Waley, trans., *The Book of Songs: The Ancient Chinese Classic of Poetry* (New York: Grove Weidenfeld, 1987), 221.

78. *Sansheng* 三牲 (three domestic animals): cattle, sheep, and pigs, which were used as sacrificial offerings.

79. Warmth and tenderness village (*wenrou* [*xiang*] 溫柔[鄉]): place where a man can find solace in feminine charms.

80. Dragon Gate (Longmen 龍門): reference to the front gate of the imperial examination hall. *Tiao longmen* 跳龍門 (leap over the dragon gate) indicates those passing the metropolitan examination held in the imperial capital who might then appear before the emperor for the final oral test.

81. Cold window (*shou hanchuang* 守寒窗): description of the suffering of a poor student.

82. Master Zhou's standards (from Zhou *lang guqu* 周郎顧曲 [Master Zhou turns to look at the songs]): allusion to Zhou Yu 周瑜 (175–210), of the Three Kingdoms period (220–280), who was especially knowledgeable about music. If there was any error in a performance, he would notice even if he had been drinking, and he would surely shoot a glance at the musician.

83. Metal walls and boiling moats (*jincheng tangchi* 金城湯池 [simplified to "metal and boiling" 金湯]): idiom for an impregnable fortress.

84. *Chengwen* 程文: originally, a reference to model essays of the imperial examinations, approved and released by the government. Here, it refers to performance movements for emulation.

85. The god Erlang imprisoned his own sister below Mount Hua because of her affair with a mortal student. On Erlang as a guardian of (female) sexual propriety, see Glen Dudbridge, "Goddess Huayue Sanniang and the Cantonese Ballad *Chenxiang Taizi*," in *Books, Tales and Vernacular Culture: Selected Papers on China* (Leiden: Brill, 2005), 307–308. See also Wilt Idema, "The Precious Scroll of Chenxiang," in *The Columbia Anthology of Chinese Folk and Popular Literature*, ed. Victor Mair and Mark Bender (New York: Columbia University Press, 2011), 380–405.

86. Lingers onstage (*diaochang* 吊場): indicates that the scene is coming to an end, leaving only one actor or a small number of actors on stage to perform a brief soliloquy or dialogue that sets up a later scene.
87. *Thousand Pieces of Gold* (*Qianjin* 千金): a Ming period *chuanqi* play by Shen Cai 沈采 about Xiang Yu (232–202 B.C.E.), the hegemon-king of Western Chu, and his consort, Lady Yu. While the main thread concerns Han Xin, the brilliant general who served Liu Bang, the king of Han, Xiang Yu is played as a *jing* or *huamian* role. Fairy Liu wishes that she and Tan Chuyu could stage this play so that Tan, as a *jing* actor, and she, as a *dan*, might play a couple. Double Pupils (*chong tong* 重瞳): two pupils in each eye, a feature that Xiang Yu was said to have had. The key scene, in which Xiang Yu takes his leave from Lady Yu, is now fairly well known from the film *Farewell My Concubine* (*Bawang bie ji* 霸王別姬, 1993), directed by Chen Kaige 陳凱歌.
88. Great king (*daiwang* 大王): a term of address for a bandit chief.
89. We (*gujia* 孤家): literally, "person in solitary splendor," a term used by ancient princes that corresponds to the English "royal we."
90. Eat raw flesh (*rumao yinxue* 茹毛飲血): originally meant that primitive humans ate the raw flesh of birds and beasts, with the hair and blood.
91. Limbs (*bie* 弰): the parts of a bow at both ends that curve outward.
92. Golden goblet (*jin'ou* 金甌): national territory.
93. Searching the mountains [for demons] (*soushan* 搜山): an important motif in traditional Chinese painting. See, for example, *Soushan tujuan* 搜山圖卷 (*Searching the Mountains for Demons*), a "picture scroll" by Li Yu's contemporary Zheng Zhong 鄭重 (fl. 1612–1648), an artist from Anhui, at the Metropolitan Museum of Art (https://www.metmuseum.org/art/collection/search/44630). See also Carmelita Hinton, "Evil Dragon, Golden Rodent, Sleek Hound: The Evolution of *Soushan Tu* Paintings in the Northern Song Period," in *The Zoomorphic Imagination in Chinese Art and Culture*, ed. Jerome Silbergeld and Eugene Y. Wang (Honolulu: University of Hawai'i Press, 2016), 171–214.
94. Defeat the dragon, subdue the tigers (*xianglong fuhu* 降龍伏虎): to overcome powerful adversaries, here presented somewhat literally.
95. Stirred up a fire just to burn themselves (*huo bu shaosheng zi re* 火不燒身自惹): here understood to be the same as the idiom *rehuo shaoshen* 惹火燒身 (stir up a fire, only to burn oneself), which means "to court disaster" and "to ask for trouble."
96. The moat fish's disaster (*chiyu da jie* 池魚大劫 or *chiyu zhi yang* 池魚之殃): trouble not of one's own making. This originates from the idiom

chengmen shihuo, yang ji chiyu 城門失火, 殃及池魚 (when the city gate catches fire, the fish in the moat come to grief), which refers to innocent people suffering from what happens to others.

97. A guest with a burned head (*jiaotou shangke* 焦頭上客): reference to the idiom *jiaotou lan'e* 焦頭爛額 (burned head and mashed forehead), which indicates being in a sorry state. According to the biography of Huo Guang 霍光傳 in *Hanshu* 漢書, a chimney in a house was very straight, and lots of firewood was stacked nearby. A guest suggested that the owner bend the chimney and remove the firewood in order to take precautions against the possible danger of its catching fire. The owner would not listen, and soon the house caught fire as expected. All his neighbors came to put out the fire. Thereupon, the owner thanked his neighbors and treated them to meat and wine; those who were badly burned took the seats of honor, but the guest who had cautioned him was not invited. Somebody said to the owner: "If you had listened to that guest, there would not have been a fire that has cost you meat and wine. Now you are inviting people according to their contributions; do you bestow no bounties on the one having given you advice while those with burned heads and mashed foreheads become your distinguished guests?" These allusions in *Bimuyu* mean that the burned beasts will not be able to get out of the fire alive.

98. Moye (鏌邪): name of an ancient double-edged sword.

99. Demon star (*yaoxing* 妖星): a strange star that presages a disaster, often referring to comets.

100. At dusk, the sunset glow shines over mulberry and *Cudrania*. Hence, this line refers to sunset.

101. Precious pearl (*Sui zhu* 隋珠): a legend has it that the Marquis of Sui resuscitated a wounded snake, and afterward the snake brought a bright pearl in its mouth and gave it to him. It was called *Suihou zhi zhu* 隋侯之珠 (pearl of the Marquis of Sui) in later ages. The third line of the aria also refers to the idiom *Sui zhu tan que* 隋珠彈雀 (shoot a pearl at the sparrow), which means "the loss outweighs the gain" or "one's talent is wasted on a petty job." For the source of the allusion, see *Zhuangzi* 莊子 18.

102. Shadows may be close but bodies far apart (*ying ji xing pianli* 影即形偏離): reverses the idiom *xing ying bu li* 形影不離 (be inseparable as body and shadow).

103. Stone drums (*shiguwen* 石鼓文): inscriptions on drum-shaped stone blocks of the Warring States period (475–221 B.C.E.). This is the earliest extant Chinese text carved on stone.

104. A thousand in gold (*yi zi qianjin* 一字千金): a highly finished literary product. This idiom refers to offering a huge sum of money to anyone who could improve on a literary masterpiece.
105. Spring dreams (*chunmeng* 春夢): transient joy.
106. Petition (*ju ti* 具題): present a memorial to the emperor, here referring to the request for the *zhengsheng* role.
107. Transfer (*liangyi* 量移): transferring an official from a distant place to a post nearer the capital as the result of an amnesty.
108. Empty title (*sanzhi* 散職): sinecure, a nominal government post having no regular duties. Using the terms "petition," "transfer," "sinecure," and *gaowei* 高位 (high position), Tan Chuyu compares the change of his theatrical roles with the promotion of an official.
109. Knotting our hearts (*jie tongxin* 結同心): to become husband and wife.
110. *Poems* or *Documents*: the Confucian classical texts *Shijing* 詩經 (*The Odes* or *The Book of Songs*) and *Shangshu* 尚書 (*Book of Documents*). Both were basic texts memorized in preparation for the civil service examinations.
111. Switch (*jiachu* 夏楚): switch used in ancient Chinese schools to discipline students.
112. Rod (*jiefang* 戒方): teacher's ruler for beating pupils.
113. Blue simurgh (*qingluan* 青鸞): bird messenger of the mythical Queen Mother of the West 西王母, which came to signify a messenger for immortals or lovers.
114. Yellow dog (*huang quan* 黃犬 or Huang'er quan 黃耳犬 [Yellow Ear, the dog's name]): swift dog belonging to Lu Ji 陸機 (261–303) that he could send for long distances to bring him news from home. These two lines (越越的青鸞信杳, 黃犬音乖) are quoted from act 1, play 4 of the fourteenth-century romantic play *The Story of the Western Wing*; a more literal translation is: "In utter silence, the blue-green simurgh brings no letter,/The yellow dog carries no news" (Wang Shifu, *The Story of the Western Wing*, ed. and trans. Stephen H. West and Wilt L. Idema [Berkeley: University of California Press, 1995], 226). The marginal commentary by Qinhuai zuihou 秦淮醉侯 on Tan's verse reads: "Curses" 罵. This suggests that Tan attacks his foolish classmates by innuendo, hoping that they will not intercept his letter to Miaogu and deliver it to her parents.
115. To salute one of equal status, the hands were cupped before the chest, but were raised higher when saluting people of higher status.
116. We are to assume that these lines are delivered as an aside.
117. *Red Whisk* (*Hongfu ji* 紅拂記): *chuanqi* play by Zhang Fengyi 張鳳翼 (1527–1613).

118. *Washing Silk* (*Huan sha ji* 浣紗記): *chuanqi* play by Liang Chenyu 梁辰魚 (1519–1591).
119. *The Golden Pellet* (*Jinwan ji* 金丸記): historical play from the Ming dynasty.
120. This line comes from the aria "Jie san cheng" 解三酲, in scene 37 of Gao Ming's 高明 (ca. 1305–1359) famous play *The Lute* (*Pipa ji* 琵琶記). See Kao Ming, *The Lute: Kao Ming's "P'i-p'a chi,"* trans. Jean Mulligan (New York: Columbia University Press, 1980), 256.
121. Simurgh (*luan* 鸞): miraculous bird more colorful than a phoenix. See note 113.
122. Wind and clouds (*fengyun hui* 風雲會): favorable turn of events.
123. This line garbles a line from poem 184 in *Shijing*, which hints at a noble recluse. See Waley, *Book of Songs*, 314.
124. Guan Yu 關羽 (Guan Yunchang 關雲長, d. 220): heroic general of the kingdom of Shu Han (221–263) during the Three Kingdoms period. Xiang Yu 項羽 (232–202 B.C.E.), a warlord, proclaimed himself hegemon-king of Western Chu following the downfall of the Qin dynasty (221–206 B.C.E.). See the discussion of the *jing* role in note 87.
125. Flower face (*huamian* 花面): *jing* role (painted face) or a beautiful face. This line, 終不然倒因為我面似蓮花也，特將花面題, plays with those two meanings of the term.
126. Fine name (*jiaming* 佳名): name of the role *huamian*.
127. In this play, the young female lead is called *zhengdan* 正旦 or *dan*.
128. Wen Qiao 溫嶠 (288–329) of the Jin dynasty used a jade mirror stand as a betrothal gift, claiming to arrange an engagement for another man. He turned out to be the bridegroom and married himself to the bride. Wen Qiao as his own matchmaker 溫嶠自媒 thus refers to recommending oneself as the son-in-law. The source of the allusion is Liu Yiqing's 劉義慶 *Shi shuo xin yu* 世說新語, sec. "Jiajue" 假譎. During the Yuan period, Guan Hanqing 關漢卿 (ca. 1240–1320) wrote a play on this story, *Wen Taizhen Yujingtai* 溫太真玉鏡台. See Guan Hanqing, *The Jade Mirror Stand*, in *Selected Plays of Kuan Han-ch'ing*, trans. Hsien-yi Yang and Gladys Yang (Beijing: Foreign Languages Press, 1958), 153–177.
129. Freckle-faced wife (*huamian qi* 花面妻): ugly wife, as well as a pun on the clownish *huamian* role.
130. These two lines refer to reliance on an able and virtuous person for one's success and fame. Sima Qian 司馬遷 writes in "Boyi liezhuan" 伯夷列傳 of *Shiji* 史記: "Although Yan Yuan 顏淵 [Yan Hui 顏回, Confucius's favorite disciple] was diligent in study, he relied on a thoroughbred horse's tail so that his conduct became more illustrious" 顏淵雖篤學，附驥尾而行

益顯. Sima Zhen's 司馬貞 annotation to the line makes it clear: "This implies that Yan Hui became well known because of Confucius" 以喻顏回因孔子而名彰.

131. Thorn trees (*zhi ji* 枳棘): trifoliate orange and thorn bushes that are called vicious trees because of their thorns, making them a metaphor for villains or a hard and dangerous environment.

132. The two historical analogies describe Tan Chuyu in straitened circumstances. *Wu shi chui xiao* 吳市吹簫: before becoming chief minister of Wu, Wu Zixu 伍子胥 (d. 484 B.C.E.) was forced to play the bamboo flute for handouts at the market of Wu after his father, a minister in Chu, had been executed. This became an allusion for a noble-minded person who meets with misfortune. See "Fan Sui Cai Ze liezhuan" 範睢蔡澤列傳, in *Shiji*. Han Xin 韓信 (d. 196 B.C.E.) was believed to be from a noble family but lived in destitution as a child. When Liu Bang became the emperor of the Han dynasty, he enfeoffed his general Han Xin as prince of Chu. For the story of Han Xin's begging for food, see "Huaiyin Hou liezhuan" 淮陰侯列傳, in *Shiji*.

133. Chu captive (Chu *qiu* 楚囚): during the Spring and Autumn period, Zhong Yi 鍾儀 from the state of Chu became a captive in the state of Jin, still wearing the hat of his native land. The term came to refer to someone who stays in a strange land but does not forget the customs of his native place, or to someone in a predicament. A hat of the Chu captive (*Chu qiu guan* 楚囚冠) here refers to a scholar's hat. For the original reference, see *Zuozhuan*左傳, Chenggong 成公 9.

134. Official's black hat (*wusha* 烏紗): black gauze hat worn by officials in the past.

135. The fox that borrowed the tiger's might is a parable from the ancient *Intrigues of the Warring States* (*Zhanguo ce* 戰國策): a fox claims to a tiger that all other animals fear him and that the tiger need only follow him around to see. The tiger does not realize that the other animals are fearful of only the tiger himself rather than the clever fox he follows.

136. —— Wharf (Ling O): unspecified place or Nowheresville, following on the manager's comment about satirizing officialdom. Wanguan means "Ten Thousand Strings of Cash," and his surname Qian literally means "Money." Other equivalents in English might be Richie Cash or Cassius Rich.

137. Do not laugh if I'm bad at drawing tigers: Moneybags Qian's twist of a one-line idiom—"failing in drawing a tiger and ending up with the likeness of a dog" (*hua hu bu cheng fan lei quan* 畫虎不成反類犬 [to attempt something overly ambitious and end in failure])—into a two-line saying.

With the term "fangs and claws" (*yazhao* 牙爪), meaning "lackeys," Qian transforms the "dog" of the idiom into "running dogs."

138. Story from the *Mencius*: also a twist of the original source. In *Mengzi* 孟子 4B.33, a man from Qi 齊 told his wife and concubine that every time he went out, he ate meat and drank wine to his heart's content with all the rich and powerful. One morning, his wife tailed him to a graveyard, where he begged handouts from those offering sacrifices. His wife returned home and told his concubine about it: "A husband is whom we look up to and spend our remaining years with till death, yet now he is like this" 良人者, 所仰望而終身也, 今若此. They mocked their husband and wept. Not aware of it, the husband came back looking happy and contented, and remained arrogant toward his wife and concubine. See *Mencius*, trans. D. C. Lau (Harmondsworth: Penguin 1979), 137. Moneybags Qian suggests that if a beggar can have a wife and a concubine and be arrogant toward them, a man of wealth should be even more so.

139. *Juren* 舉人: successful candidate in the provincial examination under the Ming–Qing civil service examination system. *Jinshi*: highest, or metropolitan, degree. See note 55.

140. Local functionary (*dianshi* 典史): district jailor, an unranked minor official who served as the county magistrate's police agent and presided over the county jail.

141. Contribution of grain (*na su* 納粟): in premodern China, men of wealth could pay millet to obtain an official post or to atone for a crime. During the Ming–Qing period, sons of wealthy families paid the government money and goods to become students at the Imperial Academy and to directly take the imperial examinations at the provincial level without the usual preliminary preparation and testing.

142. Came home in silken robes (*yi jin huanxiang* 衣錦還鄉): conventional term of praise for an official who returned home in glory after acquiring wealth and honor.

143. His subordinate (*zhisheng* 治生): self-deprecating name used by a subordinate when speaking to a senior official or by a sojourning government official when talking to a senior official of his ancestral home, which started from the Ming dynasty,

144. *Ge* 合 (0.1 *sheng*, or 0.845351 gill) and *sheng* 升 (1.8 pints [1 liter]): units of dry measure for grain. *Qian* 錢 (mace) and *fen* 分 (penny); traditional units of weight for silver: 10 *fen* equal 1 *qian*, and 10 *qian* equal 1.7 ounces (50 grams, in modern terms).

145. Grandpas (*gongzu* 公祖) and moms and dads (*fumu* [*guan*] 父母[官]): during the Ming–Qing period, terms of respect for local officials above

prefects as well as for prefects and county magistrates, respectively. Those of a fairly high position were called *gongzu fumu*, combining both terms.

146. Black gauze hat (*shamao* 紗帽) and round collar (*yuanling* 圓領): common formal attire worn by government officials of the Ming dynasty.
147. Neighborhood watch (*baojia* 保甲): administrative system initiated by Wang Anshi 王安石 (1021–1086) of the Song dynasty (960–1279). According to the Qing period system, each *pai* 牌 was made up of ten households, each *jia* of ten *pai*, and each *bao* of ten *jia*. The official indicated here by the term *sanya* 三衙 (assistant county magistrate; literally, "third [in the] *yamen*") is the third most senior county officer, or *zhubu* 主簿 (registrar).
148. Press them for repayment (*zhuibi* 追比): local officials pressured people for payment of taxes and completion of duties; those missing the deadline were flogged or put in jail as a punishment.
149. County's Third Lordship (*benxian sanye* 本縣三爺): because a colloquial term for the county magistrate is *xiantaiye* 縣太爺, this refers to the third-ranking county official, the assistant magistrate.
150. Piglets (*tun* 豚): here, slighting name for common people in arrears with taxes.
151. Memorial . . . withdraw: Using the words "present a memorial [to an emperor]" (*zou* 奏) and "withdraw [after having an audience with an emperor]" (*tui ban* 退班), Moneybags Qian compares the locals' meeting with him to an imperial court session, an arrogant practice to be found in vernacular fiction as well.
152. Guardian god (*xianghuo* 香火): literally, "incense and candles [for ritual sacrifices]," so by extension, the gods themselves.
153. Rush rain cape and bamboo hat (*suoyi ruoli* 蓑衣箬笠 or *yan suo yu li* 煙蓑雨笠): rustic gear worn by peasants and fishermen, as protection against rain and sun. This idiom can refer to the clothing of a hermit or his life of carefree leisure; Li Yu referred to himself as Liweng (old man in the [broad-rimmed conical] bamboo hat).
154. A tiny boat (*yiye pianzhou* 一葉扁舟): literally, "a single leaf of a boat."
155. Eating pulse leaves (*huoshi* 藿食): eating coarse food. "Those who eat pulse leaves" (*huoshi zhe* 藿食者) refers to common people.
156. Take off His Honor's boots (*tuo xue* 脫靴): for common people to take off a local official's boots is to stop him from leaving. The story originated in "Cui Rong zhuan" 崔戎傳, in Liu Xun's 劉昫 (887–946) *Jiu Tang shu* 舊唐書 (*Former History of the Tang*).

157. Wings (*shuang chi* 雙翅): the two stiff ribbons projecting from the sides of an official's black gauze hat.
158. Wind and waves (*fengbo* 風波): turmoil, difficulties.
159. Committed to the east-flowing river (*fu [zhu] dongliu* 付[諸]東流): generally, all one's efforts were wasted, but it is used here for its literal meaning.
160. Phoenix coronet (*fengguan* 鳳冠): formal hat decorated with phoenix images that was worn by noblewomen in ancient China. In later ages, titled ladies of the imperial court could also wear phoenix coronets.
161. Allied myself with gulls (*ou meng* 鷗盟): to live as a hermit in the region of rivers and lakes, or "gulls and egrets are free from schemes" (*ou lu wang ji* 鷗鷺忘機): retire to be a hermit without worldly cares. The second phrase refers to the Daoist text *Liezi*, in which a man who is "free from schemes" does not frighten these birds.
162. Flicked the dust off . . . hats (*tan guan* 彈冠): reference to a story of a man who dusted off his own hat and prepared to take up a post when a friend had become an official. See "Wang Ji zhuan" 王吉傳, in *Hanshu* 漢書 72.
163. Fishing net (*zeng* 罾): square net with poles to hold it open.
164. Longed for watershield and perch (*chunlu zhi si* 蓴鱸之思): longing for home and the resignation to live in seclusion. Watershield (*chun* 蓴) is an edible water plant of the genus *Brasenia*. According to "Zhang Han zhuan" 張翰傳, in *Jinshu* 晉書, when autumn winds began to blow, Zhang Han would long for the watershield soup and sliced perch of Wuzhong, saying: "In life one values being comfortable and contented; how could I hold office far from home for the sake of fame and rank?" 人生貴得適志, 何能羈宦數千里以要名爵乎? Thereupon, he left for home.
165. Put the turtle in the proper place (*cuobie* 錯鱉): vulgar expression referring to having sex. A synonym, *guitou* 龜頭 (literally, "head of tortoise or turtle"), refers to the glans of the penis.
166. Although Mo 莫 is a standard surname, its literal meaning is "no one" or "nothing."
167. Yelang 夜郎: According to "Xi'nan yi liezhuan" 西南夷列傳, in *Shiji*, Yelang was a small state in the southwest during the Han dynasty. Ludicrously conceited, its king asked the envoy from the Han Empire which was larger: Han or Yelang; so did the Marquis of Yelang. This allusion means "parochial arrogance."
168. Yan Ziling 嚴子陵 (39 B.C.E.–41 C.E.): a recluse in the first years of the Eastern Han dynasty. When Emperor Guangwu 光武 (Liu Xiu 劉秀) ascended the throne, Yan Ziling refused to take up the official post that

the emperor conferred on him, and instead lived in seclusion and went angling in the Fuchun 富春 (Yanling) Mountains of Zhejiang Province. The rock on which he sat to fish, called Yan Ziling's Fishing Terrace, was in Seven Mile Brook (Qilixi 七里溪).

169. Hills are high and the rivers long (*shangao shuichang* 山高水長): signifies the lasting influence of nobility of character. It is a quotation from Fan Zhongyan's 范仲淹 (989–1052) essay "Yan xiansheng citang ji" 嚴先生祠堂記 which praises Yan Ziling.

170. It is said that fully grown crows feed their mothers in repayment for having nurtured them, so the expressions "feeding in return" (*fanbu* 反哺), "crow feeding" (*wubu* 烏哺), and "compassionate crows" (*ciwu* 慈烏) signify repaying one's parents for having brought one up.

171. The rose-gold pussy willow (*puliu* 蒲柳) is a metaphor for suffering from poor health because it withers early (at the approach of autumn).

172. Rootless magic fungus (*Zhicao wugen* 芝草無根): metaphor for relying on nothing but one's own great efforts for one's achievements.

173. Precious pearl in trade for rice (*zhenzhu dang mi xun ren tiao* 珍珠當米尋人糶): sustain serious losses in business.

174. Pepper apartments (*jiaofang* 椒房): private apartments of the empress and imperial concubines (so-called from the pepper-mud mixture painted on the walls to preserve warmth and provide a pleasant aroma for the rooms). It is also a synonym for "empress" and "imperial concubines." Here, it is a metaphor for riches and rank.

175. A beauty . . . rich (*jiaowa he yu cailang bao* 嬌娃合與財郎抱): parody of the idiom "a fine couple" (*langcai nümao* 郎才女貌 [a brilliant young scholar and a beautiful woman]).

176. Flower star (*huaxing* 花星): constellation in charge of romance.

177. [Red] string (*hongxian* 紅線): The god of marriage has a record of the marriage fates of those on Earth, and he attaches betrothed couples together with red cords that bind them for life.

178. Mandarin ducks (*yuanyang* 鴛鴦): affectionate couple.

179. Rainbow skirt (*nishang* 霓裳): In legend, immortals take clouds as their clothes (*nishang*), which has by extension come to mean "dance garment." See note 3.

180. *Zushou* 組綬: silk ribbon used in ancient times to tie jade on a jade pendant. *Shou* 綬: silk ribbon attached to an official seal or a medal. Here, it refers to actors' costumes and paraphernalia in playing such roles as emperors, nobles, and senior officials.

181. *Yike qianjin* 一刻千金 (one moment is worth a thousand pieces of gold): time is golden. Su Shi's 蘇軾 poem "Chunye" 春夜 (Spring Night) says:

"One moment of a spring night is worth a thousand pieces of gold" 春宵一刻直[值]千金. Since gold was not regularly used as currency, *jin* probably means "money" more generally both in the play and in this poem.

182. Frosty brush (*shuangtu* 霜兔): writing brush made of white rabbit hair.
183. Resentful butterflies and mournful bees (*yuandie choufeng* 怨蝶愁蜂): transformation of the idiom "attracting bees and leading on butterflies" (*zhaofeng yindie* 招蜂引蝶) which describes women who are gorgeously made up in order to seduce men. Flower branch (*huazhi* 花枝): beautiful woman.
184. Nuptial cups (*jiaobeijiu* 交杯酒): wedding-ceremony rite of mutual toasting by bridegroom and bride, who drink from each other's cups, which are tied together by red thread.
185. Tossed the silk ball (*pao xiuqiu* 拋繡球): having already chosen an ideal spouse, the embroidered silk ball symbolizing happiness and auspiciousness. A legend that is often repeated in plays and stories identifies as a traditional practice the acceptance of a man into a family as a son-in-law who catches this kind of ball when it is thrown by the bride-to-be. On the fifteenth day of the first lunar month or the fifteenth day of the eighth lunar month, it is said, the men who had proposed marriage gathered beneath the young lady's bower. The young lady tossed a silk ball that stood for her heart, and the man who caught the ball could become her husband. This implies that marriage is left up to the will of Heaven, but the young lady usually tossed the ball directly to her beloved. There is no historical data to support this practice; parents seem always to have been involved in formal marriages. *Zhuixu* 贅婿: son-in-law who lives in the home of his wife's parents.
186. Scripts on . . . brocade (*jinzi* 錦字): can refer to fine verses or a wife's letter to her husband.
187. Phoenix pair (*luanhuang* 鸞凰): literally, "male and female phoenix," referring to a married couple or distinguished talents.
188. Side by side (*bingtou*[*lian*] 並頭[蓮]): literally, "twin lotus flowers on one stalk," referring to a devoted married couple.
189. Shanbo and Yingtai: lovers in a perennially favorite tale. During the Eastern Jin dynasty, the beautiful young Zhu Yingtai 祝英台 disguised herself as a boy to attend a school some distance away from her home; there, she fell in love with her classmate Liang Shanbo 梁山伯. They were devoted to each other as friends until much later, when she revealed her gender, they vowed to be married. But Zhu's parents had arranged another marriage for her, and Liang died of grief. Later his grave burst open, and Zhu jumped in to join him. They became a pair of

butterfly spirits and stayed together forever. That story also refers to the "butterfly dream" (*diemeng* 蝶夢): Chinese philosopher Zhuang Zhou 莊周 dreamed that he was a butterfly, so a fantastic dream came to be called a butterfly dream. See *Zhuangzi* 2.

190. The marginal commentary at this point reads: "The most profound words in history unexpectedly come from the mouth of this woman. 'Sense of honor' and 'name and integrity' are the guiding principles behind this play. Readers of Liweng's writing should keep in mind this uprightness."

191. Call back my soul (*zhaohun* 招魂): ritual traceable back thousands of years based on the assumption that the soul of a seriously ill or dead person might be persuaded to return to the body if loved ones made heartfelt pleas.

192. *Huantou* 換頭: The sentence pattern and prosody at the beginning of the second aria is different from that of the first aria written to that melody in a suite of Southern tunes.

193. The term "a thousand taels of silver" (*qianjin* 千金) is a polite way to refer to someone else's daughter.

194. The original idiom is "When enemies come face to face, their eyes get particularly red [with rage]" (*chouren xiangjian, fenwai yanhong* 仇人相見, 分外眼紅).

195. That is, he acts going off the stage within the performance so that the audience may feel that he has exited, although he remains on the stage.

196. Fairy Liu's performance of the revised scene from *The Thorn Hairpin* begins here.

197. Implacable hatred (*bugong daitian zhi chou* 不共戴天之仇), more literally, "hatred such that both of us cannot live under the same sky."

198. Senseless stones nod in agreement (*wanshi diantou* 頑石點頭): description of persuasive powers. According to legend, when he failed to move a human congregation, the Buddhist monk Daosheng 道生 went to Tiger Hill 虎丘山 in Suzhou and assembled large rocks as his audience. As he explained the Buddhist scripture, all the stones nodded in agreement.

199. This line derives from the idiom "a phoenix mated with a crow" (*cai feng sui ya* 彩鳳隨鴉), referring to a beautiful woman married to a worthless man. "Owl" (*chixiao* 鴟鴞): metaphor for an insatiably evil person. Simurgh: see note 113.

200. In others' shoes (*jiang xiong bi du* 將胸比肚): more literally, "compare your bosom with someone else's belly," which is derived from "compare your heart with someone else's heart" (*jiang xin bi xin* 將心比心).

201. Tortoise (*wugui* 烏龜): cuckold.

202. Northern [scale]: reference to the entire suite of this scene, not only the first aria.
203. Mere insects (*louyi* 螻蟻): literally, "mole crickets and ants." "Five lakes and four seas" (*wuhu sihai* 五湖四海): all corners of the land; all parts of the country.
204. Seas into mulberry fields (*canghai sangtian* 滄海桑田): great transformations made through time, such as oceans changing to dry land and vice versa.
205. *Linggu bianqian* 陵谷變遷 (exchange of mountains and valleys): vicissitudes.
206. Meat offerings (*tailao* 太牢): three domestic animals (cattle, sheep, and pigs) provided as grand sacrificial offerings
207. Talismans (*lingfu* 靈符): magic figures drawn by Daoist priests to invoke or exorcise spirits and thus bring good or ill luck.
208. Paper horses (*zhima* 紙馬): paper painted with images of the gods and burned at the altar after sacrifices are offered.
209. Drumhorns (*gujiao* 鼓角): usually understood as battle drums and bugle-like instruments, but Li Yu uses the two terms together as though they were one. What this instrument might have looked like is unclear.
210. *Saishen qu* 賽神曲 (sacrificial songs): songs that accompany sacrifices and are not part of the song suite that includes the arias.
211. Soak up the wine ([*zhiji*] *xujiu* [只雞] 絮酒): idiom that means "a small oblation." Cotton wadding that has been soaked in wine is used to wrap a roast meat (chicken) offering.
212. Rustic song and border music (*tuqu Manyin* 土曲蠻音): ambiguous phrase, especially the latter part. The word *Man* had been used for the tribal peoples of the south and southwest mountainous areas; here, it may mean simply "local" and unfamiliar to the deity—and probably to Li Yu's contemporaries as well.
213. *Xiaoshao* 簫韶: piece of ancient music. According to legend, it was the music of Shun, a legendary sage-king in ancient China.
214. Ancient times (Huang Yu 黃虞): the time of Huang Yu 黃虞, which refers to Huangdi 黃帝 (Yellow Emperor), regarded as the first ancestor of all the ethnic groups in the Central Plain, and Yu Shun 虞舜 (Shun of the kingdom of Yu), a legendary sage-king in ancient China. Here, the allusion means that local traits are simple and honest, as were the remote ages of Huangdi and Yu Shun.
215. Zhu Chen 朱陳: ancient village in which the Zhus and the Chens were related by marriage for generations. Later, the term meant "to form an alliance by marriage."

216. Demon of floods: The *jiao* 蛟 is a mythical creature capable of invoking storms and floods, sometimes called a "flood dragon" (*jiaolong* 蛟龍).
217. Leaped over the Dragon Gate (*tiao longmen* 跳龍門): succeeding in the imperial civil service examinations. See note 80.
218. Footsteps (*xiang chen* 香塵): literally, "fragrant dust," referring to women's steps.
219. Such seemingly exotic costumes would be available to most troupes that performed the more popular White Snake plays. See Wilt L. Idema, ed. and trans., *The White Snake and Her Son: A Translation of the Precious Scroll of Thunder Peak with Related Texts* (Indianapolis: Hackett, 2009).
220. Soles (*bimuyu* 比目魚): flatfish. It is said that this kind of fish is one-eyed and can move about only side by side in pairs, so it is used as a metaphor for inseparable couples. For a discussion of the symbolic relevance of this type of fish, see Jing Shen, *Playwrights and Literary Games in Seventeenth-Century China: Plays by Tang Xianzu, Mei Dingzuo, Wu Bing, Li Yu, and Kong Shangren* (Lanham, Md.: Lexington Books, 2010), 182.
221. Branches intertwined (*lianlizhi* 連理枝): romantic image of two trees whose branches intertwine, sometimes growing from two graves of separated lovers. The phrase connotes a loving couple.
222. Stringed pearls or belts of jade (*zhulian bihe* 珠聯璧合): perfect pair; happy combination.
223. Like fish and water (*ruyu sishui* 如魚似水): congenial mate.
224. Taking over the chopping board . . . chef (*yue zu dai pao* 越俎代庖): allusion from *Zhuangzi* 1 that means "to take over somebody else's job."
225. Old Man of the Moon (*yue lao* 月老): god of marriage. See note 177.
226. Here ends the first half of the play, the first day's performance, if all the scenes were performed continuously.
227. Yamen runners (*zaoli* 皂隸): minor functionaries at local or regional courts, conventionally regarded as easily bribed and abusive to any who did not bribe them.
228. Fat (*zhujia* 朱價): money extorted when accepting a petition to the authorities.
229. Soliciting complaints (*fanggao* 放告): Under the Qing Empire, prefects and county magistrates periodically put up notices inviting people who had suffered injustice to file lawsuits at the local courthouse. The prefect and magistrates accepted these cases directly.
230. Cattle (*ma niu* 馬牛): literally, "horses and oxen," referring to beasts of burden.

231. Frog: from the idiom *jingdi zhi wa* 井底之蛙 (a frog in a well), a person with a very limited outlook. The idea derives from the Daoist text *Zhuangzi* 17.
232. "Borrow flowers . . ." (*jie hua xian fo* 借花獻佛): make a gift of something given by another.
233. This line derives from the expression "A wise man will not fight when the odds are against him" (*haohan bu chi yanqiankui* 好漢不吃眼前虧).
234. Sheep's wool (*yangmao chu zai yang shenshang* 羊毛出在羊身上): in the long run, whatever you're given, you have to pay for.
235. Marked the criminal (*zhubi* 朱臂): tattoo the face of a criminal for public humiliation.
236. Father–mother official (*fumuguan* 父母官): Local officials were supposed to treat the people as their children, making this a popular term for a county magistrate. See note 145.
237. A few words to settle a lawsuit (*pian yan zhe yu* 片言折獄): idiom used to praise an official for being wise and able. Here, it is used sarcastically.
238. *Lingzhuang* 領狀 (written pledge): receipt for collecting money from local authorities.
239. *Yingquan* 鷹犬 (eagles and dogs) and *zhaoya* 爪牙 (talons and fangs): lackeys; hired thugs.
240. Ingot (*yuanbao* 元寶): shoe-shaped silver ingot
241. Bites: One could get an approximate sense of the quality of silver by biting it to test its hardness.
242. The marginal commentary at this point reads: "Truly money is something that circulates—just consider these ill-gotten gains: Fallen Angel and the rest could not keep them, and they fell to the assistant magistrate. The assistant could not keep them, and they fell to the magistrate. At this point, the reader cannot help but fervently admire the magistrate, yet he does not know that above the magistrate there are others, so this circulation just does not end."
243. Thousand-League-Eyes and Ears-That-Follow-the-Wind (Qianli yan, Shunfeng er 千里眼, 順風耳): deities that assist the city gods in watching for misdeeds committed in their area of jurisdiction.
244. Stealing food for the dog (*tigou duoshi* 替狗奪食): going to a lot of trouble for nothing.
245. Sharp-eyed enough to see 10,000 *li* and wise enough to perceive an autumn hair: elaborates on the idiom "have eyes sharp enough to perceive an animal's autumn hair" (*ming cha qiuhao* 明察秋毫), which means "perceive the minutest detail."

246. Wash our feet (*zhuozu* 濯足): being aloof from the "muddy" mundane world.
247. Hundredweight (*dan* 擔): unit of weight, about 110 pounds (50 kilograms).
248. Milky Way (Hehan 河漢); literally, "River of Stars." In ancient legend, the Herd-boy and the Weaving-girl (lovers identified with the stars Altair and Vega) are separated by the Milky Way and are permitted to meet only once a year, on the seventh day of the seventh lunar month, when magpies form a bridge for them to pass over the barrier.
249. Great dream (*dameng* 大夢): Daoist philosophers called death the "great awakening" (*dajue* 大覺) and life the "great dream."
250. Repayment for a meal: Han Xin 韓信 (230–196 B.C.E.), one of the founding generals of the Han dynasty, was very poor in his youth. An old woman once gave him a meal but rebuffed his promises to repay her in the future. After he became powerful, he found her and rewarded her with a thousand pieces of gold. For his biography, see *Shiji* 92; and *Hanshu* 34.
251. The wedding rites (*Qin Jin zhi hao* 秦晉之好): the amity between Qin and Jin sealed by a marriage alliance between the two royal houses during the Spring and Autumn period.
252. Decorated candles (*huazhu* 花燭): candles with dragon and phoenix patterns used in the bridal chamber on the wedding night.
253. A rustic presents celery (*yeren xianqin* 野人獻芹): the gift is humble, but the good wishes are sincere.
254. Offering sacrifices . . . fields (*saishe* 賽社): harvest festival after the completion of the season's work. Farmers laid out food and drink as sacrifices to the field gods and enjoyed themselves drinking together.
255. The shepherd boy's performance takes on metatheatrical significance as he performs in this role.
256. Ceremonies (*cuizhuang* 催妝): kind of nuptial etiquette and custom in old times. The groom presented the bride with wedding gifts, such as cosmetics and clothing, a couple of days ahead to urge her to get ready for their wedding. On the wedding day, a party sent by the groom to escort her to the groom's home played music and set off firecrackers outside the bride's house while urging her to get in the sedan chair.
257. Bracken powder (*jue fen* 蕨粉): made from the roots of the *Pteridium*, or bracken fern, a starch used throughout East Asia. It can be added to flour or rice to make it stickier.
258. Soft fragrance and warmth (*ruanyu wenxiang* 軟玉溫香 or *yuruan xiangwen* 玉軟香溫): feminine charm.

259. Flowers lovely (*jiaohua* 嬌花): metaphor for a beautiful woman. Willows tender (*liunen* 柳嫩): may derive from "willowy waist" (*liuyao* 柳腰), which describes a woman's slender waist.
260. Drink the nuptial cup (*hejin* 合卺): Bride and groom shared a cup of wine during the wedding ceremony.
261. Pine flowers ([*mawei*] *song hua* [馬尾]松花): flowers of the horsetail pine, which are small, egg-shaped, and purple. Here, they take the place of jewels to decorate the bride's hair.
262. Bantering in celebration (*chaoxi* 吵喜 or *nao xinfang* 鬧新房): form of warm-hearted but perhaps naughty joking and teasing at a wedding, meant to embarrass the couple and heighten the joyful atmosphere.
263. Ceremonial bows (*baitang* 拜堂): Stage convention was to have the couple make three bows: to Heaven and Earth, to their parents, and to each other. Real practice would be much more complex.
264. Turtle's head (*zhan aotou* 占鰲頭): literally, "occupying the head of the turtle," which refers to heading the list of successful civil service examination candidates.
265. Dragon Gate (Longmen 龍門): see note 80.
266. Rule (*wenfa* 文法): normally, rules of composition and rhetoric; laws and decrees.
267. Head (*tou* 頭): implies the head of the penis (*guitou* 龜頭). See note 165.
268. Savage fighters (*pixiu* 貔貅): literally, a mythical, hybrid wild animal, here referring to his beasts of prey.
269. Chen Ping 陳平 (d. 178 B.C.E.): an expert in strategy who assisted Liu Bang 劉邦 to establish the Han Empire. Zhuge Liang 諸葛亮 (181–234): a brilliant statesman and strategist during the Three Kingdoms period who helped establish the state of Shu Han.
270. Presumably, this "tiger" was represented by an actor in tiger's clothing, as was the pair of attached soles. Horses generally were represented by the rider carrying a symbolic horse whip. For a discussion of such properties, see James I. Crump, *Chinese Theater in the Days of Kublai Khan* (Ann Arbor: Center for Chinese Studies, University of Michigan, 1990), 109–114, 119–120.
271. Hang a new hat (*jiaguan* 加冠): literally, "putting on a hat," a possible pun on another expression of the same pronunciation that means "being promoted to a higher office" (*jiaguan* 加官).
272. Mount Tai . . . egg (Taishan *ya luan* 泰山壓卵): literally, "like Mount Tai bearing down on an egg," referring to overwhelmingly superior force.
273. A distinguished robe (*qingzi* 青紫): rich purple, the color of the dress and ribbon attached to an official seal for high officials in ancient times.

274. Drinking funds (*zhang tou qian* 杖頭錢): money to buy wine or liquor. According to his biography in *Jin shu* 晉書, Ruan Xiu 阮修 (270–311) often walked along with a string of copper coins hanging from his staff. When he got to a wine shop, he bought wine with the money and drank to the full.

275. Tied my hair . . . thigh (*xuanliang cigu* 懸樑刺股): the expressions "tie one's hair to a beam to keep from nodding off" and "prod oneself awake with an awl in the thigh" mean "to study assiduously." The allusion comes from *Zhanguo ce* 戰國策, "Qin ce" 秦策, sec. 1; and *Hanshu* 漢書 (quoted in *Taiping yulan* 太平御覽, *juan* 363).

276. Inkstone: reference to the idiom "wearing out an iron inkslab" (*mochuan tieyan* 磨穿鐵硯), which means "to study assiduously." Bronze peacock inkstones (*Tong que yan* 銅雀硯) are famous. The Bronze Peacock Terrace (Tongque tai 銅雀台), built by Cao Cao 曹操 (155–220) during the Three Kingdoms period, is located in Linzhang 臨漳 in Hebei, where ancient inkstones have been excavated.

277. Roc's path (*pengcheng wanli* 鵬程萬里): literally, "roc's flight of 10,000 *li* (3,100 miles [5,000 kilometers])," which means "to have a bright future." "Path to the clouds" (*yunlu* 雲路): illustrious official career. "Roc in the clouds" (*yunpeng* 雲鵬) is a metaphor for lofty aspirations and a bright future.

278. Head south (*tu nan* 圖南): In *Zhuangzi* 1, the great roc rises high in the air and flies to the faraway southern sea, becoming a metaphor for lofty aspirations and a bright future.

279. Valuables (*xiruan* 細軟): literally, "what's slender and soft," referring to jewelry, fine clothing, and other valuables that are easy to carry about.

280. Gain wealth and . . . high rank: from the phrase: "to be loaded and fly to Yangzhou on a crane's back" (*yaochan shiwan guan, qihe shang* Yangzhou 腰纏十萬貫, 騎鶴上揚州). In a story from Yin Yun 殷芸, *Xiaoshuo* 小說 (Southern Dynasties [420–589]), some travelers were talking to one another about their ambitions. One wanted to be the governor of Yangzhou, one wanted to have lots of money, and one wanted to ride on a crane's back. Yet another one wished for all three. Thus the idiom refers to the desire to be an official, get rich, and become an immortal simultaneously.

281. Jasper Pool (Yaochi 瑤池): dwelling place of the Queen Mother of the West, Xiwangmu.

282. Stench (*shan* 膻): literally, "smell of mutton," a metaphor for worldly rank and wealth.

283. Second Heaven: In the Eastern Han dynasty, Su Zhang 蘇章, the inspector of Jizhou 冀州, entertained the governor of Qinghe 清河, who was his subordinate and old friend. The governor said happily: "Everybody has one Heaven; only I have two Heavens." Because Heaven bestows favors to humans, "two Heavens" (or "a second Heaven" [*ertian* 二天]) is an appellation for benefactors, an expression of thanks. The allusion comes from Fan Ye's 範曄 *Hou Hanshu* 後漢書, *juan* 31. Here, it means that Tan Chuyu acknowledges help from both the deity Lord Yan and Old Fisherman Mo.

284. Divine beauty: Chang'e 嫦娥 is the Chinese moon goddess figuring prominently in legend and literature. In mortal life, she stole the herb of immortality and fled to the moon, where she became immortal but was cloistered forever. Later, she became a metaphor for a beautiful woman.

285. Eye to eye (*bimu* 比目): referring to a couple deeply in love, puns on "sole" (*bimuyu*).

286. Spring of Avarice (Tanquan 貪泉): name of a spring in Nanhai 南海 County of Guangdong, and another in Chen 郴 County of Hunan. Drinking the spring water there allegedly makes one greedy.

287. Acquainted with Jingzhou (*shi* Jing 識荊): Jing refers to Han Chaozong 韓朝宗 (686–750), who was the administrator of Jingzhou. In his letter to Han, poet Li Bai (701–762) wrote, "A man does not need to be made a high official in life, if only he could know Administrator Han" 生不用封萬戶侯，但願一識韓荊州. The term became a polite expression for meeting a person for the first time.

288. Martial music (*naoge* 鐃歌): ancient martial melodies played on horseback while on the march.

289. Guest star (*kexing* 客星): reference to Yan Guang 嚴光, who once was a classmate of Liu Xiu 劉秀, the founder of the Eastern Han dynasty. After Liu Xiu ascended the throne, Yan Guang concealed his identity and became a recluse. Later, it was reported that a man wearing a sheepskin coat was seen fishing in a pond. Some poets of later ages questioned his sincerity in living in seclusion because nobody could have recognized him if he had worn a rush rain cape instead of a sheepskin coat. The imposter wears a rush cape precisely to make it easy to be "found."

290. Blue robe (*lanpao* 藍袍): robes worn by officials of the eighth or ninth rank.

291. Prefecture of Tingzhou: established in the early Ming, its administrative center was Changting 長汀 in present-day Fujian Province. This is one of the few references to specific places in this play.

292. Hobbyhorse (*zhuma* 竹馬): stick of bamboo with a head like a horse attached to it that is held between the knees as a toy horse, or a bamboo horse used as a stage prop in a folk dance. See note 270.
293. March: these actors circle the stage to simulate marching until they "arrive" at their destination.
294. Heaven's Mandate (Tianming 天命): conquerors who succeeded in establishing an empire were traditionally regarded as having received Heaven's help in doing so.
295. Viewed flowers (*kan hua* 看花): by extension, passed the highest imperial examinations. The poem "Dengke hou" 登科後 (After Passing the Civil Service Examinations), written by Meng Jiao 孟郊 (751–814), says: "Flushed with spring breezes on a flying horse,/I look at all the flowers of Chang'an in one day" 春風得意馬蹄疾，一日看盡長安花. It was the custom during the Tang dynasty (618–907) that successful candidates in the highest imperial examinations gathered at banquets in the capital Chang'an when the spring flowers were in bloom, as examination results were published in the spring. One of the entertainments at gathering was that the candidates went out on horses to visit various famous gardens there to pick rare flowers and bring them back to the banquet. It was also said that the candidates celebrated with the courtesans ("the flowers").
296. Smooth my worried brows (*zhanmei* 展眉): beam with joy.
297. Gilded announcement (*nijin* 泥金): card coated with powdered gold or gold paint. Here, it refers to the gilded card that reported a candidate's success in the imperial examinations.
298. Autumn examinations (*qiushi* 秋試): imperial examinations at the provincial level in the Ming and Qing dynasties as preliminaries for the capital, highest-level, examinations.
299. Wind and dust (*fengchen* 風塵): metaphor for an official career. Blue clouds (*qingyun* 青雲): reference to rapid advancement to high office.
300. This line is a variation on the "pretty face, poor fate" (*hongyan boming* 紅顏薄命) aphorism, which suggests that pretty women inevitably suffer unhappy fates.
301. Prince Teng's Pavilion (Teng Wang *ge* 滕王閣): Wang Bo 王勃 (650–676) was invited by Commander in Chief Yan Boyu 閻伯嶼 to a banquet at Prince Teng's Pavilion by the Ganjiang River in Jiangxi. On the way there, his boat was delayed. According to legend, a water god came to his aid with wind, so that he could travel 700 *li* (220 miles [350 kilometers]) a day and arrive on time.

302. *Register of Successful Candidates* (*Timing lu* 題名錄): From the Tang and Song onward, lists circulated of the names, ages, and native places of all new graduates of the highest level examination.

303. Feng Fu 馮婦: from the expression "being Feng Fu again" (*zai zuo* Feng Fu 再作馮婦). *Mengzi* 7B.23 tells of a man named Feng Fu in the state of Jin 晉 who could capture tigers with his bare hands. Later, he became a gentleman and gave up the sport. On seeing a crowd pursuing a tiger in the open country, however, he readily took up his old practice. Here, Murong Jie expresses his concern that he will be forced by circumstances to give up his life of seclusion and again take up an official post. See *Mencius*, trans. Lau, 198.

304. Path to Zhongnan (Zhongnan (*jie*)*jing* 終南(捷)徑): high road to fame and success. According to *Xin Tangshu* 新唐書 123, because Lu Cangyong 盧藏用, a successful candidate in the highest imperial examinations, was not appointed to an important position, he went into seclusion in the Zhongnan Mountains to seek fame. Later, he was summoned to be an official, as expected.

305. Earl of Shao's pear (Shao Bo *tang* 召伯棠): Earl of Shao was the son of King Wen of Zhou (1152–1056 B.C.E.). According to *Shiji* 史記 34, when the earl toured town and country, he often handled lawsuits and conducted government affairs under a birch-leaf pear tree. After he passed away, thinking of his effective administrative work, the people did not want to cut down the tree and instead composed an ode to it. The reference has been used to laud achievements in one's official career.

306. This line means that when you help someone, you should make a thorough job of it and not leave it unfinished. A stupa (*futu* 浮屠) lower than seven stories might not be efficacious.

307. Wrapped in the hide of a horse (*mage guoshi* 馬革裹屍): die on the battlefield.

308. Bingzhou 并州: the ancient name of Taiyuan in Shanxi Province, far from Tingzhou. Bingzhou, linked to the region north of the Great Wall, was always an important place of national defense. It enjoyed topographical advantages and connected with the capitals of the Han and Tang Empires; some emperors and warlords of those dynasties built their power in that area. This reference may be meant to suggest the military importance of the region rather than a specific geographical location. Bingzhou and Tingzhou, however, were related to each other in Hakka history. When northern tribes made border raids, many Han people moved south from Bingzhou. During the Tang and Song

dynasties, many of these migrants settled in Tingzhou, in present-day Fujian Province and became known as Hakkas 客家 (guest families).

309. Magic wonderland (*huajiang* 化疆): suggests the transformation lands of bliss, *huacheng* 化城, the Buddhist concept of temporary or incomplete Nirvāṇa.

310. Good administration by man . . . law (*You zhi ren, wu zhi fa* 有治人, 無治法): From the "Jun dao" 君道 (The Rule of the True King) chapter of *Xunzi* 荀子, this line means that social tranquility depends on moral leadership, not just laws.

311. The gourd at hand: from the idiom "drawing a dipper using a gourd as a model" (*zhao hulu hua piao* 照葫蘆畫瓢), which means "to copy or imitate."

312. This couplet makes use of the idiom "to purchase fame and fish for compliments" (*guming diaoyu* 沽名釣譽).

313. Wicker gate (*chaimen* 柴門): indicates a poor family.

314. Chao and You 巢由: Chao Fu 巢父 and Xu You 許由, famous recluses during the reign of sage-king Yao (by legend, ca. 2333–2234 B.C.E.). Here, the names refer to Old Fisherman Mo himself. Yi and Lü 伊呂: Yi Yin 伊尹, who assisted King Tang of the Shang dynasty 商湯 (r. ca. 1675–1646 B.C.E.), and Lü Shang 呂尚, who assisted King Wu of the Zhou dynasty 周武王 (r. 1027–1025 B.C.E.), were virtuous and able ministers to the founders of the states.

315. Forests and springs (*linquan* 林泉): place for a recluse.

316. Yang Pass (Yangguan *sandie* 陽關三疊, or Yangguan *qu* 陽關曲): Yang Pass was an important point of departure on the land route across Central Asia. This poem by Wang Wei, also known as "The Song of Weicheng" 渭城曲, was sung to express sad feelings at parting; its second couplet is more famous: "Please, sir, drink just one more cup of wine,/West out the Yang Pass, you'll find no more friends" 勸君更盡一杯酒, 西出陽關無故人. The chorus is repeated three times, hence *sandie* (three reiterations).

317. Vermilion gates (*zhumen* 朱門): In late imperial China, the gates of the residences of nobles, officials, and the wealthy were painted red.

318. Retirement (*mai shan* 買山): literally, "to buy a mountain," metaphor for going into retirement.

319. Gibbons and cranes (*yuanhe* 猿鶴): by legend, animal companions of the recluse.

320. Cuckoo (literally, *duyu* 杜宇 or *zijuan* 子鵑): named for Duyu, the legendary king of the state of Shu (modern Sichuan), who assisted in the founding of the Zhou dynasty (ca. 1050 B.C.E.). Later, he abdicated to

live in seclusion during the second lunar month when cuckoos sang. People of Shu thought of him and so called cuckoos *dujuan* 杜鵑 or *duyu* thereafter. Their call was interpreted as "better return" (*buru guiqu* 不如歸去).

321. Shi-You wind (Shi You *feng* 石尤風): strong headwind. According to *Jianghu jiwen* 江湖紀聞, quoted in Yi Shizhen's 伊世珍 (fourteenth century) *Langhuan ji* 琅嬛記, a woman named Shi married a man named You, and they had a deep affection for each other. You planned to travel far away from home for business, ignoring Shi's attempts to stop him. He never returned, and his wife died of grief. On her deathbed, she wished to turn into a gale to prevent traveling merchants from going on long journeys.
322. Charcoal in snowy weather: from the idiom "to send charcoal in the snow" (*xue zhong song tan* 雪中送炭), which means "to provide timely help."
323. Add flowers: from the idiom "to add flowers to a brocade" (*jin shang tian hua* 錦上添花), which means "to make what is good still better."
324. Wu and Yue 吳越: see note 13.
325. *Fengliu dan* 風流旦 (coquettes): role type that portrays teenage girls who are clever, fluent, and playful.
326. A real splash: more literally, "a great wave" (*bolan* 波瀾). This will be a smaller "reunion scene" for mother and daughter, not the "grand reunion scene" (*da tuanyuan* 大團圓) that conventionally concludes a play of this form.
327. Stage right: should be from the perspective of the actors, according to David Rolston, "Jingju juben zhong wutai zhishi yanhua yu leibie chutan: Yi *Silang tanmu* lidai gezhong banben weili," in *Jingju de wenxue yinyue biaoyan*, ed. Fu Jin (Beijing: Wenhua yishu, 2016), 810. But in an edition for emperors to read, stage right would be the west side of the stage because it was from the emperor's perspective, and he faced south while watching a performance. See David Rolston, "Yi Ōsaka cangben *Shengping baofa* zhong de wutai zhishi kan Qingchao gongting daxi de wutai yishu mouxie cengmian" (manuscript, 2018), 4.
328. Intertwining: shortened from "branches intertwined" (*lianlizhi* 連理枝). See note 221.
329. That is, in scene 1 when this performer introduced the play.
330. "Offering a Sacrifice to the River": scene 30 of *The Thorn Hairpin*, although the performance that follows selects arias from scene 35, with small modifications. It omits the arias sung by the mother that are interspersed among the husband's arias and the husband's memorial

statement, with the mother's role wholly relegated to comments from backstage. The commentator at this point observes how difficult it would be to construct a stage on a stage, given the limited room, but praises the playwright for the idea.

331. Gold-lion (*jinni* 金猊): one of the mythical dragon's sons that looks like a lion. Because he likes smoke, his image often decorates incense burners.

332. Jasper Pool (Yaochi 瑤池): see note 281. Here, it refers to a pond in a palace garden or to the imperial palace.

333. Wife of chaff and husks (*zaokang qi* 糟糠妻): wife who has shared a life of poverty with her husband. This is a prominent theme in scene 21, "Zaokang zi yan" 糟糠自咽 (Chaff and Husks for Myself to Swallow), of the older play *The Lute* (*Pipa ji* 琵琶記), in which the female protagonist feeds her parents-in-law rice while eating husks herself because of their poverty. She calls herself the chaff-and-husk wife of their son. See Kao Ming, *Lute*, 156–160. Peach and apricot (*tao xing* 桃杏): peach blossoms are pink and apricot blossoms are white, so they often are used to describe a woman's beautiful face.

334. Chaoyang 潮陽: southwest of the city of Shantou in present-day Guangdong Province.

335. This translation is the original line from *The Thorn Hairpin*, which uses the word "reminisce" (*zhuisi* 追思) instead of "follow" (*zhuisui* 追隨) in the line in *A Couple of Soles*.

336. Dyed . . . cuckoos cry aloud (*xuelei ran, dujuan ti* 血淚染, 杜鵑啼): When Duyu, the legendary king of the state of Shu, died, his soul turned into a cuckoo (*dujuan*) that cried (*ti*) plaintively all day until its mouth bled. See note 320; and "Shu zhi" 蜀志, in *Huayang guo zhi* 華陽國志 (*Chronicles of Huayang*) by Chang Qu 常璩 (ca. 291–361). *Dujuan* can also refer to the azalea, its red blossoms by legend stained (*ran*) by tears of blood (*xuelei*).

337. Pepper apartment (*jiaofang* 椒房): see note 174. Here, it refers to Fairy Liu.

338. Sunset glow (*yuhui* 餘輝): giving preferential treatment in bestowing benefits.

339. Ox- and horse-headed monsters are guardians of the Underworld. A "ghost mask" suggests similar demonic associations, although the term colloquially denotes a child's mask used as a toy.

340. Chicken head and phoenix tail (*jitou fengwei* 雞頭鳳尾): may derive from the idiom "better be the head of a chicken than the tail of a phoenix" (*ning wei jitou, bu wei fengwei* 寧為雞頭,不為鳳尾). It alludes playfully to the earlier line "We mistook simurgh and phoenix for mere

pheasants," in which Liu Wenqing and Fallen Angel reprove themselves for having failed to recognize Tan Chuyu's distinguished talent.
341. Mold a statue: create a god's image to receive their regular thanks for the god's intervention.
342. God Erlang: see notes 31 and 85.
343. Grab the official's cart shafts . . . (*panyuan wozhe* 攀轅臥轍): literally, "cling to cart shafts and lie down in the ruts," measures for urging a good official to stay. According to the biography of Hou Ba 侯霸 in *Hou Hanshu* 後漢書, when a messenger was dispatched to summon Hou Ba, the common people blocked the messenger's cart or lay in the middle of the road to keep Hou from leaving for one more year.
344. Sky might start to fall (*Qiren youtian* 杞人憂天): like the man from Qi who had this worry, to entertain imaginary or groundless fears. *Youtian* can also indicate concern that one's country is in peril. Here, it means that they are worried about Tan Chuyu.
345. Gong and Huang 龔黃: allusion from the preface to the biographies of the upright officials (*Xunli zhuan xu* 循吏傳序) in *Hanshu* 89, two of whom were Gong Sui 龔遂 and Huang Ba 黃霸. As a term, "Gong Huang" also refers to law-abiding officials in general.
346. Cart has overturned up ahead: derives from the saying "The overturned cart ahead is a warning to the ones behind" (*Qianche zhi fu, houche zhi jian* 前車之覆, 後車之鑒), which means "to learn from others' mistakes."
347. Lingyan portrait (*tuhua* Lingyan 圖畫凌煙): According to their annals in *Jiu Tangshu* 舊唐書, Emperor Taizong and, later, Emperor Daizong of the Tang dynasty had the images of those who rendered outstanding service portrayed on the Lingyan Pavilion 凌煙閣, inside the Taiji Palace of Chang'an, to commend them as well as to provide models for later generations.
348. Tianshan arrows (Tianshan *jian* 天山箭): Xue Rengui, a famous Tang general, led troops on a punitive expedition to the Tianshan Mountains to suppress the Turkish peoples who were making incursions across the frontiers. After he killed three enemies by shooting only three arrows, the Turks were reportedly awed into surrender. See the biography of Xue Rengui in *Xin Tangshu* 新唐書.
349. Clear sky (*qingtian* 青天): respectful sobriquet for an honest and upright official.
350. Tiger's might: from "sheep in a tiger's skin" (*yangzhi hupi* 羊質虎皮), which means "outwardly strong, inwardly weak."
351. Yang Hu 陽虎 and Confucius (Zhongni 仲尼): Yang Hu, who physically resembled Confucius, held a position of power in the state of Lu for

three years during the Spring and Autumn period. According to *Shiji* 史記 47, when Confucius was passing through the place called Kuang 匡, he was mistaken for Yang Hu, who had offended the people there, so they detained Confucius for five days. The line means that although Yang Hu and Confucius looked very much alike, that was where the similarities ended.

352. A wily hare . . . three burrows (*jiaotu sanku* 狡兔三窟): crafty person has more than one means of escape; elaborate precautions are made for self-protection.

353. Straddling two boats (*jiao ta liangzhi chuan* 腳踏兩隻船): having a foot in each camp.

354. *Xian'ge* 弦歌 (sing to the accompaniment of stringed instruments): music in a general sense. The term also can be a metaphor for educating the masses with rites and music, as indicated in the allusion from *Lunyu* 17.4: in Wucheng 武城 of the state of Lu, Confucius heard that his disciple Ziyou used songs with string accompaniment to enlighten the people.

355. *Gupi* 鼓鼙: big and small drums used in the armies of ancient China, a metaphor for military affairs and warfare.

356. Leaden blade (*qiandao* 鉛刀): self-deprecating remark made as a gesture of politeness, meaning that a person may be lacking in ability but does his or her best.

357. Medley (*daiguoqu* 帶過曲): In this medley, *Dui yuhuan* with *Qingjiang yin*, the *Dui yuhuan* tune is bound to that of *Qingjiang yin*. For information on this form of medley, see the appendix.

358. Times are all against me (*yunjian shiguai* 運蹇時乖): derives from the idiom "be born under an evil star" (*shiguai mingjian* 時乖命蹇), which means "to fall on bad times."

359. This line derives from the idiom "no road up to Heaven and no door into Earth" (*shangtian wu lu, ru di wu men* 上天無路, 入地無門), which means "no way out of a predicament."

360. Captive sacrifice (*xianfu* 獻俘): ancient military ritual. Having returned in triumph, the army offered captives for sacrifice at the Imperial Ancestral Temple to announce their victory to the emperor's forebears.

361. Eating the emperor's food . . . land (*shimao jiantu* 食毛踐土): in traditional thinking, since both food and land belong to the ruler, one is obligated to show gratitude by being obedient. The phrase derives from *Zuo zhuan* 左傳, Duke Zhao 昭公, seventh year.

362. Common man (*caomang* 草莽): literally, "rank grass," referring to the people in contrast to the imperial government.

363. Unrestricted arrest warrant (*guang bu* 廣捕): warrant with no restriction on time and locale.
364. Deer-and-firewood (*jiaolu* 蕉鹿): *Liezi* 列子 3 tells that during the Spring and Autumn period, a woodcutter from the state of Zheng killed a deer. Afraid that other people might see it, he concealed it in a dry trench and covered it with firewood. Afterward, when he went to fetch the deer, he could not remember where he had hidden it. Thereupon, he thought that was a dream. Later, the allusion came to signify a dream or a negative opinion that regards real events as an illusion.
365. Come out of the mountains (*chushan* 出山): come out of retirement to return to official service.
366. Heaven's high and the emperor far away (*Tiangao diyuan* 天高帝遠): lacking official protection, outlaws may do whatever they wish without fear of legal reprisals.
367. Jie Zhitui 介之推 to come out: While Chong'er 重耳 (later, Duke Wen of Jin) was in exile from the state of Jin, Jie Zhitui rendered great service by feeding flesh that he cut from his own thigh to Chong'er when he was starving. Later, when Chong'er regained power and became king of Jin (r. 636–628 B.C.E.), Jie Zhitui went into retirement in the mountains. To force him out of hiding, Duke Wen had the mountains set on fire. Jie Zhitui did not leave and died in the fire while clasping a willow tree.
368. Bringing fire down on his head (*elan toujiao* 額爛頭焦): literally, "festering forehead and scorched head," paraphrase of an idiom that means "a sorry plight" (*jiaotou lan'e* 焦頭爛額), but here may also allude to the story of Jie Zhitui's death by fire.
369. Whales (*jing ni* 鯨鯢): literally, "male and female whales", a metaphor for a ferocious enemy.
370. Shields and city wall (*gancheng* 干城): metaphor for a defending army. "Our south:" Tingzhou of Fujian Province is in the south of China.
371. Volunteered (*qingying* 請纓): literally, "request a cord [from the emperor] to bind [the enemy]," referring to submitting a request for a military assignment.
372. Burn beanstalks to cook beans (*zhudou ranqi* 煮豆燃萁): fratricidal strife, referring to Cao Zhi's 曹植 (192–232) "Seven-Pace Song" (Qibu shi 七步詩): Beans in flame that beanstalks feed, /Out from the pan cry, /Sprung from the same stalk, what need/Each the other anxiously fry? 煮豆燃豆萁, 豆在釜中泣. 本是同根生, 相煎何太急 (*Beijing Waiguoyu Daxue yingyu xi cidianzu* 北京外國語大學英語系詞典組, *A Chinese-English Dictionary* 漢英詞典 [Beijing: Waiyu jiaoxue yu yanjiu chubanshe, 1997],

1652; its translation is modified with the addition of the word "anxiously"). This version of the poem, from the novel *Romance of the Three Kingdoms* (*Sanguo zhi yanyi* 三國志演義, 1522), is more popular than its original in the "Wenxue" 文學 section of Liu Yiqing's 劉義慶 (403–444) *Shishuo xinyu* 世說新語: when Cao Pi 曹丕 (187–226) ascended the throne of Wei, he regarded his gifted younger brother Cao Zhi as a threat and thus ordered Zhi to finish composing a poem within seven steps; otherwise, he would put Zhi to death. The younger brother's "Seven-Pace Song" made Cao Pi feel extremely ashamed. Murong Jie uses this allusion to criticize Tan Chuyu for betraying their friendship.

373. To fry me (*xiang jian tai ji* 相煎太急): no love lost between brothers.

374. Zhang Xun 張巡 (708–757) and Xu Yuan 許遠 (709–757): government officials who sacrificed their lives to defend Suiyang 睢陽 in Henan during the An Lushan Rebellion, according to the standard histories of the Tang. They were regarded as exemplars of loyal and righteous officers ready to die for their country and were worshiped as gods in many areas of China.

375. Hair lifts . . . cap ([*nu*] *fa chong guan* [怒] 髮衝冠): become so angry that the hair stands on end.

376. Yue Fei 岳飛 (1103–1142): loyal general who defended the territorial sovereignty of the Song dynasty against the Jurchen invasion, but the treacherous minister Qin Gui 秦檜 (1090–1155) trumped up a charge against him and had him executed. Qin Gui is considered a traitor in Chinese history.

377. Tian Guang 田光 (d. 227 B.C.E.): chivalrous man from the state of Yan who recommended his friend Jing Ke to Crown Prince Dan to assassinate the king of Qin. To assure the prince that he would not leak his secret, Tian Guang cut his own throat. See *Shiji* 86, "Biographies of the Assassins" 刺客列傳.

378. Today we drink wine . . . law (*jinri yinjiuzhe siqing, mingri anzuizhe gongfa* 今日飲酒者私情, 明日按罪者公法): expression of opposition between feelings and legal requirements that derives from *Comprehensive Mirror for Aid in Governing* (*Zizhi tongjian* 資治通鑑), entry 44 of the Han records: When Su Zhang served as regional inspector, he was required to punish his friend, a governor, for crimes that included taking bribes. Su Zhang invited the man to his home; enjoyed snacks and wine with him as friend; and the next day, in his official capacity, executed him. See note 283.

379. Boren: Zhou Yi 周顗 (269–322), chief administrator during the time of Emperor Yuan of the Jin dynasty. According to his biography in *Jinshu*

晉書, Zhou Yi was on intimate terms with Wang Dao (276–339). In 322, Wang Dao's cousin Wang Dun (266–324), regional inspector of Jiangzhou, staged an armed uprising. Wang Dao waited at the imperial palace to be dealt with by the emperor. Zhou Yi spoke to Emperor Yuan in defense of Wang Dao, and the emperor accepted his opinion, but Wang Dao did not know about it. Later, Wang Dun came to control the court administration and asked Wang Dao how to deal with Zhou Yi. Wang Dao did not respond, and thereupon, Wang Dun executed Zhou Yi. After the incident, Wang Dao learned that Zhou Yi had once saved him, and he wept bitter tears of remorse, saying: "Although I did not kill Boren, he died because of me. In the netherworld, I have betrayed this good friend" 吾雖不殺伯仁, 伯仁由我而死. 幽冥之中, 負此良友.

380. According to *Mengzi* 孟子 4B.24, Peng Meng learned archery from Hou Yi and mastered the skill. Now only Hou Yi was a better archer than Peng Meng in the whole world, so he killed Hou Yi. Here, the allusion means that things turn out contrary to one's wishes, which implies that Mo regrets having given Tan *The Handbook of Essential Knowledge*.

381. Divine talisman (*yinfu* 陰符): from the title of a book on the art of war, *The Grand Duke's Divine Talisman* (*Taigong yinfu* 太公陰符), attributed to Grand Duke Jiang Shang 姜尚 (fl. eleventh century B.C.E.). Later, the term was used to refer to books on the art of war in general.

382. Master Yuan: Yuan Gong 猿公, a recluse known for his brilliant swordsmanship. See "Goujian yinmou waizhuan" 勾踐陰謀外傳, in Zhao Ye's 趙曄 *Wu Yue chunqiu* 吳越春秋 dating to the Han dynasty.

383. Skinning and stuffing with rice straw (*baopi xuancao* 剝皮楦草): legendary cruel torture practiced during the Ming dynasty that involved flaying a convict while he was still alive, making the skin into a sack, and stuffing the bag with rice straw to be publicly exposed. It is said that Zhu Yuanzhang often tortured corrupt officials extrajudicially using this method.

384. Clear mirror hung on high (*Qin jing gao xuan* 秦鏡高懸): epithet for an impartial and perspicacious judge.

385. Meetings of wind and clouds (*fengyun* 風雲會): meetings of the emperor with his ministers.

386. Obsession . . . vitals ([*bing ru*] *gaohuang* [病入] 膏肓): literally, "the disease has attacked the vitals," which means "beyond cure." Springs and rocks (*quan shi* 泉石): mountains and rivers. The poem "Song Liu Huiqing" 送劉惠卿 by Yang Wanli 楊萬里 (1127–1206) says: "Poetry and wine maniacs are the old complaints; a new disease of spring and rock has also

attacked the vitals" 舊病詩狂與酒狂, 新來泉石又膏肓. Chronic infection . . . clouds (*yanxia guji* 煙霞痼疾): deep love for the beauty of nature. The two expressions reveal his ardent love for mountains and rivers, which indicates his determination to retire and live in seclusion.

387. Bow and banner (*gong jing* 弓旌): ancient tokens used to call men of worth to service. The bow is for calling literati, and the banner is for summoning senior officials. Prisoner's escort (*ti ji* 緹騎): literally, "scarlet cavalry," alluding to the red uniforms worn by court guards and accompanying cavalry in ancient China. It is also a general name for government officials who arrested criminals.

388. Blow to the head . . . shout (*dangtou banghe* 當頭棒喝): the teaching tool of Chan Buddhist masters. In many accounts of sudden enlightenment, during intense meditation, an unexpected shout or blow to the head or shoulders from the master triggers enlightenment in the disciple.

389. In loyal pairs (*duidui* 隊隊): allusion to a kind of insect that looks like lice. The male and female always come out in pairs. In times past, people would put a pair in a small silver box and place it inside a hollow pillow to help husband and wife become reconciled.

390. Peeping ghosts (*gui kan gaoming* 鬼瞰高明): reference to the ghosts and gods who spy on the households of those in high positions to destroy their complacency. The source of the idiom is the biography of Pei Su 裴蕭 in *Suishu* 隋書. The message is that haughtiness invites disaster, and humility receives benefit.

391. Cool breezes . . . bright moon (*qingfeng mingyue* 清風明月): companions of leisure.

392. Peach Blossom Land (Taoyuan 桃源): fictitious utopia. This refers to the hidden haven of peace conceived by Tao Yuanming 陶淵明 (365–427) in his essay "A Record of the Peach Blossom Spring" (Taohuayuan ji 桃花源記), where common people live and work in peace and contentment, having left behind the political upheavals and misery of the outside world.

393. Filled in (*tian* 填): new words written to existing melodies, as were the arias of this play and poetry in the *ci* (song lyrics) form.

394. Handsome Master Zhou: see note 82. Here, the playwright refers in a general sense to those who understand music and opera.

395. Tied the bell . . . off: reference to an idiom based on an anecdote in the Buddhist collection *Linjian ji* 林間集 by Huihong 惠洪 (1070–1128), a famous poet-monk of the Northern Song. The abbot Fayan 法眼 asked his disciples, "Who can untie the golden bell from the tiger's neck?" Nobody was able to answer the question. Then the monk Taiqin 泰欽

appeared, and Fayan asked the question again. Taiqin said, "The one who tied the bell on can untie it" (*Jieling xiling* 解鈴繫鈴). Hence the idiom means that whoever started the trouble should end it. Here, Li Yu teases his readers by suggesting that he has promoted conventional morality in this play, after having written a series of romantic comedies.

APPENDIX

1. For a broader range of areas in which Li Yu showed expertise, see Zhang Xiaojun, *Li Yu chuangzuo lungao: Yishu de shangye hua yu shangye hua de yishu* (Beijing: Wenhua yishu, 1997), 223.
2. For a more complete list of writing forms Li Yu used, see Shen Xinlin, *Huashuo Li Yu* (Nanjing: Jiangsu renmin, 2012), 50.
3. "[L]ike the first eight already circulating in print as well as an additional eight written but not yet printed" 如已經行世之前後八種及已填未刻之內外八種 (Li Yu, *Xianqing ouji*, juan 1, "Yinlü disan" 音律第三, in *Li Yu quanji* [1991; rpt., Hangzhou: Zhejiang guji chubanshe, 2010], 3:30).
4. "Piliye shi zaji" 毗梨耶室雜記, in *Xiaoshuo kaozheng*, ed. Jiang Ruizao (Shanghai: Shanghai guji, 1984), juan 2 of the continuation, "Huang qiu feng" item, 461.
5. Zhou Xinhui, "Ji Suizhong Wu shi zhencang de gu banhua," in *Wu Xiaoling xiansheng zhencang gu banhua quan bian* (Beijing: Xueyuan chubanshe, 2003), 1:6.
6. Aoki Masaru, *Zhongguo jinshi xiqu shi*, trans. Wang Gulu, ed. Cai Yi (Beijing: Zhonghua shuju, 2010), 245.
7. Li Yu, "Yu Zhao Shengbo wenxue," in *Liweng yijia yan wenji*, in *Li Yu quanji*, 1:167–168.
8. Li Yu, *Xianqing ouji*, juan 4, "Jianjian" 賤簡, 229. It was common during the Ming–Qing period for publishers to try to protect an exclusive right to print their books, but copyright laws were not even contemplated until the end of Qing. On copyright in premodern China, see Cynthia J. Brokaw, "On the History of the Book in China," in *Printing and Book Culture in Late Imperial China*, ed. Cynthia J. Brokaw and Kai-Wing Chow (Berkeley: University of California Press, 2005), 19; and Hok-lam Chan, *Control of Publishing in China, Past and Present* (Canberra: Australian National University, 1983), 22–25.
9. Shen Xinlin, *Huashuo Li Yu*, 131–132.
10. Li Yu, *Xianqing ouji*, juan 3, "Jifu" 肌膚, 109–110. The quotations are from a comment on Li Yu's *Random Repository of Idle Thoughts* by his friend Zhou Binruo 周彬若.

APPENDIX

11. Shen Yinbo, in *Li Yu quanji*, 2:495. This comment is attached to the end of "Guo Ziling Diaotai."
12. Li Yu, "Shengri kouhao," in *Li Yu quanji*, 2:276.
13. Yitang 繹堂 is Shen Quan's 沈荃 (1624–1684) literary name.
14. Qinnü 秦女 was Duke Mu of Qin's (682–621 B.C.E.) daughter Nongyu 弄玉. According to *Liexian zhuan* 列仙傳, Xiao Shi 蕭史, expert in playing the *xiao* (a vertical bamboo flute), could imitate the singing of the simurgh and phoenix with his flute. Nongyu also liked playing the *xiao* flute, so Duke Mu married her to Xiao Shi. Every day, she practiced playing the flute and making the sound of the phoenix. A few years later, they ascended to Heaven, with Nongyu riding a phoenix and Xiaoshi, a dragon. Wu Wa 吳娃 (d. 301 B.C.E.), the queen consort of King Wuling of Zhao (ca. 340–295 B.C.E.), was very beautiful. Wu *wa* can also mean "beautiful women of the Wu area."
15. *Jian* 賤 (humble) can also mean "base." The busybody plays on the two meanings of *jian* (humble; base) to mock Li Yu's libertine relationship with female entertainers.
16. Liu Tingji, *Zaiyuan zazhi* (Beijing: Zhonghua shuju, 2005), 40.
17. Abstract of the play *Yi zhong qing* 一種情, in *Quhai zongmu tiyao*, ed. Dong Kang (Beijing: Renmin wenxue chubanshe, 1959), 21:995.
18. "Huazhaosheng biji" 花朝生筆記, in *Xiaoshuo kaozheng*, ed. Jiang Ruizao, *juan* 6, "Naihetian" item, 167. Allegedly, the protagonist Que Lihou in his *chuanqi* play *You Can't Do Anything About Fate* (*Naihetian* 奈何天, 1657) refers to Yansheng Gong 衍聖公 (Confucius's descendant). The first half of the play portrays him as hideous. Then Yansheng Gong bribes Li Yu with a large sum of money so that the character was miraculously transformed into a good-looking man when Li wrote the second half.
19. Li Yu, "Yu Zhuji mingfu Liu Mengxi," in *Li Yu quanji*, 1:218.
20. Du Fu (712–770) and Li Bai (701–762): great poets of the Tang dynasty (618–907).
21. Wang Qiang (Zhaojun; 52–19 B.C.E.) and Xi Shi (b. 506 B.C.E.): two of the four famous beauties in ancient China.
22. Western Paradise (Xitian 西天): the Land of Ultimate Bliss in Buddhism; Penglai (Pengdao 蓬萊): a fabled abode of immortals.
23. Li Yu, *Xianqing ouji*, *juan* 2, "Yu qiu xiaosi" 語求肖似, 47. Yao (ca. 2356–2255 B.C.E.) and Shun (r. 2233–2184 B.C.E.): sage-kings; Peng Zu 彭祖, surnamed Jian 籛: a legendary figure who lived for about 140 years during the time of Yao and Yu (ca. 2200–2100 B.C.E.).
24. In the early Qing, literati such as Wu Weiye 吳偉業 (1609–1671) wrote drama as allegorical, serious literature to convey their feelings about the

APPENDIX 315

dynastic change. Meanwhile, professional dramatists of the Suzhou school created socio-historical plays. See Huang Guoquan, *Yasu zhi jian: Li Yu de wenhua renge yu wenxue sixiang yanjiu* (Beijing: Zhongguo shehui kexue, 2004), 234–235; and Wan Qingchuan, *Fengliu daoxue: Li Yu zhuan* (Hangzhou: Zhejiang renmin chubanshe, 2005), 96–97. For more information on Li Yu 李玉 (1591?–1671?) and other dramatists of the Suzhou school, see Wu Xinlei, "Li Yu," in *Zhongguo da baike quanshu: Xiqu quyi* (Beijing: Zhongguo da baike quanshu chubanshe, 1983), 203–204. While historical plays stood out during the dynastic transition, many writers continued to compose romantic plays to seek consolation in the imaginary fulfillment of desires, as Wang Ayling notes in "Mingmo Qingchu caizi jiaren ju zhi yanqing neihan jiqi suo yinsheng zhi shenmei gousi," *Zhongguo wen zhe yanjiu jikan* 18 (2001): 175–176.

25. Wan Qingchuan, *Fengliu daoxue*, 92–93; Zhang Xiaojun, *Li Yu chuangzuo lungao*, 70; Huang Guoquan, "Neirong tiyao," in *Yasu zhi jian*, 1–2.
26. Most of Li Yu's plays portray real-life material on contemporary issues, as Xiao Rong observes in *Li Yu pingzhuan* (Hangzhou: Zhejiang guji chubanshe, 1987), 75.
27. Li Yu, "Fanli," in *Li Yu quanji*, 3:2.
28. Shen Xinlin, *Huashuo Li Yu*, 38.
29. Li Yu, *Xianqing ouji*, juan 4, "Fangshe diyi" 房舍第一, 156.
30. Li Yu, *Xianqing ouji*, juan 6, "Xiaji xingle zhi fa" 夏季行樂之法, 318–319.
31. For a study in Li Yu's experience and theory of gardens, see Zhu Liangjie, "Li Yu de yuanlin shenghuo ji yinyi siwei," *Zhongguo wenxue yanjiu* 22 (2006): 93–132.
32. Li Yu, *Xianqing ouji*, juan 4, "Fangshe diyi" 房舍第一, 157.
33. Li Yu, *Xianqing ouji*, juan 4, "Fangshe diyi," 156.
34. Li Yu, *Xianqing ouji*, juan 4, "Lingxing xiaoshi" 零星小石, 200.
35. Scholar-artists often exchanged "gifts" with patrons that were tantamount to commercial transactions, although the amateur-art ideal promoted in literati writings to differentiate amateurism from professionalism played down the material motivation of the creative process and the reality of artists' economic need. See James Cahill, *The Painter's Practice: How Artists Lived and Worked in Traditional China* (New York: Columbia University Press, 1994), 1–31.
36. Li Yu, *Shen luanjiao*, in *Li Yu quanji*, 5:424. That the two aspects are merged in Li Yu's works was the outcome of his time when Neo-Confucianism temporarily became tempered by "decadent public morals" 淫靡的世風, according to Guo Yingde, *Ming Qing chuanqi shi*

(Nanjing: Jiangsu guji, 1999), 394. The dramatic conflict in Li Yu's plays takes the form of love opposed to disruptors rather than be presented as confrontation between *qing* (feelings) and *li* (reason), as noted in Wang Ayling, "Mingmo Qingchu caizi jiaren ju," 147.

37. Li Diaoyuan, "Yucun quhua," *juan* 2, in *Zhongguo gudian xiqu lunzhu jicheng* (Beijing: Zhongguo xiju, 1959–1960), 8:26, 27; Liang Tingnan, "Quhua," *juan* 3, in *Zhongguo gudian xiqu lunzhu jicheng*, 8:267.
38. Yang Enshou, "Ciyu conghua," *juan* 2, in *Zhongguo gudian xiqu lunzhu jicheng*, 9:265.
39. Li Yu, *Xianqing ouji, juan* 1, "Ji tiansai" 忌填塞, 24.
40. Ingenuity is Li Yu's idea of a refined taste, which can be shown in popular work, as Zhu Liangjie suggests in "Li Yu de yuanlin shenghuo," 24.
41. Zhang Xiaojun thinks that Li Yu's compromising and contradictory way of conducting himself was a "relatively complicated existence in Chinese cultural history" (*Li Yu chuangzuo lungao*, 221).
42. Li Yu named himself Yu 漁 (fisherman). Li Yu changed his name during the time he lived at his secluded Yiyuan in Lanxi, out of a desire for a reclusive life as well as for sons because fishermen are known for having many sons, according to Shen Xinlin, *Huashuo Li Yu*, 17–18.
43. Li Yu, "Shanju man xing," in *Li Yu quanji*, 2:387.
44. Li Yu, "Yin bian," in *Li Yu quanji*, 2:312. Penglai 蓬萊 is a fabled abode of immortals. Small Penglai 小蓬萊 is a tranquil, exquisite scene just like the fairyland of Penglai.
45. Li Yu, "Bimuyu," in *Li Yu quanji*, 5:201.
46. Li Yu's short story "Tan Chuyu xi li chuanqing, Liu Miaogu qu zhong sijie," on the same subject matter, has fisherman Mo live in Yanling, according to Zhu Liangjie, "Li Yu de yuanlin shenghuo," 121.
47. Li Yu, "Bimuyu," 146.
48. Li Yu, "Bimuyu," 161.
49. Li Yu, "Yanling jishi," in *Li Yu quanji*, 2:371.
50. Li Yu, "Guo Ziling Diaotai," in *Li Yu quanji*, 2:494.
51. In *A Couple of Soles*, see note 304.
52. Li Yu, "Bimuyu," 187.
53. Tan Chuyu and Fairy Liu's love story concludes in scene 24 when he has succeeded in civil service examinations and she will accompany him to his official post, according to the analysis of Shen Xinlin, *Li Yu xin lun* (Suzhou: Suzhou Daxue, 1997), 264. The remaining eight scenes focus on the subject of seclusion.
54. The *Bimuyu* illustrations here (figures 1–6) are from a copy of Li Yu, *Bimuyu chuanqi er juan*, in *Liweng shizhong qu*; this Kangxi era

(1662–1722) print is in the National Library Rare Collection in Beijing. The illustrations in *Liweng shizhong qu*, made during the Shunzhi–Kangxi period (1644–1722), are among the best woodcuts of the early Qing, according to Chinese book illustration historian Zhou Xinhui, "Ji Suizhong Wu shi zhencang de gu banhua," 6.

55. Li Yu, *Xianqing ouji*, *juan* 1, "Jie fengci" 戒諷刺, 5–8. Li Yu checked the desire to satirize in *chuanqi* creation because suspicion of satire would be detrimental to his business as a professional writer, according to Huang Guoquan, *Yasu zhijian*, 232.

56. Wan Qingchuan, *Fengliu daoxue*, 95–96. For examples from Li Yu's other plays that satirize corrupt practices in the system of civil service examinations and government-personnel placement, see Shen Xinlin, *Li Yu xin lun*, 227–228.

57. Wang Shih-pe, "Tuxiang xushi duzhe fanying: Lun Li Yu de 'Tan Chuyu' yu *Bimuyu*," *Zhongzheng Daxue Zhongwen xueshu niankan* 1 (2010): 131–133. In Wang's analysis, Qian Wanguan portrayed by the *jing* role becomes more a villain than his counterpart of the story version who acts as a buffoon. Qian Wanguan, mediating between government officials and country folks, is employed as a locus to expose county officers' savage oppression of the people, as Shen Xinlin notes in *Li Yu xin lun*, 266.

58. For a study of elder landlords as local leaders in the early Ming and rural gentry after the mid-Ming, see Si-yen Fei, *Negotiating Urban Space: Urbanization and Late Ming Nanjing* (Cambridge, Mass.: Harvard University Asia Center, 2009), 36–37, 47.

59. Shen Xinlin, *Li Yu xin lun*, 266.

60. Cai Dongmin has listed the scenes that are added in the dramatic adaptation and the details from the original story that are deleted by the adaptation, in "Li Yu xiqu bianju yanjiu" (Ph.D. diss., Shanghai Xiju Xueyuan, 2013), 51. Jing Shen compares the incorporation of *The Thorn Hairpin* in the story and the play in "Ethics and Theater: The Staging of *Jingchai ji* in *Bimuyu*," *Ming Studies* 57 (2008): 86–87.

61. In the beginning narrative passage of the story, it says: "Whereas other stories [in this collection] relate an anecdote as a prologue to the story proper, this one will follow a different course. It has no need to play the host ushering in the guest, for it will generate the child from the mother. To begin with the dunghill and go on from there to tell of the magic mushroom—that is something entirely new in literary composition" (Li Yu, *Silent Operas*, trans. Patrick Hanan [Hong Kong: Chinese University Press, 1990], 163; see Li Yu, "Liancheng bi," in *Li Yu quanji*,

8:252). The way in which the narrator contrasts the Tan and Miaogu story with the other pieces of the collection indicates that it was not the first one in the original *Silent Operas, Second Collection*, as Xiao Xinqiao observes in "Li Yu *Wusheng xi Liancheng bi* banben shanbian kaosuo," in *Li Yu quanji*, 20:344.

62. Shan Jinheng, "Li Yu nianpu," in *Li Yu quanji*, 19:30; Xiao Xinqiao, "Li Yu *Wusheng xi Liancheng bi* banben shanbian kaosuo," 349; Sun Kaidi, "Li Liweng yu *Shi'er lou*," in *Li Yu quanji*, 20:41. Zhu Ping examines the comparability between the Zhang Jinyan incident and Li Yu's story "Fengxian lou" from his *Shi'er lou* 十二樓 collection, in "Li Yu xiaoshuo *Fengxian lou* yu *Wusheng xi er ji* ji yi," *Zhengzhou Daxue xuebao* 48, no. 4 (2015): 107–110. The story is also set in the Ming–Qing dynastic transitional period: the female protagonist—a married woman—is captured by Li Zicheng's bandits and later passed on to a Qing general. To protect her baby boy, she submits to sexual aggression. After returning the boy to her former husband, she hangs herself but is resuscitated. The story makes the controversial argument that this attempted suicide, in effect, restores her chastity. Zhu Ping infers that "Fengxian lou" may originally have been collected in the lost *Silent Operas, Second Collection* and that the "chaste wife who did not die" 不死節婦 could be seen as an allusion to Zhang Jinyan, the "hero who did not die."

63. Xiao Xinqiao, "Li Yu *Wusheng xi Liancheng bi* banben shanbian kaosuo," 344, 347; Shan Jinheng, "Li Yu nianpu," 32. No complete edition of *The Combined Volume of Silent Operas* exists.

64. For the commentator Shuixiangjijiu's 睡鄉祭酒 critique, see Li Yu, *Silent Operas*, 200–201. For the original, see Li Yu, "Liancheng bi," in *Li Yu quanji*, 8:279–280.

65. Wang Shih-pe, "Tuxiang xushi duzhe fanying," 139–147; Shen Xinlin, *Li Yu xin lun*, 262, 272.

66. Li Yu, "Bimuyu," 122.

67. Li Yu, "Bimuyu," 139.

68. Li Yu, *Xiuxiang hejin huiwen zhuan*, in *Li Yu quanji*, 9:326. This is quoted from Suxuan's 素軒 comment at the end of chapter 2 of Li Yu's novel *Xiuxiang hejin huiwen zhuan*. It is generally believed that Suxuan is Li Yu himself, according to Shen Xinlin, *Li Yu xin lun*, 261.

69. For the years and context in which Li Yu wrote his plays, see Shan Jinheng, "Li Yu nianpu," 23–66.

70. Shen Xinlin, *Li Yu xin lun*, 272.

71. Wang Shih-pe, "Tuxiang xushi duzhe fanying," 112. In the contents of *Silent Operas*, an advertising notice on forthcoming adaptations is seen

below the titles of the first, second, and twelfth stories: "A *chuanqi* play based on this story will be put out instantly (later on)" 此回有傳奇即(嗣)出. See Li Yu, "Wusheng xi," in *Li Yu quanji*, 8:3.
72. The other three plays are *Naihe tian* 奈何天, *Huang qiu feng* 凰求鳳, and *Qiao tuanyuan* 巧團圓.
73. For an exposition of the story illustration, see Wang Shih-pe, "Tuxiang xushi duzhe fanying," 115–116.
74. Li Yu, *Silent Operas*, 185, and "Liancheng bi," 268.
75. Three other plays that have been adapted as novellas are *Naihe tian*, *Fengzheng wu* 風箏誤, and *Yi zhong yuan* 意中緣, according to Shen Xinlin, *Li Yu xin lun*, 269. See Aiyuezhuren, *Bimuyu*, in *Zhongguo gudai zhenxi ben xiaoshuo*, ed. Sui Fenghua et al. (Shenyang: Chunfeng wenyi, 1994), 2:1–93. This novella is composed of two parts: a seven-chapter *Play Within the Play* (*Xi zhong xi* 戲中戲) and a nine-chapter *Bimuyu*.
76. Shen Xinlin holds that the novella was designed for "middle- and lower-level readers" (*Li Yu xin lun*, 269).
77. Wang Shih-pe, "Tuxiang xushi duzhe fanying," 112.
78. Yang Enshou, "Ciyu conghua," 265.
79. Wu Mei, *Zhongguo xiqu gailun* (Nanjing: Jiangsu wenyi chubanshe, 2008), 203–204.
80. Yang Enshou's *Xu Ciyu conghua* 续词余丛话 and Wu Mei's *Guqu chentan* 顧曲塵談 quote from Li Yu's *Random Repository of Idle Thoughts*, according to Du Shuying, *Li Yu meixue sixiang yanjiu* (Beijing: Zhongguo shehui kexue, 1998), 3. See also Helmut Martin, *Li Li-Weng über das Theater: Eine chinesische Dramaturgie des siebzehnten Jahrhunderts* (Heidelberg, 1966; Taipei: Mei Ya Publications, 1968); and George Hayden, "Li Liweng: A Playwright on Performance," *CHINOPERL Papers* 9 (1979–1980): 80–91.
81. *Random Repository of Idle Thoughts* drew on Li Yu's experiments with his household troupe, according to Shen Xinlin, *Huashuo Li Yu*, 26.
82. Li Yu, *Xianqing ouji, juan* 2, "Xuan ju diyi" 選劇第一, 66.
83. Li Yu, *Xianqing ouji, juan* 1, "Jiegou diyi" 結構第一, 1. See David Pollard's translation of this section in "Li Yu on the Theatre: Excerpts from *Pleasant Diversions*," *Renditions* 72 (2009): 33–36.
84. Li Yu, *Xianqing ouji, juan* 1, "Li zhunao" 立主腦, 8–9. See Faye Chunfang Fei's translation of the section "Li zhunao" 立主腦 (The Central Brain) in *Chinese Theories of Theater and Performance from Confucius to the Present* (Ann Arbor: University of Michigan Press, 1999), 79–80.
85. Li Yu, *Xianqing ouji, juan* 1, "Li zhunao" 立主腦 and "Jian touxu" 減頭緒, 9, 12.

86. Li Yu, *Xianqing ouji, juan* 1, "Jian touxu," 12–13. There are six extant editions of the complete *Thorn Hairpin*, all of which are prints from the Ming dynasty, according to Yu Weimin, "*Jingchai ji* de zuozhe yu banben kaoshu," *Gudian wenxian yanjiu*, January 2003, 391.

87. For Li Yu's discussion on a prologue, see *Xianqing ouji, juan* 2, "Jiamen" 家門, "Chongchang" 冲場, and "Chu juese" 出脚色, 60–62.

88. Li Yu, *Xianqing ouji, juan* 2, "Chu juese," 62.

89. Li Yu, *Xianqing ouji, juan* 1, "Tuo kejiu" 脫窠臼, 9.

90. Li Yu, "Bimuyu," 111. This commentator Qinhuai zuihou is identified as Du Jun (杜濬) (1611–1687) by scholars including Guo Yingde (*Ming Qing chuanqi shi*, 342), Du Shuying (*Xi kan renjian: Li Yu zhuan* [Beijing: Zuojia, 2014], 155), and Huang Qiang (*Li Yu yanjiu* [Hangzhou: Zhejiang guji, 1996], 349–351). Du Jun was one of Li Yu's closest friends and wrote prefaces and commentaries for a number of his works. While living in Hangzhou, Li Yu often traveled south of the Yangzi River; he met Du Jun in Jiangning (modern Nanjing), where Du made his home for forty years. Du Jun was a celebrated poet and a Ming loyalist who lived in seclusion after the fall of Ming (Du Shuying, *Xi kan renjian*, 153–159).

91. Li Yu, *Xianqing ouji, juan* 2, "Biandiao di'er" 變調第二 and "Bian jiu cheng xin" 變舊成新, 69–70, 72–73, 75. For translations, see Jing Shen, "Ethics and Theater: The Staging of *Jingchai ji* in *Bimuyu*," *Ming Studies* 57 (2008): 65–68.

92. Zhao Shanlin, "Shi lun *Jingchai ji* de chuanbo jieshou," *Yishu bai jia* 1 (2011): 143. For a list of collections that include highlights of *The Thorn Hairpin* and their titles, see Yu Weimin, "*Jingchai ji* de zuozhe yu banben kaoshu," 398–399. For a study of the editions and dissemination of *The Thorn Hairpin*, see Tanaka Issei, "Nanxi *Jingchai ji* gu juben de jieceng fenhua yiji qi jindai yihou de chuanbo fangshi," *Renwen Zhongguo xuebao* 16 (2010): 1–36.

93. Liu Nianzi, "Mingdai Jiangnan nongcun yanju tu," in *Zhongguo xiqu tongshi*, ed. Zhang Geng and Guo Hancheng (Beijing: Zhongguo xiqu, 1980–1981), 2:9.

94. Li Yu, "Bimuyu," 158.

95. Zheng Zhenduo, *Chatu ben Zhongguo wenxue shi* (Beijing: Zhongguo shehui kexue chubanshe, 2009), 873.

96. Li Yu, *Xianqing ouji, juan* 2, "Xiao shousha" 小收煞, 63. On the climax in the middle of a *chuanqi* play and the development of its second half up to the ending, see Yu Weimin, *Li Yu pingzhuan* (Nanjing: Nanjing daxue chubanshe, 1998), 103.

97. Cai Dongmin clearly lists scene 16 as the "small ending," in "Li Yu xiqu bianju yanjiu," 28. Li Huei-Mian also regards scene 16 as the small

ending, in "Li Yu juzuo zhong de shenyi qingjie," *Zhongguo wenxue yanjiu* 5 (1991): 287. However, Hu Yuanling assigns scenes 16 through 19 as the "section that brings (the play) to a temporary close" (*Li Yu xiaoshuo xiqu yanjiu* [Beijing: Zhonghua shuju, 2004], 250–251), although she holds that scene 16 is important in connecting what comes before and what goes after by portraying the image of paired fish for the first time, showing Lord Yan's rescue of the young couple from drowning, and hinting at a recluse's later assistance with their wedding and official rank.

98. Li Huei-Mian lists all the roles and characters in scene 16 of *Bimuyu*, in "Li Yu juzuo zhong de shenyi qingjie," 296.
99. Zhang Xiaojun, *Li Yu chuangzuo lungao*, 93–94.
100. "Where the streams and hills end" (*shuiqiong shanjin* 水窮山盡 [*shanqiong shuijin* 山窮水盡]): at the end of one's rope.
101. Li Yu, *Xianqing ouji, juan* 2, "Da shousha" 大收煞, 64.
102. Li Yu, *Xianqing ouji, juan* 2, "Da shousha" 大收煞, 63. Some readers or audience members may have been fooled into thinking that scene 28, "A Coincidental Reunion," was the big ending of the play because it does reunite, at least temporarily, Fairy Liu and her mother.
103. Li Yu, *Xianqing ouji, juan* 2, "Kehun diwu" 科諢第五, 55.
104. Li Yu, *Xianqing ouji, juan* 2, "Zhong guanxi" 重關係, 57.
105. Li Yu, *Xianqing ouji, juan* 2, "Ji su'e" 忌俗惡, 56. See Pollard's translation of the section "Gui ziran" 貴自然 (Naturalness), on the naturalness of comic relief, in "Li Yu on the Theatre," 67–69.
106. Li Yu, "Bimuyu," 174, 175.
107. Li Yu, *Xianqing ouji, juan* 2, "Binbai disi" 賓白第四, 44.
108. Li Yu, *Xianqing ouji, juan* 2, "Binbai disi," 44–45.
109. Li Yu, *Xianqing ouji, juan* 2, "Ci bie fanjian" 詞別繁減, 48.
110. Li Yu, *Xianqing ouji, juan* 2, "Ci bie fanjian," 49.
111. Li Yu, *Xianqing ouji, juan* 2, "Yu qiu xiaosi," 47–48. *Outlaws of the Marsh* (*Shuihu zhuan* 水滸傳): one of the four masterworks of the Ming novel; Wu Daozi 吳道子 (680–760?): a renowned painter.
112. Li Yu, "Bimuyu," 134.
113. Zhang Xiaojun, *Li Yu chuangzuo lungao*, 15–16, 71, 79–81; Huang Guoquan, *Yasu zhijian*, 234–235.
114. Li Huei-Mian, "Li Yu juzuo zhong de shenyi qingjie," 296; Zhang Jing, "Lun Li Liweng shizhong qu," *Youshi wenyi* 41, no. 5 (1975): 142–150; Xu Huiya, "Li Yu shizhong qu paichang yanjiu" (M.A. thesis, Furen Daxue, 1998), 172–173.
115. Cai Dongmin, "Li Yu xiqu bianju yanjiu," 47.
116. *A Couple of Soles* vanished from the Kunqu stage for three centuries, and its traditional music notation was lost except for the two tunes included

APPENDIX

in *Jiu gong dacheng nan bei ci gongpu* from the Qianlong reign (1736–1796), according to Liu Youheng, "Tan Kunju chuantong juben zhi chong bian yu xin pu: Yi chong bian xin pu Li Yu *Bimuyu* chuanqi wei li" *Minsu quyi* 55 (1988): 117–119. There is no record of the staging of *A Couple of Soles* by the Kunqu troupes performing in Shanghai toward the end of the Qing dynasty, as indicated in the "Qingmo Shanghai Kunju yanchu jumu zhi" 清末上海昆劇演出劇目志, in Lu Eting, *Kunju yanchu shigao* (Shanghai: Shanghai jiaoyu, 2006), 344–357.

117. Xiao Li, *Chinese Kunqu Opera*, trans. Li Li and Liping Zhang (San Francisco: Long River Press, 2005), 216, 248–289.

118. Cong Zhaohuan's "Daoyan de hua," in *Bimuyu* program (Fourth Chinese Kunqu Opera Art Festival, Suzhou, June 24, 2009). This production, however, focuses on the romance of Fairy Liu and Tan Chuyu, and leaves out the scenes on Murong Jie's public service and retirement, as the lovers are assisted by only Old Fisherman Mo.

119. Chen Duo, "Li Yu," in *Zhongguo da baike quanshu*, 202; Luo Bing, "Li Yu xiqu zai guonei de chuanbo," *Zhonghua xiqu* 31 (2004): 288.

120. Xie Boliang, *Li Yu chuanqi chuangzuo ji* (Shanghai: Shanghai guji, 2011).

121. Liu Jinyun, *Fengyue wubian*, directed by Lin Zhaohua and Li Liuyi (Beijing: Beijing dianshi yishu zhongxin yinxiang chubanshe, 2001), VCD.

122. Lin Zhaohua, "Fengyue wubian," https://www.douban.com/location/drama/11538337/.

BIBLIOGRAPHY

Aiyuezhuren 愛月主人. *Bimuyu* 比目魚. In *Zhongguo gudai zhenxi ben xiaoshuo* 中國古代珍稀本小說, edited by Sui Fenghua 隋鳳花 et al., 2:1–93. Shenyang: Chunfeng wenyi, 1994.

Aoki Masaru 青木正儿. *Zhongguo jinshi xiqu shi* 中國近世戲曲史. Translated by Wang Gulu 王古魯, edited by Cai Yi 蔡毅. Beijing: Zhonghua shuju, 2010.

Birch, Cyril. *Scenes for Mandarins: The Elite Theater of the Ming.* New York: Columbia University Press, 1995.

———. "Tragedy and Melodrama in Early *ch'uan-ch'i* Plays: 'Lute Song' and 'Thorn Hairpin' Compared." *Bulletin of the School of Oriental and African Studies* 36, no. 2 (1973): 228–247.

Brokaw, Cynthia J. "On the History of the Book in China." In *Printing and Book Culture in Late Imperial China*, edited by Brokaw and Chow, 3–54.

Brokaw, Cynthia J., and Kai-Wing Chow, eds. *Printing and Book Culture in Late Imperial China.* Berkeley: University of California Press, 2005.

Bussotti, Michela. *Gravures de Hui: Étude du livre illustré chinois de la fin du XVIe siècle à la première moitié du XVIIe siècle.* Paris: Ecole française d'Extrême-Orient, 2001.

Cahill, James. *The Painter's Practice: How Artists Lived and Worked in Traditional China.* New York: Columbia University Press, 1994.

Cai Dongmin 蔡東民. "Li Yu xiqu bianju yanjiu" 李漁戲曲編劇研究. Ph.D. diss., Shanghai Xiju Xueyuan, 2013.

Carlitz, Katherine. "Printing as Performance: Literati Playwright-Publishers of the Late Ming." In *Printing and Book Culture in Late Imperial China*, edited by Brokaw and Chow, 267–303.

Chan, Hok-lam. *Control of Publishing in China, Past and Present.* Canberra: Australian National University, 1983.

Chang, Chun-shu, and Shelley Hsueh-lun Chang. *Crisis and Transformation in Seventeenth-Century China: Society, Culture, and Modernity in Li Yü's World*. Ann Arbor: University of Michigan Press, 1992.

Chen Duo 陳多. "Li Yu" 李漁. In *Zhongguo da baike quanshu: Xiqu quyi* 中國大百科全書: 戲曲曲藝, 201–203. Beijing: Zhongguo da baike quanshu chubanshe, 1983.

Chuang Tzu (Zhuangzi 莊子). *The Complete Works of Chuang Tzu*. Translated by Burton Watson. New York: Columbia University Press, 1968.

Confucius (Kongzi 孔子). *The Analects*. Translated by D. C. Lau. Harmondsworth: Penguin, 1979.

Cong Zhaohuan 叢兆桓. "Daoyan de hua" 導演的話. In *Bimuyu* program, Fourth Chinese Kunqu Opera Art Festival 第四屆中國崑劇藝術節, Suzhou, June 24, 2009.

Crump, James I. *Chinese Theater in the Days of Kublai Khan*. Ann Arbor: Center for Chinese Studies, University of Michigan, 1990.

———. *Song-Poems from Xanadu*. Ann Arbor: Center for Chinese Studies, University of Michigan, 1993.

Dolby, William. *A History of Chinese Drama*. New York: Barnes and Noble, 1976.

———. "Yuan Drama." In *Chinese Theater*, edited by Mackerras, 32–59.

Dong Kang 董康, ed. *Quhai zongmu tiyao* 曲海總目提要. Beijing: Renmin wenxue chubanshe, 1959.

Du Shuying 杜書瀛. *Li Yu meixue sixiang yanjiu* 李漁美學思想研究. Beijing: Zhongguo shehui kexue, 1998.

———. *Xi kan renjian: Li Yu zhuan* 戲看人間: 李漁傳. Beijing: Zuojia, 2014.

Dudbridge, Glen. "Goddess Huayue Sanniang and the Cantonese Ballad *Chenxiang Taizi*." In *Books, Tales and Vernacular Culture: Selected Papers on China*, 303–320. Leiden: Brill, 2005.

Durrant, Stephen W., Wai-yee Li, and David Schaberg, trans. *Zuo Tradition/ Zuozhuan: Commentary on the "Spring and Autumn Annals."* 3 vols. Seattle: University of Washington Press, 2016.

Fei, Faye Chunfang, ed. and trans. *Chinese Theories of Theater and Performance from Confucius to the Present*. Ann Arbor: University of Michigan Press, 1999.

Fei, Si-yen. *Negotiating Urban Space: Urbanization and Late Ming Nanjing*. Cambridge, Mass.: Harvard University Asia Center, 2009.

Guo Yingde 郭英德. *Ming Qing chuanqi shi* 明清傳奇史. Nanjing: Jiangsu guji, 1999.

Hanan, Patrick. *The Invention of Li Yu*. Cambridge, Mass.: Harvard University Press, 1988.

Hayden, George. "Li Li-weng: A Playwright on Performance." *CHINO-PERL Papers* 9 (1979–1980): 80–91.

Henry, Eric. *Chinese Amusement: The Lively Plays of Li Yü*. Hamden, Conn.: Archon, 1980.

Hinton, Carmelita. "Evil Dragon, Golden Rodent, Sleek Hound: The Evolution of *Soushan Tu* Paintings in the Northern Song Period." In *The Zoomorphic Imagination in Chinese Art and Culture*, edited by Jerome Silbergeld and Eugene Y. Wang, 171–214. Honolulu: University of Hawai'i Press, 2016.

Hsiao, Li-ling. *The Eternal Present of the Past: Illustration, Theater, and Reading in the Wanli Period, 1573–1619*. Leiden: Brill, 2007.

Hu, John. "Ming Dynasty Drama." In *Chinese Theater*, edited by Mackerras, 60–91.

Hu Yuanling 胡元翎. *Li Yu xiaoshuo xiqu yanjiu* 李漁小說戲曲研究. Beijing: Zhonghua shuju, 2004.

Huang Guoquan 黃果泉. *Yasu zhi jian: Li Yu de wenhua renge yu wenxue sixiang yanjiu* 雅俗之間: 李漁的文化人格與文學思想研究. Beijing: Zhongguo shehui kexue, 2004.

Huang Qiang 黃強. *Li Yu yanjiu* 李漁研究. Hangzhou: Zhejiang guji, 1996.

Huo Xianjun 霍現俊 and Zhang Guopei 張國培, annot. "Bimuyu" 比目魚. In *Liweng chuanqi shizhong jiaozhu* 笠翁傳奇十種校注, edited by Wang Xueqi 王學奇 et al., 667–760. Tianjin: Tianjin guji, 2008.

Idema, Wilt. "The Precious Scroll of Chenxiang." In *The Columbia Anthology of Chinese Folk and Popular Literature*, edited by Victor Mair and Mark Bender, 380–405. New York: Columbia University Press, 2011.

——, ed. and trans, *The White Snake and Her Son: A Translation of the Precious Scroll of Thunder Peak with Related Texts*. Indianapolis: Hackett, 2009.

Jiang Ruizao 蔣瑞藻, ed. *Xiaoshuo kaozheng* 小說考證. Shanghai: Shanghai guji, 1984.

Kao Ming (Gao Ming 高明). *The Lute: Kao Ming's "P'i-p'a chi."* Translated by Jean Mulligan. New York: Columbia University Press, 1980.

Ko, Dorothy. *Every Step a Lotus: Shoes for Bound Feet*. Berkeley: University of California Press, 2001.

——. *Teachers of the Inner Chambers: Women and Culture in Seventeenth-Century China*. Stanford, Calif.: Stanford University Press, 1994.

Kuan Han-ch'ing (Guan Hanqing 關漢卿). *Selected Plays of Kuan Han-ch'ing*. Translated by Hsien-yi Yang and Gladys Yang. Beijing: Foreign Languages Press, 1958.

Kwa, Shiamin. *Strange Eventful Histories: Identity, Performance, and Xu Wei's "Four Cries of a Gibbon."* Cambridge, Mass.: Harvard University Asia Center, 2013.

Lao Tzu (Laozi 老子). *Tao Te Ching.* Translated by D. C. Lau. Harmondsworth: Penguin, 1963.

Li, Wai-Yee. "Early Qing to 1723." In *The Cambridge History of Chinese Literature*, edited by Kang-I Sun Chang and Stephen Owen. Vol. 2, *From 1375*, 152–244. Cambridge: Cambridge University Press, 2010.

Li, Xiao. *Chinese Kunqu Opera.* Translated by Li Li and Liping Zhang. San Francisco: Long River Press, 2005.

Li Diaoyuan 李調元. "Yucun quhua" 雨村曲話. In *Zhongguo gudian xiqu lunzhu jicheng*, edited by Zhongguo Xiqu Yanjiuyuan, 8:1–29. Beijing: Zhongguo xiju chubanshe, 1959–1960.

Li Huei-Mian 李惠綿. "Li Yu juzuo zhong de shenyi qingjie" 李漁劇作中的神異情節. *Zhongguo wenxue yanjiu* 中國文學研究 5 (1991): 277–302.

Li Yu 李漁. "Bimuyu" 比目魚. In *Li Yu quanji*, 5:105–211.

———. *Bimuyu chuanqi er juan* 比目魚傳奇二卷. In *Liweng shizhong qu* 笠翁十種曲. Kangxi era (1662–1722) edition. National Library Rare Book Collection, Beijing.

———. *Bimuyu chuanqi er juan* 比目魚傳奇二卷. In *Liweng shizhong qu* 笠翁十種曲. Kangxi era edition. National Taiwan University Library Rare Book Collection, Taipei.

———. *Li Yu quanji* 李漁全集. 20 vols. 1991. Reprint, Hangzhou: Zhejiang guji chubanshe, 2010.

———. "Liancheng bi" 連城璧. In *Li Yu quanji*, 8:247–439.

———. *Silent Operas.* Translated by Patrick Hanan. Hong Kong: Chinese University Press, 1990.

———. *Wusheng xi* 無聲戲. In *Li Yu quanji*, 8:1–246.

———. *Xianqing ouji* 閒情偶寄. In *Li Yu quanji*, 3.

———. "Xiuxiang hejin huiwen zhuan" 繡像合錦回文傳. In *Li Yu quanji*, 9:293–566.

———. "Yu Zhao Shengbo wenxue" 與趙聲伯文學. In *Liweng yijia yan wen ji* 笠翁一家言文集, in *Li Yu quanji*, 1:167–168.

———. "Yu Zhuji mingfu Liu Mengxi" 與諸暨明府劉夢錫. In *Li Yu quanji*, 1:218.

Liang Tingnan 梁廷枏. "Quhua" 曲話. In *Zhongguo gudian xiqu lunzhu jicheng*, 8:233–295.

Lin Zhaohua 林兆華. "Fengyue wubian" 風月無邊. https://www.douban.com/location/drama/11538337/.

Liu Jinyun 劉錦云. *Fengyue wubian* 風月無邊. VCD. Directed by Lin Zhaohua 林兆華 and Li Liuyi 李六乙. Beijing: Beijing dianshi yishu zhongxin yinxiang chubanshe, 2001.

Liu Nianzi 劉念玆. "Mingdai Jiangnan nongcun yanju tu" 明代江南農村演劇圖. In *Zhongguo xiqu tongshi* 中國戲曲通史, edited by Zhang Geng 张庚 and Guo Hancheng 郭漢城, 2:9. Beijing: Zhongguo xiqu, 1980, 1981.

Liu Tingji 劉廷璣. *Zaiyuan zazhi* 在園雜誌. Beijing: Zhonghua shuju, 2005.

Liu Xin 刘昕 and Xiao Jieran 肖洁然, eds. *Zhongguo gu banhua: Renwu juan, Xiaoshuo lei* 中国古版画: 人物卷, 小说类. Changsha: Hunan meishu, 1998.

Liu Youheng 劉有恆. "Tan Kunju chuantong juben zhi chongbian yu xinpu: Yi chongbian xinpu Li Yu *Bimuyu* chuanqi wei li" 談崑劇傳統劇本之重編與新譜: 以重編新譜李漁《比目魚傳奇》為例. *Minsu quyi* 民俗曲藝 55 (1988): 113–145.

Lu, Tina. "Drama." In *The Cambridge History of Chinese Literature*, edited by Kang-I Sun Chang and Stephen Owen. Vol. 2, *From 1375*, 127–148. Cambridge: Cambridge University Press, 2010.

Lu Eting 陸萼庭. *Kunju yanchu shigao* 崑劇演出史稿. Shanghai: Shanghai jiaoyu, 2006.

Luo Bing 駱兵. "Li Yu xiqu zai guonei de chuanbo" 李漁戲曲在國內的傳播. *Zhonghua xiqu* 中華戲曲 31 (2004): 273–292.

Mackerras, Colin, ed. *Chinese Theater: From Its Origins to the Present Day*. Honolulu: University of Hawai'i Press, 1983.

Mao, Nathan K., and Liu Ts'un-yan. *Li Yü*. Boston: Twayne, 1977.

Martin, Helmut. *Li Li-Weng über das Theater: Eine chinesische Dramaturgie des siebzehnten Jahrhunderts*. Heidelberg, 1966. Reprint, Taipei: Mei Ya Publications, 1968.

Mencius (Mengzi 孟子). *Mencius*. Translated by D. C. Lau. Harmondsworth: Penguin, 1979.

Meng Chengshun 孟稱舜. *Mistress and Maid (Jiaohongji)*. Translated and edited by Cyril Birch. New York: Columbia University Press, 2001.

Nienhauser, William H., Jr., ed. *The Indiana Companion to Traditional Chinese Literature*. 2 vols. Bloomington: Indiana University Press, 1986, 1998.

Ouyang Hsiu. "A Record of the Pavilion of an Intoxicated Old Man," translated by Robert E. Hegel. In *The Columbia Anthology of Traditional Chinese Literature*, edited by Victor H. Mair, 590–591. New York: Columbia University Press, 1994.

Pollard, David. "Li Yu on the Theatre: Excerpts from *Pleasant Diversions*." *Renditions* 72 (2009): 30–70.

Rolston, David 陸大偉. "Jingju juben zhong wutai zhishi yanhua yu leibie chutan: Yi *Silang tanmu* lidai gezhong banben weili" 京劇劇本中舞臺指示演化與類別初探: 以《四郎探母》歷代各種版本爲例. In *Jingju de wenxue yinyue biaoyan* 京劇的文學, 音樂, 表演, edited by Fu Jin 傅瑾, 793–817. Beijing: Wenhua yishu, 2016.

———. "Yi Ōsaka cangben *Shengping baofa* zhong de wutai zhishi kan Qingchao gongting daxi de wutai yishu mouxie cengmian" 以大阪藏本《升平寶筏》中的舞臺指示看清朝宮廷大戲的舞臺藝術某些層面. Manuscript, 2018.

Shan Jinheng 單錦珩. "Li Yu nianpu" 李漁年譜. In *Li Yu quanji*, 19:1–130.

Shen, Jing. "Ethics and Theater: The Staging of *Jingchai ji* in *Bimuyu*." *Ming Studies* 57 (2008): 62–101.

———. *Playwrights and Literary Games in Seventeenth-Century China: Plays by Tang Xianzu, Mei Dingzuo, Wu Bing, Li Yu, and Kong Shangren*. Lanham, Md.: Lexington Books, 2010.

———. "Role Types in *The Paired Fish*, a *Chuanqi* Play." *Asian Theatre Journal* 20, no. 2 (2003): 226–236.

Shen Xinlin 沈新林. *Huashuo Li Yu* 話說李漁. Nanjing: Jiangsu renmin, 2012.

———. *Li Yu xin lun* 李漁新論. Suzhou: Suzhou Daxue, 1997.

Sieber, Patricia. *Theaters of Desire: Authors, Readers, and the Reproduction of Early Chinese Song-Drama, 1300–2000*. New York: Palgrave Macmillan, 2003.

Sun Kaidi 孫楷第. "Li Liweng yu *Shi'er lou*" 李笠翁與《十二樓》. In *Li Yu quanji*, 20:5–65.

Swatek, Catherine. *"Peony Pavilion" Onstage: Four Centuries in the Career of a Chinese Drama*. Ann Arbor: Center for Chinese Studies, University of Michigan, 2002.

Tanaka Issei 田仲一成. "Nanxi *Jingchai ji* gu juben de jieceng fenhua yiji qi jindai yihou de chuanbo fangshi" 南戲《荊釵記》古劇本的階層分化以及其近代以後的傳播方式. *Renwen Zhongguo xuebao* 人文中國學報 16 (2010): 1–36.

Volpp, Sophie. *Worldly Stage: Theatricality in Seventeenth-Century China*. Cambridge, Mass.: Harvard University Asia Center, 2011.

Waley, Arthur, trans, *The Book of Songs: The Ancient Chinese Classic of Poetry*. New York: Grove Weidenfeld, 1987.

Wan Qingchuan 萬晴川. *Fengliu daoxue: Li Yu zhuan* 風流道學: 李漁傳. Hangzhou: Zhejiang renmin chubanshe, 2005.

Wang Ayling 王瑷玲. "Mingmo Qingchu caizi jiaren ju zhi yanqing neihan jiqi suo yinsheng zhi shenmei gousi" 明末清初才子佳人劇之言情內涵及其所引生之審美構思. *Zhongguo wen zhe yanjiu jikan* 中國文哲研究集刊 18 (2001): 139–188.

Wang Shifu 王實甫. *The Story of the Western Wing*. Edited and translated by Stephen H. West and Wilt L. Idema. Berkeley: University of California Press, 1995.

Wang Shih-pe 汪詩佩. "Tuxiang xushi duzhe fanying: Lun Li Yu de 'Tan Chuyu' yu *Bimuyu*" 圖像、敘事、讀者反應：論李漁的<譚楚玉>與《比目魚》. *Zhongzheng Daxue Zhongwen xueshu niankan* 中正大學中文學術年刊 1 (2010): 111–150.

Wu Mei 吳梅. *Zhongguo xiqu gailun* 中國戲曲概論. Nanjing: Jiangsu wenyi chubanshe, 2008.

Wu Xinlei 吳新雷. "Li Yu" 李玉. In *Zhongguo da baike quanshu: Xiqu quyi* 中國大百科全書：戲曲曲藝, 203–204. Beijing: Zhongguo da baike quanshu chubanshe, 1983.

Xiao Rong 肖榮. *Li Yu pingzhuan* 李漁評傳. Hangzhou: Zhejiang guji chubanshe, 1987.

Xiao Xinqiao 蕭欣橋. "Li Yu *Wusheng xi Liancheng bi* banben shanbian kaosuo" 李漁《無聲戲》、《連城璧》版本嬗變考索. In *Li Yu quanji*, 20:332–352.

Xie Boliang 謝柏梁. *Li Yu chuanqi chuangzuo ji* 李漁傳奇創作集. Shanghai: Shanghai guji chubanshe, 2011.

Xu Huiya 許蕙雅. "Li Yu shizhong qu paichang yanjiu" 李漁十種曲排場研究. M.A. thesis, Furen Daxue, 1998.

Yang Enshou 楊恩壽. "Ciyu conghua" 詞餘叢話. In *Zhongguo gudian xiqu lunzhu jicheng*, 9:227–286.

Yu Weimin 俞為民. "*Jingchai ji* de zuozhe yu banben kaoshu" 《荊釵記》的作者與版本考述. *Gudian wenxian yanjiu* 古典文獻研究. January 2003, 384–401.

———. *Li Yu pingzhuan* 李漁評傳. Nanjing: Nanjing daxue chubanshe, 1998.

Zhang Jing 張敬. "Lun Li Liweng shizhong qu" 論李笠翁十種曲. *Youshi wenyi* 幼獅文藝 41, no. 5 (1975): 139–162.

Zhang Xiaojun 張曉軍. *Li Yu chuangzuo lungao: Yishu de shangye hua yu shangye hua de yishu* 李漁創作論稿：藝術的商業化與商業化的藝術. Beijing: Wenhua yishu, 1997.

Zhao Shanlin 趙山林. "Shi lun *Jingchai ji* de chuanbo jieshou" 試論《荊釵記》的傳播接受. *Yishu bai jia* 藝術百家 1 (2011): 140–144.

Zheng Zhenduo 鄭振鐸. *Chatu ben Zhongguo wenxue shi* 插圖本中國文學史. Beijing: Zhongguo shehui kexue chubanshe, 2009.

Zhongguo Xiqu Yanjiuyuan 中國戲曲研究院, ed. *Zhongguo gudian xiqu lunzhu jicheng* 中國古典戲曲論著集成. 10 vols. Beijing: Zhongguo xiju, 1959–1960.

Zhou Wu 周蕪, ed. *Zhongguo gudai banhua baitu* 中國古代版畫百圖. Beijing: Renmin meishu, 1982.

Zhou Xinhui 周心慧. "Ji Suizhong Wu shi zhencang de gu banhua" 記綏中吳氏珍藏的古版畫. In *Wu Xiaoling xiansheng zhencang gu banhua quan bian* 吳曉鈴先生珍藏古版畫全編, 1:1–13. Beijing: Xueyuan chubanshe, 2003.

Zhu Liangjie 朱亮潔. "Li Yu de yuanlin shenghuo ji yinyi siwei" 李漁的園林生活及隱逸思維. *Zhongguo wenxue yanjiu* 中國文學研究 22 (2006): 93–132.

Zhu Ping 朱萍. "Li Yu xiaoshuo *Fengxian lou* yu *Wusheng xi er ji* ji yi" 李漁小說《奉先樓》與《無聲戲二集》輯佚. *Zhengzhou Daxue xuebao* 鄭州大學學報 48, no. 4 (2015): 107–110.

TRANSLATIONS FROM THE ASIAN CLASSICS

Major Plays of Chikamatsu, tr. Donald Keene 1961

Four Major Plays of Chikamatsu, tr. Donald Keene. Paperback ed. only. 1961; rev. ed. 1997

Records of the Grand Historian of China, translated from the Shih chi of Ssu-ma Ch'ien, tr. Burton Watson, 2 vols. 1961

Instructions for Practical Living and Other Neo-Confucian Writings by Wang Yang-ming, tr. Wing-tsit Chan 1963

Hsün Tzu: Basic Writings, tr. Burton Watson, paperback ed. only. 1963; rev. ed. 1996

Chuang Tzu: Basic Writings, tr. Burton Watson, paperback ed. only. 1964; rev. ed. 1996

The Mahābhārata, tr. Chakravarthi V. Narasimhan. Also in paperback ed. 1965; rev. ed. 1997

The Manyōshū, Nippon Gakujutsu Shinkōkai edition 1965

Su Tung-p'o: Selections from a Sung Dynasty Poet, tr. Burton Watson. Also in paperback ed. 1965

Bhartrihari: Poems, tr. Barbara Stoler Miller. Also in paperback ed. 1967

Basic Writings of Mo Tzu, Hsün Tzu, and Han Fei Tzu, tr. Burton Watson. Also in separate paperback eds. 1967

The Awakening of Faith, Attributed to Aśvaghosha, tr. Yoshito S. Hakeda. Also in paperback ed. 1967

Reflections on Things at Hand: The Neo-Confucian Anthology, comp. Chu Hsi and Lü Tsu-ch'ien, tr. Wing-tsit Chan 1967

The Platform Sutra of the Sixth Patriarch, tr. Philip B. Yampolsky. Also in paperback ed. 1967

Essays in Idleness: The Tsurezuregusa of Kenkō, tr. Donald Keene. Also in paperback ed. 1967

The Pillow Book of Sei Shōnagon, tr. Ivan Morris, 2 vols. 1967

Two Plays of Ancient India: The Little Clay Cart and the Minister's Seal, tr. J. A. B. van Buitenen 1968

The Complete Works of Chuang Tzu, tr. Burton Watson 1968

The Romance of the Western Chamber (Hsi Hsiang Chi), tr. S. I. Hsiung. Also in paperback ed. 1968

The Manyōshū, Nippon Gakujutsu Shinkōkai edition. Paperback ed. only. 1969

Records of the Historian: Chapters from the Shih chi of Ssu-ma Ch'ien, tr. Burton Watson. Paperback ed. only. 1969

Cold Mountain: 100 Poems by the T'ang Poet Han-shan, tr. Burton Watson. Also in paperback ed. 1970

Twenty Plays of the Nō Theatre, ed. Donald Keene. Also in paperback ed. 1970

Chūshingura: The Treasury of Loyal Retainers, tr. Donald Keene. Also in paperback ed. 1971; rev. ed. 1997

The Zen Master Hakuin: Selected Writings, tr. Philip B. Yampolsky 1971

Chinese Rhyme-Prose: Poems in the Fu Form from the Han and Six Dynasties Periods, tr. Burton Watson. Also in paperback ed. 1971

Kūkai: Major Works, tr. Yoshito S. Hakeda. Also in paperback ed. 1972

The Old Man Who Does as He Pleases: Selections from the Poetry and Prose of Lu Yu, tr. Burton Watson 1973

The Lion's Roar of Queen Śrīmālā, tr. Alex and Hideko Wayman 1974

Courtier and Commoner in Ancient China: Selections from the History of the Former Han by Pan Ku, tr. Burton Watson. Also in paperback ed. 1974

Japanese Literature in Chinese, vol. 1: *Poetry and Prose in Chinese by Japanese Writers of the Early Period*, tr. Burton Watson 1975

Japanese Literature in Chinese, vol. 2: *Poetry and Prose in Chinese by Japanese Writers of the Later Period*, tr. Burton Watson 1976

Love Song of the Dark Lord: Jayadeva's Gītagovinda, tr. Barbara Stoler Miller. Also in paperback ed. Cloth ed. includes critical text of the Sanskrit. 1977; rev. ed. 1997

Ryōkan: Zen Monk-Poet of Japan, tr. Burton Watson 1977

Calming the Mind and Discerning the Real: From the Lam rim chen mo of Tson-kha-pa, tr. Alex Wayman 1978

The Hermit and the Love-Thief: Sanskrit Poems of Bhartrihari and Bilhaṇa, tr. Barbara Stoler Miller 1978

The Lute: Kao Ming's P'i-p'a chi, tr. Jean Mulligan. Also in paperback ed. 1980

A Chronicle of Gods and Sovereigns: Jinnō Shōtōki of Kitabatake Chikafusa, tr. H. Paul Varley 1980

Among the Flowers: The Hua-chien chi, tr. Lois Fusek 1982

Grass Hill: Poems and Prose by the Japanese Monk Gensei, tr. Burton Watson 1983

Doctors, Diviners, and Magicians of Ancient China: Biographies of Fang-shih, tr. Kenneth J. DeWoskin. Also in paperback ed. 1983

Theater of Memory: The Plays of Kālidāsa, ed. Barbara Stoler Miller. Also in paperback ed. 1984

The Columbia Book of Chinese Poetry: From Early Times to the Thirteenth Century, ed. and tr. Burton Watson. Also in paperback ed. 1984

Poems of Love and War: From the Eight Anthologies and the Ten Long Poems of Classical Tamil, tr. A. K. Ramanujan. Also in paperback ed. 1985

The Bhagavad Gita: Krishna's Counsel in Time of War, tr. Barbara Stoler Miller 1986

The Columbia Book of Later Chinese Poetry, ed. and tr. Jonathan Chaves. Also in paperback ed. 1986

The Tso Chuan: Selections from China's Oldest Narrative History, tr. Burton Watson 1989

Waiting for the Wind: Thirty-Six Poets of Japan's Late Medieval Age, tr. Steven Carter 1989

Selected Writings of Nichiren, ed. Philip B. Yampolsky 1990

Saigyō, Poems of a Mountain Home, tr. Burton Watson 1990

The Book of Lieh Tzu: A Classic of the Tao, tr. A. C. Graham. Morningside ed. 1990

The Tale of an Anklet: An Epic of South India—The Cilappatikāram of Iḷaṅkō Aṭikaḷ, tr. R. Parthasarathy 1993

Waiting for the Dawn: A Plan for the Prince, tr. with introduction by Wm. Theodore de Bary 1993

Yoshitsune and the Thousand Cherry Trees: A Masterpiece of the Eighteenth-Century Japanese Puppet Theater, tr., annotated, and with introduction by Stanleigh H. Jones Jr. 1993

The Lotus Sutra, tr. Burton Watson. Also in paperback ed. 1993

The Classic of Changes: A New Translation of the I Ching as Interpreted by Wang Bi, tr. Richard John Lynn 1994

Beyond Spring: Tz'u Poems of the Sung Dynasty, tr. Julie Landau 1994

The Columbia Anthology of Traditional Chinese Literature, ed. Victor H. Mair 1994

Scenes for Mandarins: The Elite Theater of the Ming, tr. Cyril Birch 1995

Letters of Nichiren, ed. Philip B. Yampolsky; tr. Burton Watson et al. 1996

Unforgotten Dreams: Poems by the Zen Monk Shōtetsu, tr. Steven D. Carter 1997

The Vimalakirti Sutra, tr. Burton Watson 1997

Japanese and Chinese Poems to Sing: The Wakan rōei shū, tr. J. Thomas Rimer and Jonathan Chaves 1997

Breeze Through Bamboo: Kanshi of Ema Saikō, tr. Hiroaki Sato 1998

A Tower for the Summer Heat, by Li Yu, tr. Patrick Hanan 1998

Traditional Japanese Theater: An Anthology of Plays, by Karen Brazell 1998

The Original Analects: Sayings of Confucius and His Successors (0479–0249), by E.

Bruce Brooks and A. Taeko Brooks 1998

The Classic of the Way and Virtue: A New Translation of the Tao-te ching of Laozi as Interpreted by Wang Bi, tr. Richard John Lynn 1999

The Four Hundred Songs of War and Wisdom: An Anthology of Poems from Classical Tamil, The Puranāṇūru, ed. and tr. George L. Hart and Hank Heifetz 1999

Original Tao: Inward Training (Nei-yeh) *and the Foundations of Taoist Mysticism*, by Harold D. Roth 1999

Po Chü-i: Selected Poems, tr. Burton Watson 2000

Lao Tzu's Tao Te Ching: *A Translation of the Startling New Documents Found at Guodian*, by Robert G. Henricks 2000

The Shorter Columbia Anthology of Traditional Chinese Literature, ed. Victor H. Mair 2000

Mistress and Maid (Jiaohongji), by Meng Chengshun, tr. Cyril Birch 2001

Chikamatsu: Five Late Plays, tr. and ed. C. Andrew Gerstle 2001

The Essential Lotus: Selections from the Lotus Sutra, tr. Burton Watson 2002

Early Modern Japanese Literature: An Anthology, 1600–1900, ed. Haruo Shirane 2002; abridged 2008

The Columbia Anthology of Traditional Korean Poetry, ed. Peter H. Lee 2002

The Sound of the Kiss, or The Story That Must Never Be Told: Pingali Suranna's Kalapurnodayamu, tr. Vecheru Narayana Rao and David Shulman 2003

The Selected Poems of Du Fu, tr. Burton Watson 2003

Far Beyond the Field: Haiku by Japanese Women, tr. Makoto Ueda 2003

Just Living: Poems and Prose by the Japanese Monk Tonna, ed. and tr. Steven D. Carter 2003

Han Feizi: Basic Writings, tr. Burton Watson 2003

Mozi: Basic Writings, tr. Burton Watson 2003

Xunzi: Basic Writings, tr. Burton Watson 2003

Zhuangzi: Basic Writings, tr. Burton Watson 2003

The Awakening of Faith, Attributed to Aśvaghosha, tr. Yoshito S. Hakeda, introduction by Ryūichi Abé 2005

The Tales of the Heike, tr. Burton Watson, ed. Haruo Shirane 2006

Tales of Moonlight and Rain, by Ueda Akinari, tr. with introduction by Anthony H. Chambers 2007

Traditional Japanese Literature: An Anthology, Beginnings to 1600, ed. Haruo Shirane 2007

The Philosophy of Qi, by Kaibara Ekken, tr. Mary Evelyn Tucker 2007

The Analects of Confucius, tr. Burton Watson 2007

The Art of War: Sun Zi's Military Methods, tr. Victor Mair 2007

One Hundred Poets, One Poem Each: A Translation of the Ogura Hyakunin Isshu, tr. Peter McMillan 2008

Zeami: Performance Notes, tr. Tom Hare 2008

Zongmi on Chan, tr. Jeffrey Lyle Broughton 2009

Scripture of the Lotus Blossom of the Fine Dharma, rev. ed., tr. Leon Hurvitz, preface and introduction by Stephen R. Teiser 2009

Mencius, tr. Irene Bloom, ed. with an introduction by Philip J. Ivanhoe 2009

Clouds Thick, Whereabouts Unknown: Poems by Zen Monks of China, Charles Egan 2010

The Mozi: A Complete Translation, tr. Ian Johnston 2010

The Huainanzi: A Guide to the Theory and Practice of Government in Early Han China, by Liu An, tr. and ed. John S. Major, Sarah A. Queen, Andrew Seth Meyer, and Harold D. Roth, with Michael Puett and Judson Murray 2010

The Demon at Agi Bridge and Other Japanese Tales, tr. Burton Watson, ed.

with introduction by Haruo Shirane 2011

Haiku Before Haiku: From the Renga Masters to Bashō, tr. with introduction by Steven D. Carter 2011

The Columbia Anthology of Chinese Folk and Popular Literature, ed. Victor H. Mair and Mark Bender 2011

Tamil Love Poetry: The Five Hundred Short Poems of the Aiṅkuṟunūṟu, tr. and ed. Martha Ann Selby 2011

The Teachings of Master Wuzhu: Zen and Religion of No-Religion, by Wendi L. Adamek 2011

The Essential Huainanzi, by Liu An, tr. and ed. John S. Major, Sarah A. Queen, Andrew Seth Meyer, and Harold D. Roth 2012

The Dao of the Military: Liu An's Art of War, tr. Andrew Seth Meyer 2012

Unearthing the Changes: Recently Discovered Manuscripts of the Yi Jing (I Ching) and Related Texts, Edward L. Shaughnessy 2013

Record of Miraculous Events in Japan: The Nihon ryōiki, tr. Burton Watson 2013

The Complete Works of Zhuangzi, tr. Burton Watson 2013

Lust, Commerce, and Corruption: An Account of What I Have Seen and Heard, by an Edo Samurai, tr. and ed. Mark Teeuwen and Kate Wildman Nakai with Miyazaki Fumiko, Anne Walthall, and John Breen 2014; abridged 2017

Exemplary Women of Early China: The Lienü zhuan of Liu Xiang, tr. Anne Behnke Kinney 2014

The Columbia Anthology of Yuan Drama, ed. C. T. Hsia, Wai-yee Li, and George Kao 2014

The Resurrected Skeleton: From Zhuangzi to Lu Xun, by Wilt L. Idema 2014

The Sarashina Diary: A Woman's Life in Eleventh-Century Japan, by Sugawara no Takasue no Musume, tr. with introduction by Sonja Arntzen and Itō Moriyuki 2014; reader's edition 2018

The Kojiki: An Account of Ancient Matters, by Ō no Yasumaro, tr. Gustav Heldt 2014

The Orphan of Zhao and Other Yuan Plays: The Earliest Known Versions, tr. and introduced by Stephen H. West and Wilt L. Idema 2014

Luxuriant Gems of the Spring and Autumn, attributed to Dong Zhongshu, ed. and tr. Sarah A. Queen and John S. Major 2016

A Book to Burn and a Book to Keep (Hidden): Selected Writings, by Li Zhi, ed. and tr. Rivi Handler-Spitz, Pauline Lee, and Haun Saussy 2016

The Shenzi Fragments: A Philosophical Analysis and Translation, Eirik Lang Harris 2016

Record of Daily Knowledge and Poems and Essays: Selections, by Gu Yanwu, tr. and ed. Ian Johnston 2017

The Book of Lord Shang: Apologetics of State Power in Early China, by Shang Yang, ed. and tr. Yuri Pines 2017; abridged edition 2019

The Songs of Chu: An Ancient Anthology of Works by Qu Yuan and Others, ed. and trans. Gopal Sukhu 2017

Ghalib: Selected Poems and Letters, by Mirza Asadullah Khan Ghalib, tr. Frances W. Pritchett and Owen T. A. Cornwall 2017

Quelling the Demons' Revolt: A Novel from Ming China, attributed to Luo Guanzhong, tr. Patrick Hanan 2017

Erotic Poems from the Sanskrit: A New Translation, R. Parthasarathy 2017

The Book of Swindles: Selections from a Late Ming Collection, by Zhang Yingyu, tr. Christopher G. Rea and Bruce Rusk 2017

Monsters, Animals, and Other Worlds: A Collection of Short Medieval Japanese Tales, ed. R. Keller Kimbrough and Haruo Shirane 2018

Hidden and Visible Realms: Early Medieval Chinese Tales of the Supernatural and the Fantastic, compiled by Liu Yiqing, ed. and tr. Zhenjun Zhang 2018